Forty Years of Diversity

WORMSLOE FOUNDATION PUBLICATIONS
NUMBER SIXTEEN

Forty Years of Diversity

Essays on Colonial Georgia

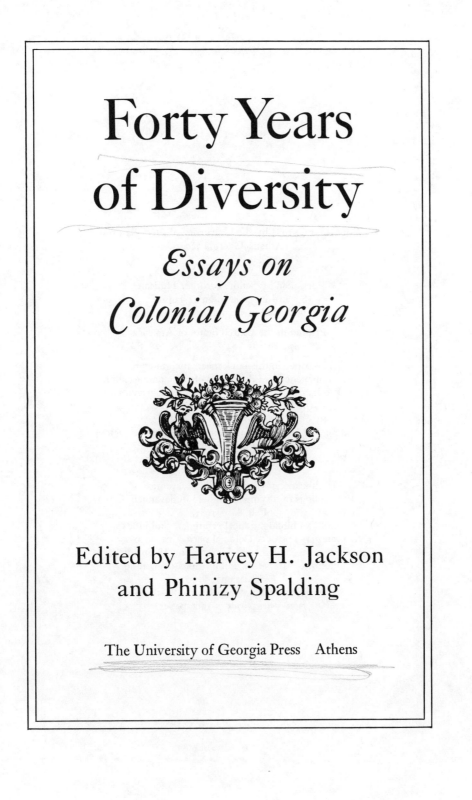

Edited by Harvey H. Jackson
and Phinizy Spalding

The University of Georgia Press   Athens

Designed by Sandra Strother Hudson
Set in Linotype 10 on 12 Janson
with Caslon 540 and 337 display

Printed in the United States of America
88 87 86 85 84   5 4 3 2 1

The paper in this book meets the guidelines
for permanence and durability of the Committee on
Production Guidelines for Book Longevity of
the Council on Library Resources.

Library of Congress Cataloging in Publication Data
Main entry under title:

Forty years of diversity.

(Publications/Wormsloe Foundation; v. 16)
Proceedings of a symposium held in Savannah, Ga.,
Feb. 8–10, 1983.
Includes bibliographical references and index.
1. Georgia—History—Colonial period, ca. 1600–1775—
Congresses. I. Jackson, Harvey H. II. Spalding,
Phinizy. III. Series: Publications (Wormsloe
Foundation); v. 16.
F289.F67 1984   975.8′02   83–18086
ISBN 0–8203–0705–X (alk. paper)

TO THE MEMORY OF

E. MERTON COULTER

Contents

Contents

Introduction

ON February 1, 1733 (old style), James Edward Oglethorpe and his first settlers clambered up Yamacraw Bluff and planted the English flag into the sandy soil that was to become the colony of Georgia. The beginning was both solemn and auspicious; the Indians were friendly, and the general guidelines that Britain's new province was to follow seemed clear and rational—albeit unique in light of the eighteenth-century experience. The Trustees in London and Oglethorpe, their representative in America, were optimistic that Georgia would benefit all the various constituencies it had been molded to enhance. As the colony settled in, however, it became apparent that the ideas it was to epitomize were not necessarily the same as those of the colonists. Internal dispute and domestic contention reared their ugly heads in the infant colony; each side drew up its battle lines and began to articulate its position. The immediate settlement period—the brief honeymoon enjoyed by Georgia's leaders and colonists—was soon over. The debate began as to what the province was to be and why.

Historians—both professional and amateur—have debated the same issue ever since. William Bacon Stevens, Charles Colcock Jones, Jr., Amanda Johnson, Lucian Lamar Knight, Verner Crane, John Tate Lanning, and a bevy of others have had their say. Closer to the colonial period, Alexander Hewat, William Gerard De Brahm, and David Ramsay expressed their opinions too. Over and above all these names, however, has hovered the scholarly work of E. Merton Coulter, whose pen touched virtually every aspect of Georgia's colonial past. It was for Georgia's two hundredth anniversary that he published *A Short History of Georgia* (Chapel Hill, 1933). It seems fitting, somehow, that fifty years later many of the ideas that Coulter first handled are being reworked. New sources and new concepts in history have found their way into the study of Georgia's past. If he were alive today Coulter, that most generous and modest of scholars, would be stimulated and flattered to see that his writings have acted as a catalyst to bring about a new examination of his beloved Georgia's colonial period.

In 1983 Georgia observed the two hundred fiftieth anniversary of its founding by Oglethorpe and the Trustees. In the welter of birthday cakes and patriotic orations it seemed appropriate that a symposium should be convened to which the scholars currently laboring in the field of colonial Georgia would be asked to contribute papers. Recognizing this, the Georgia Historical Society set out to organize such a program. It proved to be a mammoth undertaking—in fact the largest in the Society's 144-year history—but under the leadership of Director Anthony R. Dees, plans were made, participants contacted, and the many details that needed to be dealt with were handled with admirable efficiency. Savannah was the obvious choice for such a gathering, and the date was set to coincide roughly with the first landing of Oglethorpe and his colonists. The main thrust of the meeting was to extract from these scholars their newest ideas and interpretations as they related to colonial Georgia. Unlike years gone by when only a handful worked on Georgia topics, the study of colonial Georgia had branched out to include researchers all over the country and overseas as well. It was felt that it would be highly desirable to bring these people together not just for others to hear but to provide an interchange of ideas among the researchers.

Owing to the numbers involved and the distances from which they would have to come, it was clear that the symposium organizers would have to secure ample sponsorships for the meeting, as well as adequate funding to get the historians to Savannah and pay hotel expenses and honoraria. Other organizations devoted to the study of history joined the Georgia Historical Society—the Institute of Early American History and Culture at Williamsburg, Phi Alpha Theta, and the Georgia Association of Historians—and quickly offered their support. The Georgia Semiquincentenary Commission endorsed the undertaking, as did the city of Savannah; and Armstrong State College, Citizens and Southern National Bank, Inc., Days Inn, Inc., the DeSoto Hilton Hotel, the Ray M. and Mary Elizabeth Lee Foundation, the Savannah Bank and Trust Company, Robert Darrigan, Postal Instant Press, and Savannah Foods and Industries, Inc., all pitched in to assure that activities would be carried through smoothly.

Although financial contributions came from some of these supporters, the program could not have been held without a generous grant from the Georgia Endowment for the Humanities. Ronald E. Benson, who heads the Georgia Endowment, attended the sessions and was one of its most enthusiastic backers. His enthusiasm was caught by the large audiences that crowded the symposium sessions February 8–10, 1983 at the DeSoto Hilton Hotel. Average attendance at a particular meeting hovered at roughly two hundred with some sessions drawing in the neighborhood of three hundred. It did credit to both the papers and the audiences that the questions from the floor were numerous, informed, and contributed significantly to the overall impact of the program. The effect, both in the main hall where the sessions were held and in the anterooms where the registrants and the experts mingled, was electric. The give and take was so lively and the exchange of ideas so stimulating that it would not be overstating the case to claim that the symposium succeeded beyond the organizers' wildest dreams. The sponsoring groups were, of course, delighted by the success of the meeting and the Endowment looked upon the large numbers in attendance and the interaction between scholars and the general public as being precisely the sort of exchange it wants to achieve.

At the symposium many of the registrants made the point that the proceedings of the group must surely be published. The papers were of almost uniformly high caliber. The University of Georgia Press, under its astute editor, Charles East, was anxious to undertake publication of the proceedings, and the end result is the book in hand. Those who attended the sessions will, of course, recognize editorial changes within the papers themselves and will note, too, that the organization of the papers has been altered slightly to conform more appropriately to book format rather than to oral presentation. Furthermore, the comments by session chairmen, Clarence Ver Steeg, Albert Saye, Louis De Vorsey, Harold Davis, Geraldine M. Meroney, and W. W. Abbot have not been included, although their remarks are generally reflected in the revised papers.

There still remains one aspect of the symposium which should not be allowed to pass without comment. The majority of those who attended were not "scholars" in the traditional sense. They were simply people interested in history in general, and in Georgia history in particular, and the fact that they took time from other activities to attend a symposium that was clearly a gathering of academicians is a point well worth considering. Too often historians are accused of writing only for other historians, and at times that is unfortunately true. But more often such a statement reflects a tendency to define "historian" too narrowly. The attraction which history—sound, well-researched, interestingly presented—has for those outside the academic world has been too frequently ignored. This symposium, apart from its impact on scholarship, proved once again that the interested public enjoys and appreciates what takes place at these gatherings, a point future planners of such events should ponder. In this sense, everyone at the symposium was a "historian," and for them this book makes what took place permanent. For those who could not attend, it provides the information and, we hope, at least a sense of the experience.

Abbreviations of
Frequently Cited Sources

AHJ	*Atlanta Historical Journal*
AHR	*American Historical Review*
CO	Colonial Office, British Public Record Office, London
Coll. GHS	*Collections of the Georgia Historical Society*
CRG	*Colonial Records of Georgia*
Ms. CRG	Manuscript, Colonial Records of Georgia
Diary of Percival	R. A. Roberts, ed., *Manuscripts of the Earl of Egmont; Diary of Viscount Percival, Afterwards First Earl of Egmont* (London, 1920–23)
Egmont's Journal	Robert G. McPherson, ed., *The Journal of the Earl of Egmont* (Athens, 1962)
Egmont Papers	Egmont Papers, Phillipps Collection, University of Georgia Library, Athens
FHQ	*Florida Historical Quarterly*
GHQ	*Georgia Historical Quarterly*
Ga. Gaz.	*Georgia Gazette*
PRO	Public Record Office
S.C. Gaz.	*South Carolina Gazette*
SCCHJ	*South Carolina Commons House Journal*
SCHM	*South Carolina Historical Magazine*
WMQ	*William and Mary Quarterly*

Prologue

Although none of Britain's North American colonies was a simple venture, either in concept or execution, Georgia's complexity has always seemed to merit special mention. Unfortunately, that complexity has confused and continues to confuse students of the era, thus perpetuating myths and misconceptions about the settling of a province south of the Savannah River.

In the essay that follows Kenneth Coleman clears up the confusion and presents the reader with a concise explanation of the precedents for this remarkable venture. His analysis of the "plan," which her supporters claimed would make Georgia successful, and of the events that followed the founding is cogent and original. Providing the framework for the rest of the volume, this account by one of the state's most prominent historians offers insights drawn from many years of research, writing, and teaching and provides scholar and layman alike with a long-needed introduction to, and analysis of, the founding of Georgia.

KENNETH COLEMAN

The Founding of Georgia

HE STORY of the founding of Georgia very prop-
erly omits the brief occupation of the area by the
French in the 1560s and by the Spanish from the
1560s through about 1690. These people were concerned with the area that later became Georgia, not
with Georgia itself. The founding of Georgia be-
gins with a consideration of the early eighteenth-
century rivalries between European colonizing nations in southeastern
North America.[1]

About 1700 the race among France, England, and Spain for control
of the northern coast of the Gulf of Mexico increased the concern of
the Carolinians for their Indian trade. Because the English had secured
no territory on the Gulf, their entry into this area had to be from the
Atlantic Ocean; and the Altamaha River seemed the best approach.
The Altamaha was not a very good entrance because its tributaries did
not originate far enough west, but it was the best one the Carolinians
could find. Before the French secured the mouth of the Mississippi
River, there were several suggestions for English settlements in that
area to protect the Carolina Indian trade, but none of these settlements
materialized.[2]

Because of the Yamasee War of 1715–16 and the deaths it caused on
the Carolina frontier, Carolinians increased their desire to control the
land south of the Savannah River, claimed by both England and Spain
but occupied by neither. In 1717 Sir Robert Montgomery, a Scottish
baronet, proposed to the Carolina Lords Proprietors that he be allowed
to settle a new colony between the Savannah and Altamaha rivers. The
colony, to be named the Margravate of Azilia, would, Sir Robert said,
prevent Spanish and Indian invasions of Carolina and produce silk,
wine, olives, raisins, almonds, and currants—products that had to be
imported into England from the Mediterranean area. The colonists
were to be citizen-soldiers who would produce the desired items and

4

defend the area from any Spanish, French, or Indians who might invade it. Sir Robert published in London two promotional booklets, *A Discourse Concerning the Design'd Establishment of a New Colony to the South of Carolina, in the Most Delightful Country of the Universe* in 1717 and *A Description of the Golden Islands* in 1720. Neither Sir Robert nor the Carolina Proprietors had the funds to establish the Margravate, so the dream evaporated except for the two booklets and Sir Robert's ideas about the area's climate, its possible produce, and the citizen-soldiers. The approval of this settlement in London made it clear that by 1720 the British government was ready to contest the Spaniards for the area south of the Savannah River.[3]

Before the ideas of Sir Robert's Margravate were forgotten, Jean Pierre Purry, a Swiss merchant, proposed in 1724 a British settlement to the south and west of Carolina, to be named Georgia, in the climate he considered ideal for human habitation, 33° latitude north. Both the Board of Trade and the Carolina proprietors were interested, but again lack of finances prevented any settlement until 1730, after South Carolina had become a royal colony.[4]

In 1720 John Barnwell and Joseph Boone made a detailed report to the Board of Trade on South Carolina's defense. They suggested that Port Royal be made a magazine for outlying forts, the two most important of which were to be established at Savannah Town, located at the falls of the Savannah River, and at the mouth of the Altamaha River. These locations were declared to be good places for the Indian trade and surrounded by excellent agricultural land. It was suggested that several posts be established in the Alabama-Mississippi country in order to cut French contact between the lower Mississippi River and Quebec. The founding by the French of Fort Toulouse in 1717 and of New Orleans in 1718 was anathema to Carolina Indian traders who operated in the Mississippi country.

The Board of Trade agreed with this report and chose the mouth of the Altamaha as the site of the first fort, to be manned by citizen-soldiers—another indication that London was ready to extend England's claim south of the Savannah River. An independent company of one hundred men arrived in Charles Town in May 1721, but the men were too ill to build the fort and the engineer to design it did not come. Governor Francis Nicholson therefore sent Colonel John Barnwell to the Altamaha to erect a temporary fort at Carolina's expense. The Spanish protested that this fort was on their territory, and the government in London authorized direct negotiations between the governors of South Carolina and Florida. But nothing was decided. This fort, Fort King George, was always unpopular with its garrison and burned in January 1726. Temporary barracks were erected at colony expense, but in 1727 the fort was entirely abandoned.[5]

South Carolina's royal governor, Robert Johnson, was instructed to reconstruct the fort on its original site, but it was never rebuilt. Johnson, well acquainted with South Carolina and its needs, in 1729 and 1730 submitted to the Board of Trade detailed suggestions for the defense and settlement of the colony. He advocated the creation of ten townships on the frontier with a town at the center of each, surrounded by farm lots to support the citizen-soldiers. The Board of Trade endorsed Johnson's plan enthusiastically and specified that the land should be granted on the basis of fifty acres for each family member and that two of the townships should be located on the Altamaha. Township lands could be granted only to new settlers, a provision that would increase South Carolina's white population capable of bearing arms. The desired new settlers could come from two main sources: Scotch-Irish from Ulster and German Protestants fleeing from Roman Catholic persecution.[6]

By 1730 the settlement of the area south of the Savannah River had become the primary imperial concern of the British and Carolinians. Proposed new colonies since the founding of Pennsylvania in 1680 had frequently envisioned settlement south of the Savannah. By 1730 it was clear that the British would soon undertake settlement of this area. The South Carolinians who advocated settlement were much more concerned about the aggressive French penetration of the Alabama country than about the possible advance of the lethargic Spanish from St. Augustine.[7] But many Carolinians probably did not separate the French and the Spanish threats in this area. Either could get in the way of Carolina's Indian trade.

While these ideas about South Carolina's defense and imperial growth were current in South Carolina and London, the more traditional cause for Georgia's founding began. In February 1729 James Oglethorpe was appointed the chairman of a parliamentary committee to inquire into "the State of the Gaols of this Kingdom." Committee investigations in 1729 and 1730 detailed deplorable conditions in English prisons and resulted in the prosecution of several of the most notorious wardens and the freeing by Parliament of about ten thousand prisoners, mainly debtors.[8] This activity brought Oglethorpe into contact with Dr. Thomas Bray, the founder of the Society for the Propagation of the Gospel in Foreign Parts and the Society for Promoting Christian Knowledge. Bray, a leading philanthropist, had been interested in prison reform for at least twenty-five years.[9]

In 1723 Bray had joined with himself four trustees (John Lord Viscount Percival, William Belitha, the Reverend Stephen Hales, and Hales's brother Robert) to help carry out his philanthropic endeavors.[10] A little before Christmas 1729, according to Captain Thomas Coram, Bray, realizing that his death was probably near, told Coram that before he died he hoped to find a way to settle honest but poor and distressed English families and persecuted foreign Protestants in America. Bray sent for James Vernon, Dr. Stephen Hales, Viscount Percival, James Oglethorpe, and two or three others and proposed that they enter into an association with him for carrying out several of his designs: establishing a charity colony for unfortunates, Christian instruction of Negroes in the British plantations, creating parochial libraries in Great Britain, and "other good purposes."[11] On January 15, 1729/30, twenty-four new associates were named to join with Bray and the four designated in 1723.[12]

How much Bray influenced Oglethorpe's ideas on a charity colony is impossible to determine, but on February 13 Oglethorpe told Percival that he had discovered £15,000 in a charity fund left by the haberdasher Joseph King from which he hoped to secure £5,000 for founding a charity colony in America. To secure this £5,000, it would be necessary to join it to some existing charity, and Oglethorpe proposed to Percival that it be added to the legacy left by Abel Tassin D'Allone for Christianizing Negroes in America, for which Percival was one of the trustees. Oglethorpe also proposed that the enlarged Bray Associates be combined with the D'Allone trustees and the King charity to create a group to accomplish Bray's goals. Bray approved of this proposal before his death on February 15, 1729/30. Oglethorpe also told Percival of his scheme to get land from the government in the West Indies (America), to plant thereon "100 miserable wretches" let out of jail by the previous year's debtors act and now starving in London. If settled all together and properly supervised, they would increase and become a security and defense of British possessions against the French and Indians. The colonists should be employed in cultivating flax and hemp to be sent to England and Ireland to promote manufactures there.[13]

Oglethorpe was the first chairman of the expanded Bray Associates, whose minutes were titled variously but most fully "The Gentlemen

Associates for the Executing of Mr. D'Allon's will by Instructing the Negroes in the British Plantations in the Christian Religion, and for Establishing a charitable Colony in America, for settling Parochial Libraries in Great Britain, and for other good purposes."[14]

On March 21, 1729/30, the Associates agreed to Oglethorpe's proposal to forward a charity colony, and on May 12 they agreed to obtain a grant of land for this purpose and designated Oglethorpe as the leader in the action. Finally, on July 30, James Vernon laid before the Associates a draft of a petition to the king for a grant of land to the south of Carolina for a charity colony. The petition was agreed to and was to be signed by the Associates. At the same meeting Percival and Oglethorpe informed the Associates that they had received gifts to promote the proposed charity colony. On November 12 the Associates authorized Oglethorpe to begin publicity and fund-raising for the colony.[15]

All of the original Georgia Trustees came from this enlarged charity group or Associates of Dr. Bray. Eight Associates did not sign the petition for the charter and hence never became Georgia Trustees. Fourteen of the Associates were members of Parliament, and all but possibly two of these served on the gaols committee with Oglethorpe.[16] For several months before the Georgia charter was issued in June 1732, much of the time at the meetings of the Bray Associates was taken up with Georgia business.

After Georgia was chartered, the Bray Associates and the Georgia Trustees, being largely the same people, continued to meet on the same day at the same place (usually the Georgia Office in Westminster), although they kept separate minutes of their meetings. Finally on May 29, 1733, the two bodies agreed to separate, and their joint funds were divided. On May 31 the first meeting of the group, named in its minutes as the Associates of Dr. Bray, was held.[17]

It is impossible to document in detail the connections between the ideas regarding imperial defense current in London and the application for the charity colony, but it seems highly unlikely that Oglethorpe and his friends should not have known of the Carolina defense proposals. Martin Bladen and Edward Ashe, members of the Board of Trade, worked with Oglethorpe and the gaols committee in the spring and early summer of 1730. It seems more than a coincidence that Oglethorpe first mentioned Carolina to Percival as the location of the proposed colony on June 26, shortly after the Board of Trade had instructed Governor Robert Johnson of South Carolina (who was then in London) to place two of his proposed townships on the Alta-maha River.[18]

The third reason for the founding of Georgia—mercantilism—was the last one developed by the colony's backers and in many respects the least important. It was used, however, to convince many people that Georgia would be valuable to the empire. True, the predecessors of the Georgia Trustees—Thomas Nairne, Robert Montgomery, and Jean Pierre Purry—in advocating a colony south of the Savannah River all proposed production of tropical or semitropical commodities in their colonies. In fact, the Trustees undoubtedly got their ideas about producing silk, wine, spices, and other items from their predecessors.[19] In 1729, just as the Georgia movement was beginning, Joshua Gee published in London *The Trade and Navigation of Great Britain Considered*, a very popular work in which he repeated the ideas of what the Carolina-Georgia area could produce (silk, flax, and hemp) and advocated new settlements of poor from Britain in this area. What he said sounds remarkably similar to what Oglethorpe told Percival about his plans for the proposed colony in February 1730.[20] Once the Trustees adopted these ideas of what Georgia could and should produce, they clung to them throughout the early phase of Georgia's development.

The petition for the charter for a charity colony was considered by the Privy Council on September 17, 1730. It was referred routinely to the Board of Trade, which considered it in December 1730 and January 1731, with Oglethorpe and others of the petitioners present for questioning, and reported favorably to the Privy Council. The actual provisions of the charter were evolved through a series of meetings with and suggestions from the petitioners throughout 1730 and 1731. The drafting was done by the attorney general and the solicitor general. The petitioners especially wanted to be free from South Carolina, which they eventually achieved except that the Carolina governor would command the militia of the new colony.[21] On January 19, 1731/32, the Committee of the Privy Council approved the altered charter, and the petitioners agreed to it although they were not entirely satisfied. On January 26 the king informally indicated his approval.[22]

Throughout March the petitioners frequently approached Sir Robert Walpole and the Duke of Newcastle, the secretary of state, about the king's failure to sign the charter. The king was reported to object to several points, especially the appointment of the militia officers being given to the Trustees rather than the governor. The petitioners objected to this idea being brought up so late, after the charter had been approved by the Privy Council. Finally on April 21 the king signed the charter without amendment.[23]

The Privy Seal was affixed to the charter on June 9, 1732, which is taken as the date of issue. Expenses connected with signing the charter and passing it through the various offices came to £160, although the Duke of Newcastle forgave his fee. After the correction of mistakes made in transcribing the charter, Percival was able to take the oath as president of the Georgia Trustees on July 7. He then summoned the other Trustees to meet on July 20 to be sworn in. Only twelve attended their first official meeting, foreshadowing future poor attendance.[24]

The charter created "the Trustees for Establishing the Colony of Georgia in America" to govern the new colony for twenty-one years and to control the land between the Savannah and Altamaha rivers, westward from their headwaters to the Pacific. No Trustee could own land, occupy any Georgia office of profit or trust, or receive any income from his participation in the colony. The government was entirely in the hands of the Trustees, except that any governor appointed or laws passed must receive royal approval and the militia was under the command of the governor of South Carolina. This provision made Georgia different from the earlier proprietary colonies. Twenty-one Trustees were named in the charter. The best known and most important were James Oglethorpe, James Vernon, and John Viscount Percival, who became the Earl of Egmont in 1733. All Georgia settlers were to enjoy the same rights and liberties as free subjects born in Britain; but, interestingly enough, there was no provision for a legislature in the colony.[25]

Once the Trustees for Establishing the Colony of Georgia were organized as a corporate body, they began to solicit funds. On May 12 the Georgia backers intended to ask the House of Commons for permission to address the king for £10,000 to transport vagrants and beggars under the age of sixteen to Georgia, but objections in the House of Commons killed the move. Plans for Georgia were formulated and prospective settlers solicited. Frequently the Trustees' Journal bears the notation "Examined several Persons who Offered themselves to Go to Georgia, and Enter'd their Names for Further Consideration."[26]

As early as July 27, 1732, the Trustees decided that they would send over persecuted Protestant Salzburgers who were desirous of going to

Georgia as soon as funds were available. In December and January the question of sending Jewish settlers came up, and it was decided that no Jews would be sent and that deputations given to Jews to collect funds for Georgia should be recalled. Several Trustees were afraid that allowing Jewish settlers would hamper the collection of money and settlers in England.[27]

Throughout the preliminaries of the Georgia charter, best documented in the diary of Viscount Percival, it was clear that Oglethorpe was the leader in the movement. The proposed colony was always spoken of by Percival as the charity colony, "our Carolina colony," or some such phrase. The first mention of the name Georgia in his diary occurred on May 2, 1732. Nowhere has the present writer been able to find who was responsible for the naming of the colony, although Georgia was the most obvious name for any province founded at that time and it had been proposed earlier for several other colonies that were never founded.

Interestingly enough, once the Trustees organized and began work, they forgot all about debtors in the selection of colonists. Albert B. Saye, who has searched hardest for debtors among the colonists, estimates that not more than a dozen debtors released from prison by Parliament ever came to Georgia, if indeed that many came.[28] The charity colonists, those sent to Georgia at the expense of the Trustees, were usually poor tradesmen and artisans from London and other English towns. To the modern mind it seems strange that no soldiers, sailors, husbandmen, or laborers from the country were accepted for a colony where the fighting of Indians and Spaniards and support by agriculture were envisioned. There were objections in England to taking laborers out of the country, so the Trustees tried to find people who were unsuccessful in supporting themselves and whose migration would not hurt the English economy.[29] Apparently the new environment in America was supposed to make them successful farmers and soldiers, if the Trustees ever got that far in their thinking.

By mid-October 1732 Oglethorpe announced that he would go to Georgia with the first colonists; therefore, the initial settlement was made sooner than it otherwise would have been. The Trustees had collected only £2,000, certainly not enough to found a colony, and many people had advised them to delay until they had more colonists and funds. But Oglethorpe was determined to go as soon as possible, and actual settlement probably brought in more money and more favorable publicity. By the charter, Oglethorpe could not be appointed as governor—an office the Trustees never created—and he was given little specific authority by the Trustees in Georgia. But Oglethorpe was never one to quibble about technical details when he thought something needed doing. The Trustees undoubtedly understood that he would be in control in Georgia, and he certainly supplied the strong leadership needed in the infant colony.[30]

The Trustees engaged a two-hundred-ton frigate, the *Anne*, to transport the colonists to Georgia. Captain John Thomas marked down a total of 114 passengers, or 91 "heads," children under twelve being counted at less than a "head." On Sunday, November 12, 1732, the Reverend Henry Herbert, the volunteer minister to Georgia, preached to the colonists their last sermon on English soil. On Thursday, November 16, seven Trustees came to Gravesend where Oglethorpe presided at a meeting on board the *Anne*. They pronounced the vessel "Tight & Strong & well Manned" and "the People very well satisfied." The *Anne* left Gravesend on Friday, November 17, and last sighted English land on November 22. The voyage across the Atlantic was fairly routine, but there were days of celebration when flip or punch was served with a special dinner: the christening of Georgius Marinus Warren on November 23 with Oglethorpe as godfather, Oglethorpe's birthday on December 21, and Christmas Day. Two infants, described by Oglethorpe as weak and half-starved, died during the voyage. Oglethorpe's care for the colonists on board the *Anne* caused them to begin to call him "father." On the Atlantic crossing both the settlers and Oglethorpe decided he was the leader, if there had ever been any doubt.[31]

Early in the morning of January 13, 1733, land was sighted near Charles Town, South Carolina. Oglethorpe went ashore, but the colonists were required to remain on the *Anne*, lest they refuse to continue on to Georgia. Oglethorpe was received by Governor Robert Johnson and his council and given advice and material aid voted by the South Carolina Assembly and contributions of individual Carolinians. The next day the *Anne* sailed for Port Royal, where the colonists were landed and housed in the new barracks while Oglethorpe and a small party went on to pick the site for settlement. Although it cannot be documented, the location of Savannah was almost certainly suggested by South Carolinians. The spot was well known because it was the location of John Musgrove's trading post and the site of Tomochichi's small Yamacraw Indian village. Yamacraw Bluff, the first high ground upriver from the river's mouth, was undoubtedly the best location that could have been found for a settlement in the area. There is no documentary evidence that Colonel William Bull was present when the site was picked, but he did help Oglethorpe lay out the town. On February 1, 1733 (February 12, new style), the colonists landed at Yamacraw Bluff and erected the four large tents that were to house them for several weeks.[32] Oglethorpe's description of the site and town is the best early one.

I fixed upon a healthy situation, about Ten Miles from the Sea. The River here forms an Half-moon, along the South side of which the Banks are about Forty Feet high, and on the Top a Flat, which they call a Bluff. The plain High ground extends into the Country Five or Six Miles, and along the River-side about a mile. Ships that draw Twelve Feet Water can ride within Ten Yards of the Bank. Upon the River-side, in the Centre of this Plain, I have laid out the Town, opposite to which is an Island of very rich Pasturage, which I think should be kept for the Trustees Cattle. The River is pretty wide, the Water fresh, and from the Key of the Town you see its whole Course to the Sea, with the Island of Tybee, which forms the Mouth of the River, from about Six Miles up into the Country. The Landskip is very agreeable, the Stream being wide, and bordered with high Woods on both sides. . . . I have marked out the Town and Common; half of the former is already cleared, and the first House was begun Yesterday in the Afternoon. A little Indian Nation, the only one within Fifty Miles, is not only at Amity, but desirous to be Subjects to his Majesty King George, to have Lands given them among us, and to breed their Children at our Schools. Their Chief and his beloved Man, who is the Second Man in the Nation, desire to be instructed in the Christian Religion.[33]

Everyone set to work under Oglethorpe's direction to clear the town site, build houses, and clear land for planting. Luckily, the building material to be used for the houses came from the site as it was cleared. One of the best descriptions of conditions at early Savannah came from Charles Town merchant Samuel Eveleigh, who visited the town in late March.

Mr. Oglethorpe is indefatigable, takes a vast deal of Pains. . . . He is extremely well beloved by all his People; the general Title they give him is Father. If any of them is sick, he immediately visits them, and takes a great deal of Care of them. If any Difference arises, he is the Person that decides it. . . . He keeps a strict Discipline; I never saw one of his People drunk, or heard one swear, all the Time I was there.

He does not allow them Rum, but in lieu gives them English beer. It is surprising to see how chearfully the Men go to Work, considering they have not been bred to it. There are no Idlers there; even the Boys and Girls do their Parts. . . . In short, he has done a vast deal of Work for the Time, and I think his Name justly deserves to be immortalized.[34]

Friendship with neighboring Indians was important for all American colonies at their founding, but Georgia was particularly fortunate in this regard. The Yamacraws, a small, outlawed group of Creeks, were the only Indians within some fifty miles of Savannah. Tomochichi, their chieftain, was a remarkable person who probably realized that the new colony could help him and his people as much as they could help it. Oglethorpe was particularly adept at securing Indian friendship, and he and Tomochichi seem to have been friends from the beginning. Tomochichi was the Georgia entrée to the larger Creek confederation, and Mary Musgrove, the wife of the Yamacraw trader John Musgrove, became Oglethorpe's Indian interpreter and ambassador as long as he remained in Georgia. So the colony in its first few years had no fear of Indian troubles—a very fortunate circumstance.[35]

On Saturday, July 7, 1733, the colonists met to hear prayers of praise and thanksgiving. The streets, wards, and tithings were named, and the colonists drew their lots. Then a hearty dinner was held after which the Trustee-appointed officials were sworn in and the court held its first session.[36]

During the first summer, there were a number of deaths among the new colonists, which was to be expected until "seasoning" had taken place and the people had adjusted to the new climate and living conditions. Dr. William Cox, the colony's physician, was the first to die. Oglethorpe had his own theory about the causes of the deaths—rum punch. He gave no blame to the climate and drinking river water. Sometimes, but not usually, entire families were wiped out. If one parent died, the other tended to remarry as soon as possible to set up a working household. But orphans became a problem that first summer.[37]

In mid-July some sixty people were ill with little hope of recovery. Then, on July 11 a ship arrived unexpectedly with some Jews from England. One of them was Dr. Samuel Nunes, who immediately began to minister to the sick. Oglethorpe soon reported that none of Nunes's patients had died and that all sang his praises. The worst was over, and conditions were improving.[38]

Besides the sickness, the summer brought what Oglethorpe called "this Petulancy," a feeling of independence on the part of the colonists. When Oglethorpe returned from Charles Town in mid-June after an absence of six or eight weeks, he reported that some of the people had become intemperate and then disobedient, mutinous, and impatient of labor and discipline. Oglethorpe said he gradually brought the people back to discipline, but he could not stop rum drinking, which had begun during his absence. Jean Pierre Purry, the founder of Purrysburg, across the river in South Carolina, reported that Georgians were unhappy because of the system of land tenure which did not allow women to inherit, because slaves were prohibited, and because many idle people either would not or could not work. Those able to work thought it unfair that they must labor for those who did not. Oglethorpe could not see that most settlers now better understood how to succeed in Georgia and would no longer blindly follow his leadership. His tenure as "father" had ended.[39]

With Georgia founded and the people beginning to adapt themselves to the new environment, this seems a good place to stop the chronological treatment and make some analysis of the founding, even though some reference to events not described above will be necessary.

The Trustees had three main motives for the founding of Georgia: philanthropy, imperial defense, and mercantilism. Clearly, philanthropy was foremost in their minds, but the other two were of importance in their efforts to secure private and government help for Georgia.

The most obvious result of Trustee philanthropy is that released debtors were not aided by the founding of Georgia because very few of them ever came to the colony. So what of the "unfortunate poor"? It did not take long after Georgia's settlement to discover that many who were worthless in England were also worthless in Georgia. A number of historians, including the present writer, have expressed the opinion that many of the initial failures in Georgia were inevitable considering the type of settlers originally sent over. People who had failed in England and who knew nothing about agriculture could not be expected to become successful farmers immediately. Many of them never did but instead searched for nonagricultural ways to make their livings. Self-respecting artisans and merchants in the eighteenth century looked down on farm laborers as being of lower status.

But, of course, many of the unfortunates did succeed, although it often took several years before these people had adjusted to the climate and new conditions. During the early years there was a shortage of agricultural labor, and the indentured servants sent over by the Trustees or brought by colonists often did not prove satisfactory. But shortage of labor was customary in all new settlements in America. Eventually a number of unfortunates did get a new start in Georgia. Whether they could have done as well in England is something upon which we cannot even speculate.[40]

Besides the English colonists, there were also the Salzburgers, who came mainly between 1734 and 1736, and settled at Ebenezer, upriver from Savannah. They were mainly farmers in Europe and so were more successful than most of the colonists as farmers in early Georgia. Although they, too, had the usual early illnesses and deaths, they complained less and seemed to succeed earlier than most of the English colonists around Savannah. Certainly in Georgia they were free from religious persecution, which had been responsible for their leaving Salzburg. So in two aspects, they could term their migration to Georgia a success.[41]

Many of the Highland Scots who came in 1735–41 as soldiers lost their lives in the fighting against the Spanish. Once this fighting was over, they were free to develop on their own, and some succeeded and founded families that have remained important in Georgia.

The imperial defense motive was the most successful of the three. Once the colony was settled, the debatable land between the Savannah and the Altamaha became English. When the Spanish were unable to defeat Oglethorpe on St. Simons Island in 1742, Georgia remained English. The usual theory that Georgia was supposed to be a buffer colony to protect South Carolina could be a misstatement of the imperial viewpoint. Georgia was founded to secure more of the debatable land, not to protect South Carolina. Of course, from South Carolina's viewpoint, Georgia was a buffer.[42] Georgia had little, if any, effect upon the French in the Mississippi Valley and the Gulf of Mexico. Not until the British victory in a general European and American war were the French removed from this area in 1763.

It is often said that in carrying out the principles of mercantilism the Trustees experienced their greatest failure, but this is not entirely true. Silk was the most important item in the Trustees' mercantilistic designs, and silk was raised in Georgia until 1775. But neither Georgia nor other colonies that tried to produce silk ever raised enough to have any substantial effect on Britain's importation of it from the Continent of Europe. The main drawback to silk production in America was that labor was too expensive to make silk pay when compared with the cheap labor found in France and Italy, where most of Europe's silk was produced.

Wine production was the second mercantilistic item to receive the Trustees' emphasis, but they never considered wine as important as silk. European wine grapes were early brought to Georgia, and vineyards were planted until the 1740s. Secretary William Stephens was a great advocate of wine production at his plantation of Bewlie. Yet wine production was never successful in Georgia, probably because of climate or soil problems, and it was dropped about 1745. Such items as tea, coffee, olives, spices, and a few other plants seldom got beyond the Trustees' Garden in Savannah and were of no economic importance to the colony or to Britain.[43]

A negative effect of the Trustees' mercantilistic views was that they emphasized such products as silk and wine when the colony needed food. Had food production been emphasized from the first, the colony might have cost the Trustees less to feed and more colonists might have succeeded in supporting themselves sooner than they did. Oglethorpe did recognize the importance of food and offered bounties for food production from 1734 to 1739.

Another aspect of mercantilism generally ignored by historians is that although Georgia did not produce the more exotic items that the Trustees envisioned, she did contribute to the empire lumber products, naval stores, deerskins, and agricultural products which South Carolina also produced.

And finally, the Trustees brought together the various ideas about a colony south of the Savannah River and founded Georgia. It has continued and prospered ever since. That in itself is worthy of the thanks of all Georgians to the Trustees!

NOTES

1. The best treatments of this rivalry known to the author are Verner W. Crane, *The Southern Frontier, 1670–1732* (Ann Arbor, 1929; reprint, 1956), and Kenneth Coleman, "The Southern Frontier: Georgia's Founding and the Expansion of South Carolina," *GHQ* 56 (1972): 163–74. A briefer treatment is in Kenneth Coleman, *Colonial Georgia: A History* (New York, 1976), 1–12.

2. Coleman, "Southern Frontier," *GHQ*, 56:164–65.

3. Ibid., 165–66; Crane, *Southern Frontier*, 210–14.

4. Crane, *Southern Frontier*, 284–97; Coleman, "Southern Frontier," *GHQ*, 56:166–67; any reliable history of Colonial South Carolina.

5. Crane, *Southern Frontier*, 188–91, 229–52; Coleman, "Southern Fron-

tier," *GHQ*, 56:166–69; W. Roy Smith, *South Carolina as a Royal Province, 1719–1776* (New York, 1903), 192–93, 209–11, 244; *Journal of the Commissioners for Trade and Plantations from November 1718 to December 1722* (London, 1925), 197–98, 202–3; *Calendar of State Papers, Colonial Series, America and West Indies, 1717–20* (London, 1933), 143–47, 300–302, 365–68; Records in the PRO relating to South Carolina, 8:78–83, 98, South Carolina Department of Archives, Columbia.

6. Crane, *Southern Frontier*, 292–94; Coleman, "Southern Frontier," *GHQ*, 56:169–70; Richard P. Sherman, *Robert Johnson: Proprietary and Royal Governor of South Carolina* (Columbia, 1966), chap. 9.

7. Crane, *Southern Frontier*, chaps. 3–5.

8. Amos Aschbach Ettinger, *James Edward Oglethorpe: Imperial Idealist* (Oxford, 1936), 88–95.

9. Ibid., 111–12; Crane, *Southern Frontier*, 303–10, 316–18; H. P. Thompson, *Thomas Bray* (London, 1954).

10. Verner W. Crane, "The Philanthropists and the Genesis of Georgia," *AHR* 27 (1921):63–64.

11. Worthington C. Ford, ed., "The Letters of Thomas Coram," *Proceedings of the Massachusetts Historical Society* 56 (1923):20–21, 24.

12. Thompson, *Thomas Bray*, 97–100.

13. *Diary of Percival*, 1:44–46; Ford, ed., "Letters of Thomas Coram," 20–21, 24.

14. Associates of Dr. Thomas Bray Papers, 1635–1911, pt. D, Minutes, 1729–35 (reel 4 of microfilm edition), p. 21. The best account of Bray's and his Associates' actions in securing Georgia's charter is in Verner W. Crane, "Dr. Thomas Bray and the Charitable Colony Project, 1730," *WMQ*, 3d ser., 19 (1962):49–63.

15. Bray Papers, pt. D., 6, 9, 16, 29; *Diary of Percival*, 1:99.

16. Crane, "The Philanthropists and the Genesis of Georgia," *AHR*, 27: 67–68.

17. *Diary of Percival*, 1:378, 382; Bray Papers, pt. D., p. 61; *Egmont's Journal*, 23–24.

18. Crane, *Southern Frontier*, 293–94, 318–20; *Diary of Percival*, 1:98; *Calendar of State Papers, Colonial Series, America and West Indies, 1730* (London, 1937), 141; PRO, CO 5:400, pp. 283–376, esp. 290, 324–28, 357ff., 364.

19. Coleman, "Southern Frontier," *GHQ*, 56:164–66.

20. Verner W. Crane, "The Promotional Literature of Georgia," in *Bibliographical Essays: A Tribute to Wilberforce Eames* (Cambridge, Mass., 1924); Crane, *Southern Frontier*, 315–16.

21. *Calendar of State Papers, Colonial Series, America and West Indies, 1730* (1937), pp. 357–58, 383–84, 394–97; *1731* (1938), 3–4, 12–13, 369; *Journal of the Commissioners for Trade and Plantations from January 1728–9 to*

December 1734 (London, 1928), 165–69, 175, 259; *Diary of Percival*, 1:127, 128–29, 154, 157, 165, 193, 204, 209.

22. *Diary of Percival*, 1:216–17, 219.

23. Ibid., 220, 223–24, 226–27, 231, 232, 235, 240, 254, 260–61, 262.

24. *Calendar of State Papers, Colonial Series, America and West Indies, 1732* (London, 1939), 146; *Diary of Percival*, 1:282–83, 285–86; *CRG*, 1: 65–66.

25. The charter is published in *CRG*, 1:11–26, and in Albert B. Saye, *Georgia's Charter of 1732* (Athens, 1942), which gives a useful introduction.

26. *Diary of Percival*, 1:272–76, 282, 285–86ff.; Journals of the Trustees and Common Council in *CRG*, vols. 1 and 2.

27. *Diary of Percival*, 1:287–88, 301, 305, 309, 313; *CRG*, 1:67, 93–94, 98; 2:13–14.

28. Albert B. Saye, *New Viewpoints in Georgia History* (Athens, 1943), v.

29. E. Merton Coulter and Albert B. Saye, eds., *A List of the Early Settlers of Georgia* (Athens, 1949); *CRG*, vol. 1; *Diary of Percival*, 1:274, 276, and passim.

30. *Diary of Percival*, 1:278, 293, 294–95, 304; Ettinger, *Oglethorpe*, 125–28.

31. Ettinger, *Oglethorpe*, 129–30; Coleman, *Colonial Georgia*, 22–24.

32. Ettinger, *Oglethorpe*, 130–33; Coleman, *Colonial Georgia*, 24–27.

33. Oglethorpe to the Trustees, February 10, 1732–33, in *Coll. GHS*, 1:233–34, and *CRG*, 20:9–10.

34. *S. C. Gaz.*, March 24, 1732/3, reprinted in *CRG*, 3:406.

35. Ettinger, *Oglethorpe*, 133–34; Coleman, *Colonial Georgia*, 32.

36. See the description in Charles C. Jones, Jr., *History of Georgia*, 2 vols. (Boston, 1883), 1:149–51; Coleman, *Colonial Georgia*, 32–33.

37. Oglethorpe to the Trustees, August 12, 1733, *CRG*, 20:27–31; Coleman, *Colonial Georgia*, 33–35.

38. *CRG*, 20:29; Jones, *History of Georgia*, 1:152–55.

39. *CRG*, 20:27–31; Coleman, *Colonial Georgia*, 34–35.

40. The best treatment of individuals as successes or failures in early Georgia is in Sarah B. Gober Temple and Kenneth Coleman, *Georgia Journeys* (Athens, 1961).

41. On the Salzburgers see P. A. Strobel, *The Salzburgers and Their Descendants* (1855; reprint, Athens, 1953); Samuel Urlsperger, comp., *Detailed Reports on the Salzburger Emigrants Who Settled in America . . .*, ed. George Fenwick Jones et al., 7 vols. to date (Athens, 1968–).

42. On military affairs see Ettinger, *Oglethorpe*, and Larry E. Ivers, *British Drums on the Southern Frontier* (Chapel Hill, 1974).

43. On economic affairs see Coleman, *Colonial Georgia*, 111–43; Milton L. Ready, *The Castle Builders: Georgia's Economy under the Trustees, 1732–1754* (New York, 1978); Milton Sydney Heath, *Constructive Liberalism: The Role of the State in Economic Development in Georgia to 1860*

(Cambridge, Mass., 1954); Lewis Cecil Gray, *History of Agriculture in the Southern United States to 1860*, 2 vols. (1933; reprint, New York, 1941); James C. Bonner, *A History of Georgia Agriculture, 1732–1860* (Athens, 1964); Mary Thomas McKinstry, "Silk Culture in the Colony of Georgia," *GHQ* 14 (1930):225–35; Reba C. Strickland, "The Mercantile System as Applied to Georgia," *GHQ* 27 (1938):160–68; Temple and Coleman, *Georgia Journeys*.

The
Beginnings

Τ he apparent ease with which the Indians living on Yamacraw Bluff accepted the Georgia colonists and helped them during the early years, when the venture was most vulnerable, has often been pointed to as evidence of James Oglethorpe's ability to convince even simple savages of the wisdom and significance of his plan for the colony's settlement. As Charles Hudson shows in the following essay, however, the Georgia founder may have received more credit than he was due, for he was hardly working without precedents. The Indians he met and "won" knew well what to expect from Europeans, especially Englishmen—their own socioeconomic system was created largely in response to Old World pressures felt for over two centuries. Beginning even before de Soto, who saw the southeastern tribes "at the apex of their social development," Hudson traces the changes in the lives of Georgia's Indians that brought them to the point, geographically and culturally, at which Oglethorpe found them. In the process he lays the foundation necessary for our understanding of relations between the colony and her Indian neighbors.

In the second essay of this section, Milton Ready examines what many observers, then and now, consider the critical force behind the creation and conduct of the colony—the philanthropic urge among many of England's upper class during the seventeenth and eighteenth centuries. Long recognized as a major factor in the planning of the project, and sometimes blamed for the failure of that "plan," this attempt to deal with the paradox of poverty amid plenty has usually been underestimated and misunderstood. By placing the motivation and expectations behind the founding of Georgia within the broader context of contemporary ideas and ideals, and by relating them to other efforts to solve what many Englishmen perceived to be their nation's most pressing social and economic problem, Ready provides

23

new insights into the principles behind the experiment and the motives of the men who conducted the venture.

To study the origins of Georgia, however, is by necessity to study the man most identified with the colony—James Oglethorpe. Essential to its inception in England, Oglethorpe was also the only Trustee to come to the province, and there he served as general, unofficial governor, and "father" to the people. Though other Trustees were important, his imprint on the enterprise was indelible. To help us better understand the man who seemed to personify the province, Phinizy Spalding has delved into Oglethorpe's early life and the environment in which he lived to reveal the forces that moved him to such herculean efforts. An analysis of the elements that formed his vision and gave him a sense of mission is presented in this essay. The result is a unique study of a man whose view of his own society and its evils caused him to see Georgia as more than an opportunity for the worthy poor to rehabilitate themselves. James Oglethorpe was attempting to carve a place in America for an England made new, able to avoid or prohibit the evils he saw around him. In revealing this quest for a second Zion Spalding adds yet another dimension to our understanding of the Georgia James Oglethorpe sought to create.

So pervasive is the image of Oglethorpe, the "Founder of Georgia," that other Trustees are usually mentioned only in passing and in reference to their support of, or opposition to, that principal member of their body. Many of the Trustees deserve just such treatment, but in a few cases their relegation to obscurity has caused historians to neglect rich sources that would aid in comprehension of the Georgia experiment. Betty Wood's contribution to this collection corrects the most significant of these oversights by assessing the career of John Percival, first Earl of Egmont. Next to Oglethorpe, Egmont was clearly the most influential of the Trustees and perhaps was the one who remained most true to the concept of the colony as first conceived. Drawing on Egmont's diaries and extensive correspondence, Wood calls attention to the contributions of a man who was the staunchest supporter of the Georgia "plan's" most unpopular yet some would contend most significant aspect—the prohibition of Negro slavery. Egmont's efforts in this regard reveal clearly the tensions between the ideals that brought Georgia into being and the forces that worked to dismantle the "plan."

CHARLES M. HUDSON

The Genesis of Georgia's Indians

HEN JAMES OGLETHORPE and his first contingent of colonists put ashore at Yamacraw Bluff in February 1733, they pitched their tents on the edge of a territory that was to become the state of Georgia. Even though they were greeted by Tomochichi and his small Yamacraw band, the Georgia territory at that time was largely devoid of Indians; clusters of Indian villages could be found only at a few places along the margins. Yet the Indians of the Georgia territory had once been far more numerous and far more impressive than Tomochichi and his outcast Yamacraws. To appreciate fully the degree to which these and other southern Indians had been transformed by their relations with Europeans, it is necessary to go back to the time these first encounters began.

The Indians whom Oglethorpe met had already had far more experience with Europeans than he probably realized. If the Yamacraws had possessed a literate culture, complete with historians and learned societies, and if they had counted their first meeting with Europeans as an epochal event, Oglethorpe would have arrived at Yamacraw Bluff at about the time Tomochichi and his people were observing their bicentennial. They would have just celebrated—or, more probably, mourned—the coming of Lucas Vásquez de Ayllón in 1526, or if Ayllón's short-lived colony was not sufficiently epochal, they would have been accepting grant applications for a suitable remembrance of Hernando de Soto, who appeared in 1540.

The first Spaniards briefly cast anchor on the coast of the lower South between 1514 and 1516 and again in 1521, when the slave-raiders Pedro de Quejo and Francisco Gordillo tricked some Indians onto their ship and sailed away with them.[1] But the first attempt at colonization was by Lucas Vásquez de Ayllón in 1526. Ayllón first put his colonists ashore at Winyaw Bay in South Carolina, but it soon became obvious that this was not a good place for a settlement. He then moved forty to forty-five leagues down the coast to the river Gualdape, which may have been the Savannah River[2] or one of the rivers not far to the south.[3] Here Ayllón built the town of San Miguel de Gualdape, the site of which has not yet been found. Ayllón and his colonists appear not to have penetrated very far inland or to have had much sustained contact with the Indians. Within a few months, Ayllón's colonists fell ill from disease and starvation, and the survivors abandoned the colony.

The next Spaniard to walk upon the soil of the Georgia territory was Hernando de Soto, who explored far into the interior, encountering as he traveled many of the larger Indian societies of the region. After landing on the western coast of Florida, de Soto wintered in the chiefdom of Apalachee, near present Tallahassee, Florida. On March 3, 1540, he resumed his march, proceeding northward to the Flint River and crossing near Newton, Georgia.[4] From here he went to Capachequi, a cluster of villages along Chickasawhatchee Creek southwest of Albany. Capachequi appears to have been a small but bellicose chiefdom. All of its inhabitants, like those of Apalachee, evaded the Spaniards by running away from their towns and hiding in the swamps. They succeeded in ambushing a small party of de Soto's men, killing one and wounding three others.

Departing from Capachequi, de Soto and his army traveled northward through a "desert," an uninhabited area along the western side of the Flint River. They built a bridge and crossed the Flint, probably near where present Dooley, Sumter, and Macon counties come together. Soon after crossing they came to another chiefdom, Toa, which was probably located south of the town of Montezuma. They remained in Toa only briefly, and the chroniclers have very little to say about their visit.

From Toa, de Soto proceeded rapidly northeastward to the Ocmulgee River, where he came upon the first town of the chiefdom of Ichisi. This town was situated on an island in the river, perhaps near the southwestern corner of Twiggs County. Continuing their journey, they followed a trail up the west bank of the Ocmulgee River, passing through other towns of Ichisi before arriving at the main town, which was probably at the Lamar mound site just east of Macon.

Ichisi was the first chiefdom whose people received de Soto and his men in peace. Emissaries from the chief of Ichisi came out to meet them with peace offerings of dressed deerskins. As the army approached the main town, women clothed in white mantles woven from mulberry fibers brought corn cakes and bunches of wild onions for the Spaniards to eat. On a mound in the main town of Ichisi, de Soto set up a cross, which the Indians were said to have worshiped, though they could have had little understanding of what they witnessed.[5]

Heading eastward from the main town of Ichisi, de Soto came to the Oconee River just south of present Milledgeville. Here his party came to the first town of a chiefdom that was larger than Ichisi and encountered for the first time several chiefs who were under the sway of a paramount chief.[6] The first of these, Altamaha, probably had his town at the Shinholzer mound group south of Milledgeville, near where the expedition crossed the river. The paramount chief, Ocute, appears to have had his town at the large multiple-mound site on Shoulderbone Creek, northwest of Sparta. Ocute's power also extended over another chief, Patofa, who probably had his town on the Oconee River near Greensboro.

De Soto quickly learned that the entire larger chiefdom of Ocute was at war with the chiefdom of Cofitachequi, which lay to the northeast. Cofitachequi was one of de Soto's main destinations because the young Indian guide he had captured in Apalachee had persuaded him that he would find gold and silver there. But de Soto did not know when he departed from the Oconee River that the main towns of Cofitachequi lay on the Catawba-Wateree River, more than 130 miles away, and that between the Oconee River and the Catawba-Wateree River there lay a vast "desert" of unoccupied land. After departing from Ocute, de Soto and his army were on the trail for fourteen days before they reached the first town of Cofitachequi, and they were very hungry when they got there because they depended upon the Indians for food. They were so hungry, in fact, that they killed and butchered some of their precious herd of pigs, which they ate only in times of dire necessity.

The "desert" of Ocute included the middle course of the Savannah River as well as a large expanse of land on either side of the river that is today regarded as prime real estate. Earlier, Indians lived along this part of the Savannah River, but in 1540 it was abandoned and was clearly functioning as a no-man's-land between two warring chiefdoms. The uninhabited area between Capachequi and Toa through which de Soto passed earlier was tiny when compared to the desert of Ocute.

After departing Cofitachequi, de Soto set out northward following

"Trustees of Georgia." Oil painting (1734–35) by William Verelst, depicting Oglethorpe and the Trustees in London with Tomochichi and other Yamacraw Indians. (Courtesy of The Henry Francis du Pont Winterthur Museum.)

the Catawba River to its headwaters. Then he ascended the Blue Ridge Mountains and near the site of present Asheville, North Carolina, picked up a trail that ran alongside the French Broad River. He followed this trail to the other side of the mountains, rested for a time, and then proceeded southward down the Tennessee Valley and entered the northwestern corner of the territory that is now Georgia. Here, near the present town of Carters, on the Coosawattee River, he came to Coosa, whose chief was even more impressive than the chief of Ocute had been. The chief of Coosa possessed some measure of political influence, if not real power, over Indians in an immense area stretching all the way from Newport, Tennessee, in the northeast to the vicinity of Rome, Georgia, in the south, and he also was influential as far as the region around present Childersburg, Alabama.

The de Soto chronicles tell us nothing about large areas of the Georgia territory. They say nothing, for example, about the people who lived along the Chattahoochee River, about those who may have lived on the headwaters of the Savannah River, or about those on the coast. But the chronicles together with the results of several decades of archaeological research provide enough information for us to construct a general picture of the Indians of Georgia at the dawn of history. It is clear, for example, that the cultivation of corn was their most important consideration, which was why their population centers were all located near the rich alluvial soils of the larger rivers. These societies fell short of the large aboriginal states which the Spaniards found in Mexico and South America, but they were far more complex than simple egalitarian bands. They were chiefdoms, with leaders who were accorded high social honor and who possessed some political power. Moreover, these chiefdoms enjoyed a full ritual life with a priesthood and invested heavily in maintaining a skilled military organization.

It is also clear that these sixteenth-century Georgia chiefdoms were variable in size. Capachequi was small; Ichisi somewhat larger; Ocute larger still; and Coosa the largest of all. No one is prepared to hazard a guess at the size of the populations of the larger chiefdoms, but it is clear that they were considerable or they would not have been able to feed de Soto and his eight hundred or so uninvited guests for weeks or even months at a time. It is also clear that their chiefs were treated with far more deference and respect than those of the smaller chiefdoms. If the chief of Ichisi was treated with deference, the chroniclers do not mention it. But when de Soto approached Coosa, the chief, dressed in finery, came out seated upon a litter carried on the shoulders of his people. He was surrounded by his principal men and by many attendants playing flutes and singing.[7]

To de Soto and his men, Coosa was a land of plenty, the most attractive Indian society they had encountered up to that point in their explorations. It was so attractive that one of their number, a Levantine named Feryada, decided to desert the expedition and stay with the Indians. Perhaps he would not have been emboldened to do so had not de Soto left behind at Coosa another of his company, a black slave named Robles, who had become ill and could not walk.[8]

As the de Soto expedition wound its way through the Southeast, it was accompanied by a substantial number of Indians. Some of them the Spaniards seized and put in chains; others went along as burden-bearers either voluntarily or at the behest of their chiefs. Whether the Spaniards later released any of these burden-bearers is unclear. Many of the enslaved Indians died of mistreatment and starvation.

When de Soto left Coosa, he forced its chief and some of his relatives to go along as hostages. When they reached the town of Talisi, on the Coosa River in Alabama, de Soto released the chief but refused to release his sister. The chief departed in tears because of the loss of his sister and because he had been taken so far from his home.[9]

De Soto and his army were the first and the last Europeans to see the Indians of interior Georgia at the apex of their social development. During the century and a half following the de Soto expedition, these Indians were profoundly changed. The causes of this change were largely biological, particularly the epidemic diseases from the Old World for which they had little resistance. An early, perhaps the very first, outbreak of an Old World epidemic disease among the southeastern Indians occurred just before the de Soto expedition, for when de Soto reached Cofitachequi in 1540, he learned that the chiefdom had been struck by an epidemic two years earlier and that many towns were deserted. Several buildings were piled full of corpses. When Juan Pardo, the next Spaniard to explore the interior of the Carolinas, visited Cofitachequi in 1566–68, the population had declined even more.[10] By this time Cofitachequi no longer had a paramount chief as it had in de Soto's day. When a party from Tristan de Luna's Gulf Coast colony went to Coosa in 1559, the chiefdom had declined so much that it hardly seemed to be the same place de Soto had visited.[11]

European diseases such as smallpox, measles, and influenza were particularly destructive among the Indians both because they had no re-

A New Map of Georgia, with Part of Ca[rolina]

Drawn from Original Draughts, assisted by the

Collected by Eman: Bowen Geographe[r]

GULF OF MEXICO

ASCENSION BAY

A map of Georgia by
Emanuel Bowen, 1748.
(Courtesy of the
Georgia Department of
Archives and History.)

sistance and because when the germs and viruses were first introduced to a particular population everyone became infected and was ill at the same time so no one could take care of anyone else. Lack of care resulted in particularly high mortality among infants and children.[12]

Many of these diseases require a relatively numerous host population in order to become endemic. Measles, for example, may require a population as large as two hundred thousand or more to maintain itself. Indian populations quickly fell below this number. Their decimation did not rid them of the germs and viruses, however, because in the late sixteenth century Spain established a small colony in Florida and coastal Georgia, and in the early seventeenth century England established a colony in Virginia, both of which were periodically visited by infected individuals from Europe and the islands of the Caribbean. In this way, in the later sixteenth century and throughout the seventeenth century, very small numbers of Europeans in Virginia and Florida were able to wreak terrible havoc among the Indians even though they seldom visited Indian towns in the interior. If an occasional Indian living near those colonies became infected and carried his infection to inland villages, mortality rates of 50 percent or more could result, and such losses were devastating to the chiefdoms. Many of the large mound centers were abandoned, and much of the political and ritual superstructure of the Indian societies appears to have crumbled and fallen away.

Old World epidemics were one of the catastrophes that changed the Indians in the early colonial period. Perhaps an even greater catastrophe was that the Europeans brought with them a new economic system that would, in time, disrupt the cultures and societies of the Indians and ultimately alienate them from their land. Under this economic system, a small number of north European states developed the capability of sustaining a trade in necessities—raw materials—from far-flung places. These European states began competing with each other for the right to extract wealth from people in distant places, and they reinvested this wealth in ways that ensured ever more profit. It was a system whose lineaments were still vague in the early seventeenth century, but toward the end of that century it began to become clear that England's social and economic structure was carrying the day.[13]

Spain was the first European power to colonize the New World, but her fortunes had begun to slip before the end of the sixteenth century. Late in the century, with her economy in deep depression, Spain belatedly colonized Florida and Georgia. But it soon became clear that she lacked the wherewithal to extract wealth from her new colony. Operating through a ponderous, old-fashioned imperial bureaucracy, Spain was able to establish only the most tenuous toeholds along the coast. There is no doubt that Pedro Menéndez de Avilés, who lacked nothing in ambition, ability, and aggressiveness, wanted to exploit and control the interior. After extirpating the French Huguenots from their colony at the mouth of the St. Johns River and establishing several outposts of his own, in 1566–68 he sent one of his captains, Juan Pardo, to take control of the interior and to build a road to the Spanish silver mines in Zacatecas, Mexico. Pardo dutifully entered the interior and, following the trail that de Soto had followed earlier, penetrated beyond the Blue Ridge Mountains into the Tennessee Valley before the Indians forced him to turn back. On his return trip he built a string of small forts along the trail and stationed a missionary, Sebastian Montero, among the Guatari Indians, who at that time probably lived near Salisbury, North Carolina.[14] But within a few years the Indians forced the Spaniards to abandon all of these interior forts and to return to the coast.

The best the Spaniards could do was to maintain a presence on the coast so as to offer some protection for their shipping, provide a haven for shipwrecked sailors, and impede French and English colonization. They attempted to achieve this end by controlling the Indians through their mission system, converting the Indians to Christianity and controlling them by gradually transforming them into Spanish-speaking peasants. One of the main functions of the missions was to discipline the Indians.[15]

The role of the missionary was demanding, dangerous, and not infrequently fatal. Pedro Martinez, the first Spanish missionary to set foot on the coast of Georgia (actually on Cumberland Island) was met by a group of Indians who promptly brained him with their war clubs. Beginning in 1566 the Jesuits founded several missions along the coast, but after numerous setbacks they were withdrawn in 1572.[16] The Franciscans who followed them were more successful. Beginning in 1573 they established a string of missions from St. Augustine up the coast of Georgia to the Port Royal area of South Carolina. But as the friars attempted to impose their wills on the Indians, to persuade them to abandon their own customs and instead practice Catholic and Spanish customs, the Indians often rebelled. Grievances accumulated, and then a particular incident, such as being forced to surrender some of their food, would prompt them to kill their priest and sometimes soldiers as well. The most serious uprising was the Juanillo revolt of 1597, touched off by two friars who interceded when Juanillo, the son of the chief of Guale, was about to assume the office of chief. Juanillo was not compliant enough to suit the priests, and they saw to it that the chieftainship passed to an older man whom they could more easily manipulate. Other disaffected Indians collected around Juanillo, and together they killed one of the friars and then went from mission to mission killing other priests.

After the Juanillo revolt was put down, the Guale missions along the Georgia coast were gradually rebuilt, and as the seventeenth century wore on, the Indians became more docile, although the rebellions never ceased entirely. But even though the Spaniards succeeded well enough in their missions on the coast, they were never able to establish viable missions in the interior of the Georgia territory. The Indians of La Tama—no doubt the same as de Soto's Altamaha on the upper Oconee River—asked for a missionary, but none was ever sent. In 1597 Governor Gonzalo Mendez de Canço, wishing to exploit the interior, sent in a soldier who spoke the language of Guale, along with two missionaries. They visited La Tama and went on to Ocute, a day's travel away as it had been in de Soto's day.[17] The chief of Ocute remembered de Soto's visit and wept when he spoke of it, perhaps remembering the agony it had caused.

There is no doubt that the missions transformed some Indians into loyal Spanish subjects. In 1600, for example, Doña María, the chieftainess of Nombre de Dios, a village near St. Augustine, wrote to Philip III extolling the good work of Governor Canço.[18] But beyond the neighborhood of the missions the Spanish did not possess the means to intercede in the affairs of the Indians and to force them to change their way of life. The English, on the other hand, proved to be dreadfully capable of effecting changes. At first they used a method common to slavers in Africa.[19] They would provide arms to a friendly group living near their coastal settlements and set them to attacking Indians at a distance with the object of capturing them and selling them into slavery. This slave trade in Indians began in Virginia. By 1661 some Indians whom the Spaniards called "Chichumecos" were attacking Guale. The Indians told the Spaniards that these Chichumecos were cannibals, perhaps because they took prisoners away with them who were never seen again.[20] But the truth about Chichumecos became evident in 1670, when the settlers of Charles Town found that the Cussos and Cusabos who lived nearby were terrified of these same

Indians, whom they called "Westoes." The Westoes had guns supplied to them by traders in Virginia, and they were capturing coastal Indians to be taken back to Virginia and sold as slaves.[21] In an attempt to escape the Westoes, some of the Indians of Guale moved inland to La Tama.

But the economic impact of the traders from Virginia proved to be insignificant when compared to that of the traders from Charles Town. In 1674, just four years after Charles Town was founded, Henry Woodward entered into an agreement with the Westoes, who had built a fortified village on the Savannah River (called at that time the River of the Westoes). He agreed to trade guns and ammunition to the Westoes in exchange for young Indian slaves and animal skins. The English formed similar alliances with the Yuchis and with the "Chiluques."[22] This latter word is probably a variant of the Muskogean word *čilo·kkita*, meaning "people of a different speech." Hence these were probably Siouan-speaking or Cherokee-speaking people from upper South Carolina.

The Spaniards quickly began to feel the effects of these brash, aggressive Englishmen. When Marcos Delgado journeyed from the Apalachee missions to the junction of the Coosa and Tallapoosa rivers in Alabama in 1686, probably the first Spaniard to visit this area since Tristan de Luna's men over a century earlier, he found that the Qusate Indians had moved there from a great distance to the north because they were being harassed by the English and their Chichumeco and "Chalaque" allies.[23] In de Soto's day Qusate (called "Coste") had been an important town situated on Bussel Island in the mouth of the Little Tennessee River. In the late seventeenth century the Qusate Indians had fled some 260 miles to the south to escape the English and their Indian slave-catchers. The Coosas also fled from their home in the northwest corner of Georgia southward to Alabama to build a town on the Coosa River, to which they bequeathed their name. Since Delgado appears not to have made contact with the Coosas, it is possible that they had not yet arrived at the time of his visit. Other Indians, such as the Chiaha, who in de Soto's day lived to the east of present Knoxville, Tennessee, moved southward to take up residence on the Chattahoochee River. When Delgado attempted to form an alliance with the Qusate and others who had fled to the South, they let it be known that they would prefer to form an alliance with the English. Even though the English and their Indian mercenaries had run them out of their homeland, the English supplied more guns, powder, and balls than did the Spanish, and this consideration was more important than any other.

The Westoes on the Savannah River did not realize that an agreement with one Englishman was not binding on all other Englishmen, particularly if a profit might be made. But the hard truth came home to them in 1680, when a powerful faction of Carolina colonists decided to cut in on the lucrative trade. This faction armed yet another group of Indians, the Savannahs, and set them on the Westoes. When the shooting was over, only about fifty Westoes escaped. The others had been killed or enslaved.[24] For a time the Savannah Indians enjoyed the favor of the Charles Town traders, and they built a town near the falls of the great river that took their name.

The Carolinians now set their slave-catchers upon the missions of Guale, whose Indians were especially desired because many of them had already learned the rudiments of European culture and labor. By 1683 Guale was reeling from repeated slaving raids. Santa Catalina was the first to be abandoned. Zapala, St. Simons, and Tolomato soon followed; all of Guale was abandoned by 1686. And within another two decades, particularly after James Moore's raid in 1704, the Apalachee missions in western Florida had collapsed and the Spaniards were largely confined to St. Augustine.[25]

Some of the Indians who fled the missions to join the English had scores to settle with the Spaniards. Under the regimen in the missions the Indians had to labor hard, they lived in poverty, and they were often mistreated. They had accumulated grievances, and they wanted revenge. Their intimate knowledge of the missions must have provided invaluable military intelligence when the English planned their raids.

After the Charles Town traders began their economic penetration, life for Indians in the Georgia territory became hazardous for some and untenable for others. Once these merchants put guns in the hands of their slave-catchers, a grim arms race was set in motion. To avoid being killed or enslaved, other Indians had to acquire guns and ammunition, and the only way they could do so was to produce a commodity—initially Indian slaves and later deerskins. In addition, the Indians often had to move their towns further into the interior or closer to the towns of other Indians who were willing to combine forces for mutual defense.[26] If life for the Indians was hazardous before, it was doubly so now. In all the land there was no safe place. A mere walk to fetch a jug of water could expose one to capture and a lifetime of slavery.

The Genesis of Georgia's Indians

The most striking characteristic of the English colonists, particularly as contrasted with the Spanish, was the degree to which their economic system shattered, dislocated, and remade Indian societies. The English trading regime not only caused Indians to change their economic livelihood and move their towns hundreds of miles, but it also basically changed the nature of the Indians. The Spaniards converted some Indians to Christianity, but they did not totally transform them as the English did. Apalachee was Apalachee in 1539, when de Soto wintered there, and with changes it was still Apalachee in 1700. But by 1705, after Moore's raids, Apalachee was no more. An even more startling social transformation began around 1685, when some Guale Indians began deserting their missions and settling in the Port Royal area to be nearer to the English. Many other Indians quickly settled around them. Here they became known by a different name—Yamasees—by which they served the English as mercenaries in attacking the Indians in the Guale missions. They had left their missions as Guales and returned as Yamasees to attack these same missions.[27]

By about 1710 the only Indians in the Georgia territory were those who had come to terms with the Charles Town traders, as was clearly shown to be true at the small trading post whose remains were discovered in the course of the archaeological excavations on the site of Ocmulgee National Monument at Macon in the 1930s. This post, built perhaps as early as 1685, was surrounded by a five-sided stockade and a ditch, and outside the stockade were the remains of a substantial number of Indian houses. These Indians, who were called the "Ochese Creek Indians," no doubt worked for the traders as hunters, slave-catchers, mercenaries, and burden-bearers. The similarity between "Ochese" and "Ichisi"—the name of the chiefdom de Soto encountered in this area—is obvious. In time the English shortened "Ochese Creek Indians" to "Creeks" and used this word for all the Indians on the Chattahoochee and the Coosa-Tallapoosa rivers.[28]

The aggressiveness of the Charles Town trading regime stimulated a more potent and explosive resistance among the Indians than did the Spanish mission system. The traders possessed such life-or-death economic power over the Indians that they were tempted to mistreat and cheat them, and many of them did. In 1715 the Yamasees spearheaded a widespread revolt against the Charles Town traders and the entire Carolina colony. In a wide-ranging, coordinated effort, thousands of Indians rose up simultaneously. Many traders were killed, plantations along the coast were burned, and colonists who were able fled to

Charles Town for safety. Characteristically, however, the Indians were unable to sustain a far-flung alliance, just as they were unable to sustain a military siege. The Carolinians succeeded in breaking up the alliance and in driving the Indians further from their frontier. The Yamasees who started the war fled back to the Spaniards in Florida, who were by this time so desperate for allies that they embraced them again. But they found no safety there. The English slave-catchers hunted them mercilessly until, in time, they were reduced to a mere handful.[29] In addition, the Macon Trading Post was abandoned (the traders were probably killed), and the Ochese Creek Indians fled westward to the Chattahoochee and the Coosa-Tallapoosa rivers.

After the Carolina colony recovered from the Yamasee War, the Charles Town traders gradually began trafficking less in Indian slaves and more in dressed deerskins. The enslavement of Indians declined not for humanitarian reasons but because the Indian population had fallen to such low levels that the trade in Indian slaves became less and less profitable. Also, perhaps because of their vulnerability to disease, Indian slaves never brought as high prices as African slaves.

At this juncture in history, the most favorable circumstance a southern Indian could hope for was to live deep in the interior of the South and to have around himself the greatest possible number of European interests—Spanish, British, and French—contesting for supremacy. Because the Indians held the balance of power in the interior, they could use their position to play one European interest against the others to their own advantage. In exchange for arms, ammunition, and other goods, the Indians would promise to align themselves with one power or another. Perhaps the most adept at this game was Emperor Brims of the Lower Creeks, who sometimes accepted gifts from several European powers, making promises to all. But throughout the eighteenth century, as these colonial powers fell away one by one—first the Spanish, then the French, then the British—the position of the Indians in the South was progressively weakened.[30]

These, then, were some of the long-term and short-term historical forces that help account not only for the geographical locations of the small number of Indians inhabiting the fringes of the Georgia territory in 1733 but also for the nature of their societies at that time. The Indians of the Georgia territory were descended from sixteenth-century horticultural chiefdoms who had been decimated by a series of Old World diseases beginning in the sixteenth century and continuing throughout the seventeenth century. The survivors of this germ-and-

virus-caused holocaust were shattered by yet another holocaust beginning in the late seventeenth century, when they collided with traders,
soldiers, herdsmen, and frontiersmen of the oncoming modern world
system.

By 1733 the Indians of the Georgia territory were socially and economically differentiated in their relations with the Carolina colonists
in general and the traders in particular. The various Indian groups differed in the degree to which they retained social and cultural autonomy. The English referred to the most autonomous Indians as "nations."[31] Such were the Cherokees in the northern part of the Georgia
territory, who lived in towns on the Chattooga and upper Chattahoochee rivers.[32] Some of these towns, such as Estatoe, Taucoe, Chotte,
and Nacooche, were in the general vicinity of where their ancestors
had lived since perhaps A.D. 1000.[33] In fact, of all the Indians in the
Southeast, the Cherokees, despite population loss through diseases, appear to have been stronger vis-à-vis other southeastern Indians in the
eighteenth century than they had been in the sixteenth century. Their
mountain homeland conferred a decided military advantage, perhaps
even against early slave-catchers, and may have saved them from mos-
quito-borne Old World diseases such as malaria. By 1733 the Cherokees had for many years been supplying the Carolina traders with
some of their heaviest and best deerskins, and this trade was the basis
of their "nationhood."

Though less well known archaeologically, the Lower Creeks on the
Chattahoochee River near present Columbus also appear to have co-
alesced within their ancestral homeland. But the Lower Creeks were
more composite than were the Cherokees, having absorbed such far-
flung peoples as the Chiahas from the Tennessee Valley, refugees from
the Spanish missions, and, in time, the Yuchis, who lived in the Georgia
colony in the early years.[34] Like the Cherokees, the Lower Creeks in
1733 retained some of their autonomy by trading deerskins and also
by playing a role in frontier politics.

Other Indians served the traders more directly and therefore possessed less autonomy. These might properly be called "traders' Indians." For example, in 1737 a small band of Chickasaws, who had
originally settled near New Windsor in South Carolina, moved westward across the Savannah River after Fort Augusta was built. They
acted as mercenaries, interpreters, hunters, scouts, and in other capaci-
ties for the Augusta traders.[35] It is clear that these Chickasaws served
the traders more than they did frontier farmers. When some of them

moved away from Augusta to the Ogeechee River, the traders persuaded them to return to the Augusta–Fort Moore area even though the frontier settlers in the area were afraid of them and did not want them.[36]

The hundred or so Yamacraw Indians who lived near John and Mary Musgrove's trading post were also traders' Indians. They had been expelled from the Lower Creeks for some unspecified crime, but whatever the nature of their offense, they clearly owed their existence to the Musgroves and later to Oglethorpe and his colonists.

Even more detribalized and less autonomous than traders' Indians were those known as "settlement Indians." Living in and around the settlements and plantations, they served the colonists by hunting for game, destroying vermin and predators such as wolves, and tracking down runaway slaves, some of whom were Indians. They existed more as individuals and as families than as ethnic enclaves, and they had no chiefs.[37] The arrival of the Georgia colonists began the Yamacraws' transition to this status, though most of Tomochichi's people eventually rejected that fate and returned to the Creek nation.

Thus Oglethorpe's arrival at Yamacraw Bluff in 1733 did not mean the beginning of the end of Indian life in the new Georgia colony. That had been accomplished by the biological reunification of Old World and New World peoples through the agency of Spanish explorers nearly two centuries before, as well as by the ties of economic dependency more recently created by the Charles Town traders. By Oglethorpe's day Indian life had been all but eliminated in the area that would be settled by the Georgia colonists. Tomochichi was not the aboriginal chief that Coosa or Ichisi had been. Nor was he the chief that Brims was at that time. Tomochichi was a white man's Indian, and he had become so even before Oglethorpe's arrival. Oglethorpe was a visionary. He wanted to found a humane, exemplary colony with an enlightened approach to the "Indian problem" that had plagued previous British colonies.[38] Perhaps, then, we can forgive him for making a band of trading Indians appear to be more than they really were. But we cannot allow ourselves the same delusion, else we deny that Indians, as all other people, have been transformed by history many times over.

The Genesis of Georgia's Indians

NOTES

1. Paul E. Hoffman, "A New Voyage of North American Discovery: Pedro de Salazar's Voyage to the 'Island of Giants,' " *FHQ* 58 (1980):415–26; David B. Quinn, *North America from Earliest Discovery to First Settlement: The Norse Voyages to 1612* (New York, 1977), 144–45.

2. John R. Swanton, *Early History of the Creek Indians and Their Neighbors*, Bureau of American Ethnology Bulletin no. 73 (Washington, D.C., 1922), 40.

3. Paul E. Hoffman, "Why Santa Elena?" paper presented at the Forty-eighth Annual Meeting of the Southern Historical Association, Memphis, Tennessee, November 5, 1982.

4. The de Soto route presented here is based on research by myself and two colleagues, Marvin T. Smith and Chester B. DePratter, in which we have used current archaeological information in combination with a detailed analysis of the documents of the de Soto, Pardo, and Luna explorations. Especially useful has been the extensive documentation of the Pardo explorations, which included many of the same towns through which de Soto passed. For our Pardo findings, see Chester B. DePratter, Charles Hudson, and Marvin T. Smith, "The Route of Juan Pardo's Explorations in the Interior Southeast, 1566–1568," *FHQ*, in press. Our findings for de Soto's route through central and eastern Georgia are contained in an article currently submitted for publication: Charles Hudson, Marvin T. Smith, and Chester B. DePratter, "The Route of the De Soto Expedition: From Apalachee to Chiaha." The route through northwestern Georgia can be found in Chester B. DePratter, Charles Hudson, and Marvin T. Smith, "The De Soto Expedition: From Chiaha to Mabila," in Reid R. Badger and Lawrence A. Clayton, eds., *Alabama and the Borderlands: From Prehistory to Statehood* (Tuscaloosa, in press).

5. Rodrigo Ranjel, "A Narrative of de Soto's Expedition," in Edward G. Bourne, ed., *Narratives of the Career of Hernando de Soto* (New York, 1922), 87–89.

6. Marvin T. Smith and Stephen A. Kowalewski, "Tentative Identification of a Prehistoric 'Province' in Piedmont Georgia," *Early Georgia* 8 (1980): 1–13.

7. A Gentleman of Elvas, "Relaçam . . . ," in *Narratives of De Soto in the Conquest of Florida*, ed. and trans. Buckingham Smith (New York, 1866; reprint, Gainesville, Fla., 1968), 75–76.

8. Ranjel, "Narrative," 113; Garcilaso de la Vega, *The Florida of the Inca*, trans. John G. Varner and Jeannette J. Varner (Austin, 1962), 347.

9. Ranjel, "Narrative," 116.

10. DePratter, Hudson, and Smith, "Route of Pardo's Explorations."

11. Fray Augustín Dávila Padilla, *Historia de la fundación y discurso de la*

provincia Santiago de Mexico de la Orden de Predicadores (Brussels, 1625), 205–17, trans. Fanny Bandelier in Swanton, *Early History*, 231–39.

12. George R. Milner, "Epidemic Diseases in the Postcontact Southeast: A Reappraisal," *Midcontinental Journal of Archaeology* 5 (1980):39–56.

13. Immanuel Wallerstein, *The Modern World-System* (New York, 1974); L. S. Stavrianos, *Global Rift: The Third World Comes of Age* (New York, 1981).

14. Michael V. Gannon, "Sebastian Montero: Pioneer American Missionary, 1566–1572," *Catholic Historical Review* 51 (1965–66):335–53.

15. Herbert E. Bolton, "The Mission as a Frontier Institution in the Spanish American Colonies," *AHR* 23 (1917–18):42–61.

16. John Tate Lanning, *The Spanish Missions of Georgia* (Chapel Hill, 1935), 33–38.

17. Inquiry made officially before Don Gonzalo Mendez de Canço, governor of the province of Florida, upon the situation of La Tama and its riches, and the English Settlement, February 4, 1600, AGI Est. 54, Caj. 5, Lef. 9, folio 17, Mary Ross Papers, Georgia Department of Archives and History, Atlanta.

18. Doña María, Chief of Nombre de Dios, to Philip III, Archivo de Indias, Seville, Santo Domingo 231:54/5/16/, trans. in David B. Quinn, ed., *New American World*, 5 vols. (New York, 1979), 5:102–3.

19. R. W. Beachey, *The Slave Trade of Eastern Africa* (London, 1976), 182–83, 186–87.

20. Lanning, *Spanish Missions*, 209.

21. Verner W. Crane, *The Southern Frontier, 1670–1732* (Durham, 1928; reprint, 1956), 6–12; William Robert Snell, "Indian Slavery in Colonial South Carolina, 1671–1795" (Ph.D. dissertation, University of Alabama, 1972), 7–19.

22. Crane, *Southern Frontier*, 16–17.

23. Mark F. Boyd, "The Expedition of Marcos Delgado from Apalachee to the Upper Creek County in 1686," *FHQ* 16 (1937): 3–32.

24. Snell, "Indian Slavery," 25–27, 34.

25. Lanning, *Spanish Missions*, 219–28.

26. Charles Hudson, "Why the Southeastern Indians Slaughtered Deer," in Shepard Krech III, ed., *Indians, Animals, and the Fur Trade: A Critique of Keepers of the Game* (Athens, 1981), 168–70.

27. Crane, *Southern Frontier*, 25–29; Lanning, *Spanish Missions*, 227.

28. Mark Williams and Charles Hudson, *Ocmulgee* (Washington, D.C., in press).

29. Crane, *Southern Frontier*, 162–86.

30. Hudson, "Why the Southeastern Indians Slaughtered Deer," 169.

31. Charles Hudson, *The Catawba Nation* (Athens, 1970), 47–51.

32. Betty Anderson Smith, "Distribution of Eighteenth-Century Cherokee

Settlements," in Duane H. King, ed., *The Cherokee Indian Nation: A Troubled History* (Knoxville, 1979), 47–48.

33. Roy S. Dickens, Jr., "Mississippian Settlement Patterns in the Appalachian Summit Area: The Pisgah and Qualla Phases," in Bruce D. Smith, ed., *Mississippian Settlement Patterns* (New York, 1978), 132–35.

34. Swanton, *Early History*, 215ff.

35. William Stephens, *A Journal of the Proceedings in Georgia Beginning October 20, 1737* (London, 1742), 55.

36. Wilbur R. Jacobs, *The Appalachian Frontier: The Edmond Atkin Report and Plan of 1755* (Lincoln, Nebr., 1967), 45–46.

37. Ibid., 44–45.

38. Phinizy Spalding, *Oglethorpe in America* (Chicago, 1977), 76–97 and passim.

MILTON L. READY

Philanthropy and the Origins of Georgia

HE GENESIS of the colony of Georgia can be traced through Hanoverian England's concern for prison reform, imperial defense, and trade. The impulse for Georgia's founding lay in philanthropy, particularly in the behavior of altruists such as Thomas Bray and James Edward Oglethorpe. Indeed, a close study of the broader relationships between the philanthropists Oglethorpe and Thomas Coram, for example, and the great proprietors of England, men such as the first Earl of Egmont and Baron Digby, shows the Georgia plan to be more than the "detailed . . . petty specifications" of narrow-minded, paternalistic Trustees.[1]

As a representation of eighteenth-century English philanthropy, the Georgia scheme reflected the cooperation of humanitarians, politicians, and the nobility in a project that, had it succeeded, would have anticipated a twentieth-century welfare state. Rather than showing the "limited aspiration of the England of that day," the altruism of the Georgia plan exhibited an attempt to solve Hanoverian England's most pressing problems, poverty in the midst of plenty.[2]

Poverty threatened a changing, newly affluent England in the early decades of the eighteenth century. On the whole, Georgian society was diverse, characterized by dissimilar experiences of the rich and the poor, town and country, London and the provinces. Sustained by its permeability and by the adaptability of the elite, the social hierarchy remained stable and confident. The key to English unity lay in the actions of the great proprietors, the very top people of society who were, by turns, both capitalists and philanthropists, eager to innovate yet protective of the values they were helping to erode. Social arrangements, the sedative effect of constitutionalism in the political arena, and the power of the government all conspired to perpetuate the position of the great proprietors of England. It was from this group that the Georgia Trustees emerged.[3]

Hanoverian England's new affluence from increased foreign trade and commercialized agriculture created new values, new tensions, and new problems. Not surprisingly, the gulf between the rich and the poor widened from 1713 to 1760. The enormous growth in the economy, rapid increase in population, and accompanying political pressures redoubled the concern of the nation's rulers to discipline and restrain the populace and to ensure the dominance of the great proprietors.

New institutions and new methods had to be developed to sustain power. The "perils of neglect" of the seventeenth century were replaced by the "pains of attention" of the eighteenth, which became the age of confinement in England. Greater supervision and control—of children, the mad, criminals, the politically radical, and especially the unfortunate poor—were necessary to keep people in their place. Georgians wanted to isolate all deviants in their society. Voluntary associations such as the societies for the reformation of manners, for the treatment of the mad, for the defense of property, and for the relief of debtors all demonstrated willingness on the part of the leaders of society to participate in the regulation of their social inferiors.[4] One group in particular—the minority of the population that lived in dire poverty—seemed to threaten the post-Enlightenment ideals of Hanoverian England. Poverty in the midst of plenty challenged the achievements and humanitarian values of eighteenth-century Englishmen. They responded with a series of solutions that included schools, workhouses, prisons, and, in the end, colonies in far-off America and Australia. In this light, the founding of Georgia was simply an extension of the workhouse principle in early eighteenth-century philanthropy, one of the steps along England's long road to becoming a modern social welfare state.

The idea of the workhouse emerged in England as early as the 1670s. Thomas Firman, merchant, philanthropist, and an early Unitarian leader in England, initiated a project for providing work for the poor. Much like the Georgia scheme, Firman suggested putting poor children to work doing repetitive tasks such as spinning flax and silk. Firman's proposal held out the promise of doing away with beggars in the streets, reforming children's manners, and setting aside pensions for the poor. Also like the propaganda promoting Georgia, Firman saw his workhouse as a means of future prosperity for England.[5]

Firman's experiment later became the model of a public plan for the city of Bristol. Created by a special act of Parliament in 1696, the Bristol Corporation merged a new soap-and-water gospel with poor relief. Children would be taught cleanliness and godliness "by which means" they would be won over "to civility, and a love to their labor." Two years after its incorporation, John Cary, an enthusiastic supporter of the plan, proclaimed that the city of Bristol would "produce a virtuous and laborious generation with whom immorality and profaneness may find little encouragement." Supported in Parliament by grants, the Bristol experiment received wide assistance from merchants, noblemen, and the Anglican church.[6]

The comments and descriptions of the two workhouse experiments by Firman and Cary typify the confusion of purpose and attitude that characterized the concept of employing the poor. The Georgia plan did the same. Cary wanted the Bristol scheme to be economic, useful, and practical for the good of the nation, yet he justified it on moral grounds. The promotional literature of the Trustees, in like manner, was both crudely calculating and moralistic. Oglethorpe's *A New and Accurate Account of the Provinces of South Carolina and Georgia*, for example, promised that the settlement of the regions south of Carolina would "increase the trade, navigation, and wealth of these our realms." Yet no "Rum, Brandies, Spirits or Strong Waters" would be allowed in Georgia, any kegs of liquor found would be publicly staved, and the sale of liquor would be punished as a crime.[7]

In similar fashion, Firman argued that his plan would allow the poor to earn two to three pence per day, eliminate begging and profanity, encourage morality, and raise a new generation of industrious poor who would work in England's factories. Cary promoted the Bristol Corporation as a step toward making the poor self-supporting, but he still hoped for charitable donations and parliamentary grants. The Georgia Trustees also believed that England would grow rich "by sending her Poor Abroad," but they nevertheless hoped for sizable parliamentary grants and charitable donations. Even if the Bristol Corporation or the Georgia plan did not succeed, the Trustees of both organizations maintained that the money would be well spent in a charitable cause, and, into the bargain, the morality and character of the recipients improved.

In 1704 Daniel Defoe intensified the enthusiasm for employing the poor through distribution of his pamphlet *Giving Alms*. The pamphlet was a general critique of the workhouse principle, but its argument strengthened the larger cause of employing the poor. Along with John Locke, Defoe believed that poverty was caused by a defect in character. Defoe maintained that the schemes of Thomas Firman and John Cary failed because they did not address the causes of the condition. "Tis the men that won't work, not the men that can get no work, which makes the numbers· of our poor," Defoe reasoned. Locke's explanation supported Defoe's. "The growth of the poor," Locke asserted, must "have some other cause [than scarcity of provisions or want of employment] and it can be nothing else but the relaxation of discipline and corruption of manners." Thus charity was not enough.[8] The new philanthropy must discipline the poor to improve their character. As a matter of public policy, philanthropy in the early eighteenth century aimed both at relieving distress and at suppressing disorder among growing numbers of unemployed.[9] The new philanthropist must not only be a paternalist but must also act the part of the policeman. James Edward Oglethorpe became the prototype of the new philanthropist of the 1730s.

In the year that Oglethorpe first became a member of Parliament the Law of 1722 "for the greater ease . . . of the poor" was passed.[10] Commonly called the Workhouse Act, it set the tone of philanthropy in England for the rest of the century. Within ten years of its passage more than one hundred workhouses were set up in and around London. Indeed, the idea to promote a labor colony in America occurred at the height of the workhouse movement in England.

Oglethorpe was uniquely prepared for his scheme in Georgia both by his committee work in Parliament and his association with volunteer philanthropy. In the summer of 1728, Robert Castell, an architect and friend of Oglethorpe's, was confined to Fleet Prison in London for debt. Castell died of smallpox in Fleet, and Oglethorpe, moved by the young man's early death, asked for a parliamentary investigation of English jails. Appointed in February 1729 as chairman of a committee to inquire into "the State of the Gaols of this Kingdom," Oglethorpe wrote a report that led to the indictment of several wardens and the release of numerous "unfortunate poor" from prison.[11]

A national hero overnight, Oglethorpe quickly became an intimate of prominent politicians, of religious and philanthropic leaders, indeed, of some of the great proprietors of England. England now looked to him for solutions to the problem of the poor and unemployed. A labor colony in far-off America seemed appealing. As a new institution supported by philanthropy and government, Georgia would be ideal.

49

Some of the "best people" of England—the Georgia Trustees—would be regulating their social inferiors. Moreover, many of the deviant elements that seemed dangerous to Hanoverian society—Highland Scots, Irish vagrants, debtors, the unfortunate poor, even the pious German Protestants who threatened to flood into England—could be rounded up and shipped to Georgia in good conscience. Through a series of regulations and rules, the Georgia Corporation would exercise supervision and control over every facet of the colonists' lives.

The Georgia plan incorporated eighteenth-century philanthropical notions from 1714 to 1760. In his multivolume work on the history of England, William E. H. Lecky divided eighteenth-century philanthropy into three periods. Active charity first occurred as an ecclesiastical reaction by the Anglican church under Queen Anne. The initial enthusiasm "gradually subsided. . . . The philanthropic and reforming spirit . . . was almost absolutely unfelt" from 1714 to 1760.[12] On the whole, this middle period was undistinguished in philanthropic and charitable impulse. It was a time of cynicism, of misanthropy, of disbelief in the goodness and sincerity of human motives, of smallness, meanness, and of pettiness in charitable enterprises. Thus to Lecky, Oglethorpe and the Georgia plan represented a parsimonious and constricted philanthropy that did not lead to the more liberal enterprises of the nineteenth century. Once again, during the reign of George III an expansive and reforming spirit dominated.

Lecky's view is that of a nineteenth-century liberal, and, as such, has damaged the reputation of Oglethorpe and the Georgia Trustees and presented a distorted view of the Georgia enterprise. It has been repeated by writers and historians who are themselves survivors of other liberal wars on poverty. Indeed, the rise of the mid-twentieth-century welfare state in England and America coincided with the greatest criticism of Georgia as a philanthropic enterprise.[13]

Writers such as William Lecky and Daniel Boorstin have misjudged the philanthropy of the period from 1714 to 1760. Far from a falling off of warm and disinterested charity, these years saw the beginning of the London general hospitals, the justly famous Foundling Hospital, a parliamentary grant of £100,000 sterling in 1755 for relief of the Portuguese after the great earthquake, the first dispensaries, orphanages, reformatories for boys and girls, hospitals for special diseases such as fever and madness, the establishment of provincial hospitals outside London, and, from our point of view, the founding of Oglethorpe's labor colony in Georgia.[14]

The growing perception of a need for more flexible and comprehensive institutions of relief such as labor colonies indicated and was founded on a growing sensitivity to human suffering. Thus the key to the Georgia plan lay in the prohibition of slavery. An abhorrence of slavery and a concern for relief of the poor were the two dominant charitable impulses of the period. It was impossible for Oglethorpe and the Georgia Board to abandon either trust.

Heeding the purposes of the colony, the Trustees recognized Negro slavery as the greatest danger to their charitable enterprise. Especially to Oglethorpe, the acceptance of slavery would have meant a populace of unfortunate poor dominated by a plantation elite, land engrossment and consolidation, the evolution of the economy of Georgia toward a cash crop system, and the loss of discipline and loyalty among the colonists. As Oglethorpe consistently pointed out, any or all of these results would have violated the very reasons for which the Trustees associated themselves. Moreover, at the heart of the Trustees' regulation against slavery lay not only the fear of undermining the chartered principles of the corporation but also of appearing indirectly to approve of slavery as an institution in eighteenth-century life. To permit slavery, insisted Oglethorpe, would "occasion the misery of thousands in Africa by Setting Men upon using Arts to buy and bring into perpetual Slavery the poor people who now live free there."[15] Why release debtors from prison and shelter Salzburgers from an oppressive prince in Germany only to enslave Negroes? The philanthropy of the Georgia Corporation, in typical eighteenth-century fashion, extended not only to the unfortunate poor of England but also to the Negro slave in America.

Oglethorpe's views on rum and slavery represented those of the Georgia Board and of eighteenth-century philanthropy as a whole. In part, the morality behind the two prohibitions emerged in the dominance of a few philanthropists and noblemen on the Board. Although the Georgia Corporation appealed to the general philanthropic public through donations and subscription lists, it depended, like most voluntary charitable associations, on an inner circle of philanthropists and proprietors. Twenty-one men were designated as original members of the corporation; fifty others were elected to office during the next twenty years. The Common Council of the Trustees, a closed board that conducted much of the colony's business, had forty-eight members. Because the duties of a common councilman were tiresome and fatiguing, the faithfulness of its members was a gauge of the philanthropic sentiment that founded Georgia. In truth, only ten men in the history of the Trust did the lion's share of the work.[16]

The small number of Trustees who administered the corporation's affairs gave it a narrowness of vision and of purpose essential to Georgia's immediate success. The Georgia Trustees believed in their plan for planting a labor colony in America. For success in soliciting charitable donations and parliamentary grants, the Trustees must prohibit slavery, deny the unfortunates rum, order their daily affairs, carefully choose the recipients of their bounty, and see that their colonists did not fall into idleness.

By following these precepts, the Trustees placed Georgia in the mainstream of eighteenth-century philanthropy but also subjected the Georgia plan to the illusion of simplicity. A problem that was difficult was thought to be easy, an undertaking that was costly—for example, supporting large numbers of colonists for a year on relief—was regarded as cheap, a plan that would tax the resources of the nation was supposed to be within the means of casual benefactors, a few small grants from Parliament, and the leisure time of a dozen or so committeemen.

The Georgia plan suffered a weakness not found in earlier seventeenth-century proprietary schemes such as those for Pennsylvania and Carolina. Unlike earlier proprietors, the Georgia Trustees could not own land, hold office, or otherwise benefit from their association with the colony. The Trustees and the Georgia Corporation eschewed any profit motive in settling the colony. Whatever the Trustees did was solely for the benefit of the colonists and England. *Non Sibi, Sed Aliis* (not for ourselves, but for others) was their motto.

The love of power lay behind many charitable enterprises of the eighteenth century, but the altruism of the Georgia Trustees was genuine. Egmont, Vernon, and Oglethorpe held offices without pay, received little recognition, and had almost no political plums to dispense. In truth, seats on the Georgia Corporation were not highly sought after 1735. In place of patronage and power, the Trustees expected the objects of their charity "should be respectful and grateful. We think our kindness in a manner repaid, when it is thankfully received: It's a pleasure then to have done it, and an incitement to do more."[17] The Trustees needed to foster this sense of superiority, the idea that they were noble men doing good deeds, both in London and in Georgia. The letters and petitions from the hardworking Scots of Darien and the pious Salzburgers of Ebenezer substituted for power and patronage. Much like the letters of thanks children in the Foundling Hospital were instructed to write their benefactors, the letters from Johann Martin Boltzius and William Stephens fostered this sense of superiority.

The long struggle that opened between the Trust and the malcontents on the whole question of Trustee policy diminished the philanthropic sentiment that lay behind the Georgia plan. After 1740, the enthusiasm of the Trustees noticeably declined. The publication of *An Account shewing the Progress of the Colony of Georgia in America from its First Establishment* by the Trustees in 1741 is not only an answer to the malcontents and their complaints but also the epitaph for philanthropy within the Georgia plan. The two should be considered together. In the *Account shewing the Progress* the Trustees indirectly cataloged the motives behind their philanthropy and thereby placed Georgia in the mainstream of English history in the middle of the eighteenth century. Central to the Trustees' account is the elaboration of the "Rules of 1735." Declaring their intention to "lay out a County, and build a new Town in Georgia," the Trustees listed the provisions, down to "a narrow Hoe," that would be given to every man, woman, and child. Explaining why land would not be owned in fee simple, the Trustees emphatically stated that the right to sell land was "a Power not to be trusted with the People sent over." Still, only the industrious poor would be sent to Georgia. "The Trustees do expect to have a good Character of the said Persons . . . because no Drunkards, or other notoriously vicious Persons, will be taken." Such provisions smack of more than a well-run jail; they are remarkably similar, even down to the dietary restrictions of "beef days" and "pork days," to rules for the workhouses established by Firman and Cary. "Ah, Madam," Egmont told the queen, " 'tis for persons in high station, who have the means . . . to do good."[18]

Their disappointment at having failed oppressed the Trustees after 1741. In part a natural reaction from earlier visions of easy colonization, it also resulted from financial exhaustion. After 1740, charitable donations virtually ended, and the colony was almost entirely supported by parliamentary grants.[19] The difficulty in obtaining money was compounded because institutions such as the Foundling and Fever hospitals bid against the Georgia Corporation and each other in Parliament. The exhaustion further was exhibited by the difficulty in obtaining members for active committees and in the decline of Common Council attendance.[20] The criticism of the malcontents, the wide circulation of Patrick Tailfer's *A True and Historical Narrative of the Colony of Georgia* after 1742, and Thomas Stephens's attack on the Trustees in Parliament all sharpened the criticism and discontent of Georgia's philanthropists. Harman Verelst, the accountant for the Trustees, explained the constant dissatisfaction among Georgians by quoting the Latin proverb, *nema sua sorte contentus* (no man is content with his lot). As early as 1735 the Georgia Board sadly observed that "many of the poor who had been useless in England, were inclined to be useless also in Georgia."[21] Egmont's continuing illness and disenchantment finally forced his replacement in March 1743, and Oglethorpe's removal from Georgia that same year robbed the Trust of its charitable impulse. Thereafter, the Georgia plan concentrated almost entirely on military defense. After 1743, only 113 charity colonists were sent to Georgia. Egmont despondently observed that it was "a melancholy thing to see how zeal for a good thing abates when the novelty is over."[22]

Disillusionment was the outcome of the enormous charitable impulse that founded Georgia. In part, it derived from the failure to fulfill the first optimistic plans of the great proprietors. The contrast between the atmosphere in 1732 and in 1743 is striking. In the former year the Trustees described Georgia as a colony where "many families who would otherwise starve, will be provided for, and made masters of houses and lands; the people of Great Britain, to whom these necessitous families were a burden, will be relieved; numbers of manufacturers will be here employed for supplying them with clothes, working tools, and other necessaries; and by giving refuge to the distressed Salzburghers and other Protestants, the power of Britain, as a reward for its hospitality, will be increased by the addition of so many religious and industrious subjects." In a letter to the Trustees on August 10, 1740, David Douglas, William Sterling, and Thomas Baillie maintained that "the colony is reduced to one-sixth of its former number" and that "the few who remain were in a starving and despicable condition." Even James Habersham, long a supporter of the Georgia plan, despaired of success. The colonists "droop under these difficulties," he wrote Oglethorpe, "grow weary of the colony," and were losing their sense of cohesion as a separate province. The very fabric of family life seemed threatened, particularly by the allurements of drink.[23]

Even in their disillusionment, the Georgia Trustees never gave up the Trust or the cause of philanthropy. They joined still more causes—Coram's Foundling Hospital, the care of the mad, schools and orphanages for children—and voluntarily associated themselves with other charitable organizations. Their readiness to found a labor colony in America had been only a manifestation of the willingness of the "best people" in society to regulate their social inferiors. The Trustees generally explained the failure of the colony in much the same way that other philanthropists justified their own lack of success: the recipients had proved unworthy of the bounty. The colonists' moral defects betrayed the plan as a whole.

To the Trustees, charity as sentiment was inadequate, perhaps even mischievous. Before anyone would be sent to America as a charity colonist, a preparatory inquiry into the person's character would be necessary. Not all the unfortunate poor would be chosen. The character of the poor always was a concern of their benefactors in the eighteenth century, and the Trustees were no exception. To the Georgia Board, it was more important to make a man something different in Georgia than to make him prosperous there. Georgians must be industrious, diligent, respectful, prompt, and sober. The original sin of the poor was not that they were unfortunate but that they were lazy. Indeed, a close reading of the correspondence of Oglethorpe, Egmont, Habersham, and William Stephens reveals this belief. Reject the colonists' application for slaves, Oglethorpe declared, and "the Idle will leave the Province and the Industrious will fall to work." When open defiance seemed likely in 1739, Oglethorpe's response was to drive Negro sawyers out of the colony, stave such rum as he could find, and blame "Idleness and Drunkeness" for the discontent. Bounties would be given to the industrious, and new land grants were usually awarded on the basis of the person's "diligence." Moreover, the Trustees would not punish the industrious people of Georgia by granting slaves to the lazy members of the colony.[24]

Holding such sentiments as they did, the Trustees were inclined to accept the opinions of the hardworking Scots of Darien and the pious Salzburgers from Ebenezer. Indeed, the Germans occupied a special place in schemes for relieving the poor in the eighteenth century. Andrew Yarranton, a wealthy and successful merchant who visited the Continent in 1675, described the workhouses he found in Germany: "In all these parts there is no beggar, nor no occasion to beg; and in all the towns there are schools for little girls, from six years old and upwards, to teach them to spin. . . . Is it not a pity and a shame that the young children and maids here in England should be idle within doors, begging abroad, tearing hedges, or robbing orchards."[25] Always praying, working, and thanking the Trustees for their benevolence, the Salzburgers convinced the Trustees that their scheme would work.

Living as they did in a century that was devoid of psychologists, social workers, and social scientists, the Georgia Trustees believed that success was determined more by the character of the person than by the nature of his environment. The influence of the environment upon a man's character awaited another century. For this reason, the Trustees placed more importance on the prohibition of rum, a moral constraint, than upon the distribution of land, an economic one, in determining a person's success. It seemed equitable for everyone to own fifty acres of land regardless of whether it was "swamp overflowed" or "pine barren" but not to be tempted by the evils of drink. James Habersham stated the point perfectly when he said that the colony's troubles began when the ungrateful wretches turned away from the Trustees, fell into "idle and refractory company; from thence naturally to drinking . . . which perhaps ends in the total ruin of themselves and [their] families."[26] In typical fashion, William Stephens's journals depicted the colonists' personalities and town gossip more than they described Savannah's trade. Oblivious to reports of privation and suffering within Georgia, the Trustees always asked about the state of its churches, the behavior of its ministers, and the number of Bibles in the colony. For children, "young plants," to be busy at work spinning flax and silk was more important than to make products at a profit. A generation of children thus would be saved from beggary and taught discipline and order, to the benefit of the colony and nation.

Starting with an unimpressive beginning in 1733, the Georgia Trustees planned an economy whose anticipated growth seemed like the visionary increase of the one hundred drachmas in the Arabian Nights. According to the theories stated in *Reasons for Establishing the Colony of Georgia with regard to the Trade of Great Britain* and *A New and Accurate Account of the Provinces of South Carolina and Georgia*, the colonists would grow the products of other countries, especially those purchased by Englishmen from foreigners with ready cash. In this way, England would provide for her poor and "add an increase of our people by increasing their employment."[27]

The production of silk, "a luxury too prejudicial" to England, by the laboring poor in Georgia would save the £500,000 sterling spent annually for French, Italian, Indian, Turkish, and Chinese silk imported into England. Moreover, employment would be provided for twenty thousand people in Georgia during the four months of the silk season and year round for twenty thousand more in England. During late summer and early fall Georgians could also raise rice and corn and tend cattle—not for sale but for their own maintenance—and in the winter months they could offer prayers of thanks for their deliverance.[28]

From such silken threads of half-truths, vague notions of morality, and the rich enthusiasm of their own propaganda the Trustees spun the cocoon that encompassed the Georgia plan. But the scheme failed because colonists were selected on the basis of their character and their unfortunate status rather than their adaptability to the trade or craft desired by the colony. The Trustees embarked upon the manufacture of silk and exotic goods less because of a market demand than because of the existence of unemployed people. The Trustees did not succeed in providing their settlers with a profit base that would allow Georgia to prosper.

Ultimately, the Georgia plan was yet another failure in the long series of efforts to aid the unfortunate. From the poor relief laws of the 1720s to the Great Society programs of the 1960s, all the schemes to do away with unemployment and to help the poor have failed. The Georgia plan is important, however, for its expression of Hanoverian philanthropy, which tested the belief that the moral worth of a society is determined by the way it treats its more unfortunate members—the poor, the sick, and the insane. Oglethorpe and the Trustees were optimistic about the power of their society to provide remedies for human pain and suffering. The Georgia plan exemplified the morality of Hanoverian England and showed the willingness of some of its greatest men to participate in the philanthropy of their age.

NOTES

1. Daniel J. Boorstin, *The Americans: The Colonial Experience* (New York, 1958), 76. Boorstin sees little to admire and much to malign in eighteenth-century philanthropy.

2. Ibid., 73.

3. William Bacon Stevens, *A History of Georgia*, 2 vols. (New York, 1847, 1859; reprint, Savannah, 1972), 1:258–65, 463–75. For eighteenth-century England and the philanthropy of the period, see Rosamond Payne-Powell, *Eighteenth-Century London Life* (London, 1938); William E. H. Lecky, *History of England in the Eighteenth-Century*, 8 vols. (London, 1828–90); I. B. Kirkman Gray, *A History of English Philanthropy* (New

York, 1967); and Roy Porter, *English Society in the Eighteenth Century* (New York, 1982).

4. Attributed largely to Michel Foucault, the age of confinement thesis runs throughout his *Madness and Civilization: A History of Insanity in the Age of Reason* (New York, 1965).

5. Firman's plan is outlined in his *Proposals for the Imploying of the Poor, Especially in and about London* (London, 1678). See his second account in *Some Proposals for the Imployment of the Poor* (London, 1681).

6. John Cary, *An Essay toward Regulating the Trade and Employing the Poor of this Kingdom,* 2d ed. (London, 1719), 150.

7. *CRG,* 1:45; see also *Coll. GHS,* 16 vols.; and H. B. Fant, "The Indian Trade Policy of the Trustees," *GHQ* 15 (1931):207–22.

8. Daniel Defoe, *Giving Alms No Charity, and Employing the Poor a Grievance to the Nation* (London, 1704), 11; John Locke, *The Reasonableness of Charity* (London, 1704), 23.

9. George Rudé, *The Crowd in History: A Study of Popular Disturbances in France and England, 1730–1848* (New York, 1964); Gustave LeBon, *The Crowd: A Study of the Popular Mind* (New York, 1896); Lloyd I. Rudolph, "The Eighteenth-Century Mob in America and Europe," *American Quarterly* 11 (1959):447–69.

10. The 1722 law is given in *The Statutes: Third Revised Edition,* (32 vols. (London, 1950), vol. 9, 9 Geo. 1, c. 7.

11. Oglethorpe's career can be traced in Henry Bruce, *Life of General Oglethorpe* (New York, 1890); Leslie F. Church, *Oglethorpe: A Study of Philanthropy in England and Georgia* (London, 1932), an excellent work on Oglethorpe and philanthropy; Amos Aschbach Ettinger, *James Edward Oglethorpe: Imperial Idealist* (Oxford, 1936); and Phinizy Spalding, *Oglethorpe in America* (Chicago, 1977).

12. Lecky, *History of England,* 1:467, 498–503.

13. Boorstin, *The Americans,* 71–83; Lawrence Henry Gipson, *The British Empire before the American Revolution,* vol. 2, *The British Isles and the American Colonies: The Southern Plantations, 1748–1754* (New York, 1960), 152–80; and Randall M. Miller, "The Failure of the Colony of Georgia under the Trustees," *GHQ* 53 (1969): 1–17.

14. An appraisal of Georgia in eighteenth-century philanthropy is given in Gray, *History of English Philanthropy,* 221–24.

15. Oglethorpe to Trustees, January 17, 1739, Egmont Papers, 14203, pt. 2, p. 187.

16. See the tables given in James Ross McCain, *Georgia as a Proprietary Province: The Execution of a Trust* (1917; reprint, Spartanburg, 1972), 31–40.

17. *Report of the Society for Bettering the Condition of the Poor* (London, 1747), 33.

18. *The Account shewing the Progress of the Colony of Georgia,* in

Trevor R. Reese, ed., *The Clamorous Malcontents: Criticisms and Defenses of the Colony of Georgia, 1741-1743* (Savannah, 1973), 179-255. The best accounts of the disputes between the malcontents and Trustees are in Milton Ready, "The Georgia Trustees and the Malcontents: The Politics of Philanthropy," *GHQ* 60 (1976):264-81; Reese, ed., *Clamorous Malcontents*; and Stevens, *History of Georgia*, 1:262-84.

19. See Reese, ed., *Clamorous Malcontents*, 197-224.

20. McCain, *Georgia as a Proprietary Province*, 28-56.

21. Quoted in Stevens, *History of Georgia*, 1:264.

22. Quoted in Boorstin, *The Americans*, 71.

23. Quoted in Stevens, *History of Georgia*, 1:66-67, 296.

24. Oglethorpe to Trustees, Jan. 17, 1738/39, Phillipps Collection, 14203, p. 187; Oglethorpe to Trustees, July 16, 1739, ibid., 14204, p. 9; Martyn to Eveleigh, May 1, 1735, ibid., 14207, p. 138; Trustees Meeting, Aug. 7, 1742, ibid., 14213, p. 23; Trustees to William Stephens, July 14, 1739, ibid., 14210, p. 44.

25. Andrew Yarranton, *England's Improvement by Sea and Land* (London, 1677), 9.

26. Stevens, *History of Georgia*, 1:296.

27. [Benjamin Martyn], *Reasons for Establishing the Colony of Georgia* (London, 1733), reprinted in *Coll. GHS*, 1:205.

28. Ibid., 209-10.

PHINIZY SPALDING

James Edward Oglethorpe's Quest for an American Zion

HE SOCIETY of early eighteenth-century England seems, to the eyes of the twentieth century, full of contradiction. On the one hand it was a time when social movements of varied strength and longevity were slowly coming to fruition. Although not of the same dimension as some of the reform efforts that were to shake England to its core toward the end of the century, these movements possessed considerable significance for both the mother country and her colonies. Attention in the early years was concentrated upon what seemed to be achievable aims such as sailors' rights, legislation on the importation and use of various liquors, new programs and procedures for the nation's gaols, and so on. Thomas Bray founded and publicized organizations that aimed to extend the overseas arm of the Anglican church to the Indians in America through educational and missionary activities; George Berkeley experimented with the reform of manners and society and devoted several years of his life to the notion of establishing a college for Indians and colonists in Bermuda. Negro slavery, considered sacrosanct almost up to midcentury in both mother country and colonies, began to come under scrutiny—albeit somewhat timid—by the 1730s.[1]

And yet as these social movements ebbed and flowed, Robert Walpole was securely in power as the most important political figure in England other than the king. Walpole was confident that his tenure would last for the forseeable future, and he was not averse to using his appointment power to ensure that such would be the case. Nor was he averse to building up a personal fortune while holding the position of chief minister to the Hanoverian monarchs.[2] Walpole was too astute to try to stop or alter the more powerful social movements that eddied about him. Rather, as the good pragmatist he was, he watched them cautiously as a detached observer, looking for postures within these movements that might somehow threaten his hold on the government. When he felt that the advocates of a cause were strong enough to present a problem to him, Walpole knew how to give in graciously or how to offer limited cooperation. Occasionally he might seem to take on the mantle of leadership of such a movement, reckoning that he could remove any political stinger by joining and then controlling it. Essentially this appears to be the role he took in the Georgia proposals before the granting of the colony's charter in June 1732.[3]

James Edward Oglethorpe was sympathetic with and active in most of the benevolent reform movements stirring on the political surface in the 1720s. He was a close associate of Bray, worked with issues relating to sailors' rights, showed a keen concern for imperial affairs, and was a part of the political and social clique within Parliament that projected many of the ameliorative plans gaining credence at the time. Along with John Lord Viscount Percival, whose association brought Oglethorpe into touch with Berkeley and his schemes for America, he was serious, deeply moral, personally abstemious, self-sacrificing, and grimly determined to make a name for himself. Oglethorpe dealt frequently in absolutes, as did a number of his associates and friends, including Percival; he was keenly aware of his own dignity and the role he might play in English society.

But in political attitudes Oglethorpe was hard to characterize. He was not a dependable Tory and yet he loathed Walpole and everything for which he stood. Probably he considered himself an independent—a position much favored by many of the landed gentry like himself who denounced the first minister and all his works. These people found themselves badly outnumbered in Parliament during this period, but they constituted possibly the largest single group of backbenchers who sat in the House of Commons during the 1720s. Accustomed in the past to wielding considerable authority on the local level, they watched in dismay as the patronage mongers in Westminster began to work their wiles not only in London but in rural hustings as well. To them it seemed as though the bottom rail was on top and that the new politics was threatening to alter for good the old and tried configurations of British political life. Walpole, chief minister for an unprecedented two decades, was the particular bête noire of the gentry and country faction.

Oglethorpe and Walpole, however, may have had more in common than would appear on the surface. If J. H. Plumb's assessment of Walpole as a figure bridging the political gap between the Tudor-Stuart politicians and those of Victoria's day is accurate, Oglethorpe, too, may be placed in the same general transitional category, even though the two men differed markedly on specific issues.[4] The careers of both men mirror the political and economic changes that were occurring in England in the early eighteenth century. Walpole, however, represents the opportunist's effort to take advantage of these circumstances to build a personal political empire and thereby to effect an alteration in English politics that became basic to the thinking of subsequent generations. Oglethorpe, on the other hand, represents the attitudes of the group that would take advantage of the fluidity of the political situation in early Hanoverian England to return the nation to a simpler and—it was thought—purer system that had existed in the seventeenth century. Although Walpole's and Oglethorpe's attitudes and aims could hardly have been more dissimilar, the men were alike in their approaches to the system and how they hoped to use it to satisfy their own ends. They were also similar in that they are transitional figures— Walpole a link between the past and the future politics of Britain, Oglethorpe a representative of the old order, whose influence was gradually waning as the years of the century passed slowly by.

Certainly within his family circle there would be good reason to view Oglethorpe as a man of the seventeenth century. He was born in 1696, the last of a long line of children, to Eleanor Wall and Theophilus Oglethorpe. The family had fled England with James II in 1688, and although they seemed to move back and forth across the English Channel almost at will, there is no question that the Oglethorpes were among the staunchest of the Jacobites. Theophilus recanted on Jacobitism in the year of his last son's birth, but his wife and daughters made political agitation their avocation. There was rarely a plot to overthrow the early Hanoverians that did not have the female name of Oglethorpe associated with it. James, as a young man, took a passive part in these intrigues as long as he was under the dominating influences of the Oglethorpe women.[5]

James Oglethorpe's university training came at Corpus Christi in Oxford, both school and town hotbeds of sentiment for the Catholic Stuarts. By the time James had reached his majority he had decided the Jacobite cause was fruitless and, taking his cue from Theophilus, he made his peace with George I. Oglethorpe then secured election to Parliament in 1722, representing the borough of Haslemere, where his father and two brothers had preceded him. In the House of Commons he settled down to make a reputation for himself as a hardworking member of clear eye and independent mind—a man who could be trusted with affairs of state even if his name *was* Oglethorpe.[6] He nurtured a preference for the old form and the old order that makes some of his stances seem similar to the positions taken by the Whiggish country party before the overthrow of James II. Although Oglethorpe and his family were pro-Stuart in their leanings, it is mildly ironic that the Independents who aimed to reform England in the 1720s used the same tactics that the anti-Stuarts used to bring down the king in 1688. Politically difficult to categorize, Oglethorpe was very much a creature of his upbringing. Stern, self-righteous, dour, humorless, driven, quick to take offense, confident of his moral and social superiority, he plunged into the work of Parliament with all the zeal an Oglethorpe could muster. His work habits were demanding; the long hours he spent at his job became legion. He voted both for and against certain key Tory measures and, like a number of his contemporaries in Parliament, was impossible to pigeonhole. Personally fastidious and intensely moral, he probably most closely resembled in his stances the Roundheads of the mid-seventeenth century. Probably in the final analysis he was simply an Independent, a vanishing breed in the caldron of British politics—a simple fact he himself comprehended with decreasing bitterness in later life.

Although personal and individual elements are of enormous importance in judging the accomplishment and motivation of Oglethorpe, it should be underscored that he was merely a part of a general movement abroad in the England of the 1730s. Oglethorpe was not averse to using the system to bring about the ends he had in mind. It was not inconsistent, then, that in their anxiety to reform Hanoverian England, he and his colleagues held that reasonable social reforms were attainable and that it was desirable for society to pursue such goals. Generally speaking such movements were led by men from established families whose motives were above suspicion. It was a kind of Mandarin reform—self-conscious and aware of the good it wanted to do. Milton Sidney Heath saw at work "a vast organized benevolent movement" with its own body of "interlocking enterprises" and philosophies.[7] The Georgia scheme was part of this movement, but realizing themselves in a decided minority and being unable to dent even the outer defenses of the Walpolian citadel, Oglethorpe, Percival, and some of their supporters may have looked to America in the same way the early Puritans had viewed the New World: as a stage upon which to erect a model for the Zion they wished England to become. Georgia, in this sense, would be the economic and social prototype that might demonstrate the superiority of the old way to the current slough of Walpolian cynicism and materialism that seemed to dominate English life. The drunkenness, vice, and corruption that were so readily apparent, particularly in London, would be purged; the established church would be cleansed; the province would provide a haven for the unemployed and the ambitious small merchants and shopkeepers who could remake their lives in America. Their departure would also relieve the pressures on the lower and middle classes in England. Jobs would be more plentiful, alcoholism would be reduced, and public virtue would be uplifted. Prosperity for Georgia, then, also meant prosperity and improvement for the mother country.

Oglethorpe's experiences as chairman of Parliament's committee on gaols in 1729 clarified his previously disorganized thoughts on the question of overseas colonization.[8] His notion for Georgia, as it gradually emerged, was to put into reality the ambitions he had for himself—and to recreate an English society that reflected the purity of ideals more characteristic of the nation of his parents than of the England of the 1730s. Samuel Johnson's poem "London," to which Oglethorpe was one of the enthusiastic initial subscribers, sang the virtues of an earlier England, whose society had been pure and whose government was dominated by elements more answerable to the people than were the special interest groups of the 1730s. Other opposition writers— notably Jonathan Swift—also wrote of peoples and governments that had been debauched from the paths of rectitude by corruption and cynicism. The theme was familiar in the 1730s, and Oglethorpe agreed wholeheartedly with the sentiments of alienation and reconstruction.

To bring his visionary notion of Georgia to reality would require prodigious labor and dedication, but Oglethorpe, who was reared with a strong respect for the Protestant work ethic, did not quail at the challenge. He had not survived the upbringing he had from his mother, which included having holes punched in his shoes so his feet would become inured to cold and wet, without learning about determination and intestinal fortitude.[9] That he never learned quite enough about human nature was reflected in some of the unsatisfactory personal relationships he experienced with the Georgia Trustees and in the New World.

Eleanor Wall Oglethorpe, indefatigable Jacobite to the last, died in

June 1732, much mourned by many elements of London society. Her death freed her son James to lead the Georgia experiment personally, and he volunteered to take the first settlers across the Atlantic. As Henry Newman, secretary of the Society for the Promotion of Christian Knowledge (SPCK), wrote, Oglethorpe "with the Spirit of an Old Roman offer'd himself to the Trustees for settling the New Colony of Georgia to go thither with about 100."[10] He lost little time once he had received the imprimatur of the other Trustees. In spite of Percival's reservations about leaving prematurely and South Carolina Governor Robert Johnson's advice not to sail "this twelvemonths," Oglethorpe's impatience to begin the affair could not be contained.[11] He sailed with the original settlers in November of that same year.

For some time Oglethorpe had been considering the nature of the colony the Trustees should plant in America. He was well-read in current colonial literature, as was reflected in his own publication, *A New and Accurate Account of the Provinces of South-Carolina and Georgia in America*, which appeared about the same time the settlers were departing for the New World. He was familiar with the writings of Joshua Gee and John Archdale and the plans of Jean Pierre Purry, and he may have been conversant with Robert Johnson's township scheme for South Carolina. That he already had a number of the characteristics in mind that were to distinguish Georgia from other British colonies is apparent upon reading his writing. *A New and Accurate Account* denounced rum as "a fatal Liquor" to the Indians that made them all "too apt to commit Murders."[12] Another publication reflected the ideals of landholding and the slavery prohibition: "If these Trustees given Liberty of Religion, establish the People free, fix an *Agrarian* Law, prohibit the Abominable Custom of Slavery: In fine, they go upon the glorious Maxims of Liberty and Virtue, their Province, in the Age of Man, by being the Asylum of the Unfortunate, will be of more advantage to Britain than the Conquest of a Kingdom."[13] There is good reason to believe that Oglethorpe, whom the Trustees had designated as the member responsible for promoting their colonial venture, wrote those words as well.[14] The emphasis upon agrarian law and agrarian democracy at such an early date—not to mention the slave ban—would also indicate Oglethorpe's authorship. The concept of Georgia being controlled by some form of agrarian law may, in Oglethorpe's mind, have stemmed from the seventeenth century and his preference for landed interests just as his concept of rum prohibition may have harkened back to the legislation late in the same century against the importation of French brandy. It also was reflective of the current agitation against the use or importation of gin, of which William Hogarth's noted representation of "Gin Lane" was the best known. The profligacy and drunkenness of the times stirred this same reform element and culminated in the passage of a Gin Act in 1736.[15]

Oglethorpe's independent attitude and his preference for tradition are reflected in an entry in Percival's *Diary* that mentions Georgia's founder opposing a proposed Qualification Bill in Parliament on the grounds that it was "contrary to the ancient constitution of England." Oglethorpe reasoned that there should be no qualifications for election to Parliament because "the country might send up who they pleased, good sense and loyalty not being confined to fortune or estates, but to parts and education."[16] Presumably, the agrarian law of the country-side, still much influenced by the landed gentry, would winnow the wheat from the chaff and counterbalance the craven urban voters who would invariably choose a Walpole.

Oglethorpe had a literary and antiquarian bent. He read history, wrote verse of a sort, sponsored struggling young poets such as Samuel Johnson and Oliver Goldsmith, flattered and coauthored a book with James Boswell,[17] and was a good friend to the collector-antiquarian Sir Hans Sloane. He heartily disliked litigation and attorneys and, in later years, confessed to Johnson that he reflected his father's disapproval of Parliament's triumph over the king in 1688. As he saw it, Commons "usurped" the power of the purse from the executive "and used it tyranically." Government was operated by "corrupt influence, instead of [by] the inherent right of the king." Johnson mildly defended the events of 1688, but Oglethorpe put an end to the conversation with the remark that his father considered the Glorious Revolution unnecessary.[18]

James also mirrored Theophilus's preference for army life and organization in the semimilitary settlement in Georgia. To one observer the fifty-acre land grants appeared to be "more like military fiefs" than anything else because a qualification for attaining them was wartime service and peacetime guard duty.[19] The fifty-acre farms were to be the strength of the colony, and each landholding was to provide Georgia with its own Cincinnatus should trouble develop. Presumably the settlers who paid their own way over, who brought servants, and who received the maximum five-hundred-acre grants would be playing the role of the English landed gentry whom Oglethorpe and the political Independents so admired. From this group the natural leaders of the colony would be expected to emerge.

Oglethorpe's Quest for an American Zion

The more Oglethorpe is observed, the harder it is to escape the conclusion that his mind had a military cast. This leaning became an obsession during the war with Spain after 1739, when he insisted on the necessity of settling soldiers and their families on the frontier nearest Florida.[20] In fact, it was the attempted implementation of the military fief idea that caused his notion of agrarian equality to fail. Soldiers and plowshares did not necessarily go together, in spite of Oglethorpe's insistence. The war itself, of course with the political, economic, and demographic changes it brought, was the most important single factor to write *finis* to the Georgia experiment.

Oglethorpe and the Trustees ultimately evolved an interlocking plan for Georgia which, if successfully implemented, might have changed the entire face of subsequent English colonial development on the North American continent. The landholding pattern of fifty-acre grants, each with its resident farmer, was essential to the structure of trusteeship Georgia and may echo an Oglethorpian preference for England before the economic and political dislocations associated with the enclosure movement and developing industrialism. Lawyers—the scourge of the eighteenth century—were unofficially barred from the colony, and Roman Catholics were prohibited.[21] These two concepts reflected the desire by the Trustees and Oglethorpe to return to a simpler world purged of both attorney and papist. Oglethorpe thought lawyers inimical to the proper running of a new colony, and he insisted that each man make his own plea to the magistrate, as had been done in the old days. He urged the Trustees not to consent to a change in the land law, which restricted inheritance to a male heir and prevented outright sale and alienation, because it would "open [Georgia] to the Frauds of Wills, a Grievance Complained of in England, and a Yoke which neither We nor our Fathers could bear." Common law would decide land cases as the colony was then constituted, but giving freehold possession "will make a Court of Doctors Commons, and a Chancery necessary, either of which will be enough to crush a full grown, much more a young Colony." Oglethorpe's dislike of Roman Catholics was less strong than his prejudice against attorneys, possibly because he had had extensive exposure to Catholics when living on the Continent and because two of his sisters had married into the French nobility and converted to the old faith—and the Oglethorpe family ties were strong. When war with Spain loomed, however, his attitude toward Catholics became more severe. As lines between the two nations hardened, he tended to blame even domestic unrest with the Trustees' rules on Romish agitators.[22]

In many ways Georgia was an anachronism. For example, the charter did not create a representative assembly, and there were no elected officials in the colony. It was left to the ruling group in London to decide what was good for the settlers: the Trustees would provide the social and economic incentive on the southern frontier that would cause their American wards to work diligently. In turn, Georgia, with its enlightened leaders, would enjoy prosperity under the unwritten convenant between colonists and colonizers. Although they provided the proper colonial stage upon which their settlers could act out their drama, the Trustees, including Oglethorpe, could not keep their hands off the province. Their regulations seemed to be everywhere. Some have placed ultimate blame for Georgia's failure to prosper squarely at the feet of the colony's London leaders. In Milton Heath's words, they failed to let the "partnership responsibilities of the colonists" grow along with colonial life.[23] Probably the Trustees were not temperamentally capable of letting this growth occur.

Although the land restrictions and others such as the bans on Catholics and lawyers were cumulatively important, it was in the three laws passed by the Trustees that the main hopes for creating a southern Zion rested. Two of these laws related to the natives and how they were to be treated. The Georgia Board was determined that its colony would not repeat the same mistakes that had been made years before in South Carolina. Hence there was passed an act strictly controlling the Indian trade within Georgia's chartered limits. Licenses were to be bought yearly in Savannah from properly authorized officials; bond must be posted giving assurance that the traders would not traffic in forbidden commodities. A schedule was set up to be followed in negotiations between the Indians and the traders, and a commissioner was appointed to oversee Indian affairs in the province. Not surprisingly, James Oglethorpe was named the first such official under this Indian Act of 1735.[24] At the same time rum and "any other kind of Spirits or Strong Waters by whatsoever Name" were absolutely forbidden both in Savannah and in Indian country.[25] The natives had asked for legislation on both of these subjects in order to avoid misunderstandings between themselves and the British. So a decision was made to treat the Indians fairly and to heed their complaints about the most patent abuses associated with their trade with the British.

In considering why the Trustees treated the natives as they did, it should be remembered that one facet of the colony intended to provide the Church of England—long negligent in the missionary field—

with an area in which the natives might be Christianized and taught the rudiments of a proper education. Both the SPCK and its sister organization, the Society for the Propagation of the Gospel, were active in the evolution of the Georgia movement, along with the Bray Associates. Membership on the boards of these groups was overlapping and complementary, but they all shared one major goal: to proselytize and bring the Anglican cause to a position of strength in America. The ministers on the Georgia Board, then, agreed with the politicians and merchants among the Trustees in the broad outline of what the province should be: a colony where the native Americans were to be treated fairly and where, if at all possible, they were to be led to Christianity. Members such as Oglethorpe and Percival saw the colony as more of a secular Zion; for the ministers the religious overtones were paramount.[26]

But it was on the prohibition of Negroes that Oglethorpe pinned most of his hopes for the establishment of a new kind of colony on the southern frontier. By refusing entry of free blacks or Negro slaves into Georgia, he hoped to establish a work ethic among the white settlers on the banks of the Savannah River such as had been planted on the Charles far to the north in Massachusetts.[27] The land restrictions would accustom his yeoman farmers to a new environment—one free from competition to amass larger and larger landholdings and also free from competition for and with slaves. With no blacks in the colony the dignity of white yeoman labor would be established; the province could be populated with merchants, traders, and farmers of the middling sort, who contributed not only to their own families but to the empire as well. The dignity, integrity, and modest prosperity (which was all the Trustees ever promised) of the settler might not only set the mode for America but could serve as an object lesson for an England grown fat and soft at the feet of Robert Walpole and his disciples.

Oglethorpe, just as the Puritan fathers long before him, felt that he was going on a mission to America. He counseled his first settlers about the conditions they would face and the behavior that was expected of them. John Winthrop had instructed his colonists on the *Arbella* to be meek, generous, patient, and charitable toward themselves and their natural leaders; Oglethorpe aboard the *Anne* slightly more than a century later expected similar reactions from his colonists. Each made clear, both directly and implicitly, that too much liberty was an experience that should be enjoyed by the beasts of the forest only; man's individuality should be sublimated to authority, and the social structure must stay fixed. Oglethorpe's society, like Winthrop's, would be united and fired with the desire to improve not just a special few but British life in general. It was the errand of both colonies to establish societies in the New World from which the corruptions of the British politicians and their allies—notably attorneys and other negative elements—would be purged. As Massachusetts Bay was to be a counter to the court of Charles I, so Georgia was to stand in stark contrast to the abominations of the early Hanoverian years and might, if all went well, serve as an object lesson to those of independent mind to persevere in their efforts to purify the system.[28]

It may be contended that Oglethorpe and his closest associates thought of Georgia as an indirect means of ridding the old country of the Walpole sickness. The irony, however, is that Georgia, at least indirectly, brought about the fall of Walpole from power, but not the way Oglethorpe hoped it would. The War of Jenkins' Ear, which broke out in 1739, exposed the corruption and patronage that riddled England's armed forces. After an embarrassing series of setbacks at the hands of the Spanish, Walpole fell in 1742, but these hostilities also put the quietus on Oglethorpe's dream of Georgia as a self-supporting yeoman farmer colony. Alarms, invasions, border raids, and the failure of the Trustees to alter some of the more obnoxious restrictions caused a general malaise to hit the colony. Most settlers fled for safer or more congenial locations; Oglethorpe and the idea of a military buffer colony were left. Oglethorpe optimistically proclaimed, on the eve of the Spanish invasion in 1742, that his "Soldiers hold the spade in one hand and the sword in the other and both successfully," but even he must have realized that the war had ruined his final hopes for a Georgia that would show the way to a craven Britain.[29] Although Walpole's dethroning was the result at least partly of American events, the Georgia experiment as a southern Zion was destroyed by the same war.

Although agriculture was to be important, Georgia was intended to be a community of towns along the New England model. It was anticipated that each settlement would be made very carefully and that every individual town would be drawn out and surveyed before colonists were granted plots or were permitted to move in. Compact settlement with an urban focus, such as in Savannah and Ebenezer, would provide the proper social and economic milieu in which the righteous, such as the Trustees' persistent secretary, William Stephens, could gather and bolster one another's morale when times were perilous. It

would also make defensive measures easier should they become necessary. Social planning, as in the Puritan colonies, was extensive and centered upon an unspoken covenant between Oglethorpe and the Georgia magistrates rather than in the complex written covenants of New
England. But a covenant assumed reciprocal sharing of aims and responsibilities—a trust that bonded the people to their rulers. It was
perhaps Oglethorpe's major failure that he was incapable of sharing
responsibilities in such a fashion. When asked—even begged—to reform
particulars in the Georgia experiment, he bristled. Unlike the American Puritans, who trimmed their sails when they saw their strongest
efforts going the way of other seventeenth-century utopian endeavors,
Oglethorpe was adamant; he might break, but he would never bend.
Hard work, he reasoned, could save his zealous colonial experiment
and bring physical prosperity, which was an outward sign of civil justification. To him, just as to the Puritans, an individual's failure to
work diligently to pull himself up by his own bootstraps was not only
reprehensible but incomprehensible. His colonists, borne down by pes-
tilence, war, infertile land, and a myriad other problems, thought differently. They wanted slaves, rum, fee simple landholding, and other
enticing items that seemed to make life for their neighbors so easy.[30]
The Georgia colonists, in short, sought prosperity, not justification.

Oglethorpe and the Trustees, like the Massachusetts leaders one hundred years before, faced numerous dilemmas in bringing their Zion
into focus. Problems were endemic to experimental societies, and Oglethorpe coped with controversial issues about as successfully as others
in his position. The covenants governing Georgia were more secular than religious—consistent perhaps with the precepts of an evolving
eighteenth-century rationalism. The visible saints of the colony embraced only those in London and Savannah who worked to see the
Georgia experiment created in line with the notions laid down by the
Oglethorpe-Percival faction. In fact, the colony's elect were fewer
proportionately and cumulatively than the number of the chosen in
Massachusetts Bay. Sainthood Georgia style included a few outsiders
such as Governor Johnson of South Carolina and William Bull (at
least for a time). It also embraced the half-breed translator-diplomat,
Mary Musgrove, and the gentle but politic Tomochichi. William Stephens deserved initial membership owing to his position, the confi-
dence the Trustees put in him, and his long background in the House
of Commons, but Oglethorpe seemed to see Stephens as a rival, so he
was purged from the list and ostracized. Noble Jones may also have

merited the role of saint. The list is most notable, however, for the calling not represented: ministers. The quality of priest sent to the colony by the Anglicans in the early years militated against their inclusion, and although the Wesleys were old family friends of the Oglethorpes there was never any inkling that John or Charles would be taken to Oglethorpe's bosom once the brothers touched the shores of Georgia. The Salzburgers' Johann Martin Boltzius probably came closest among the ministers to being accepted within the Georgia covenant, but Oglethorpe usually took Boltzius for granted and failed to consult with him on important questions that might influence the direction the colony was to go.[31]

The dilemmas faced by Oglethorpe and the Georgia elect related particularly to the basic perversity of human nature. How could the colonists resist the dictates of those who had the insights and influence to make the colony leap off the drawing board? How, too, to express legislation and fix governmental principles for a group of settlers who would rather express the rules by which they were to be governed themselves? How to deal with a group that derided the elect by such comments as were found in *A True and Historical Narrative of the Colony of Georgia in America?* "Thus have you *Protected us from ourselves* . . . by keeping all Earthly Comforts from us: You have afforded us the Opportunity of arriving at the Integrity of the *Primitive Times*, by intailing a more than *Primitive Poverty* on us. . . . As we have no Properties, to feed Vain-Glory and beget Contention; so we are not puzzled with any System of Laws, to ascertain and establish them."[32] Indeed, how to keep people happy with a modest living—and no hopes beyond that—has brought down more than a few earthly Zions, so Georgia was far from unique in this instance.

As in Massachusetts, the basic dilemma of Georgia lay in that old insoluble problem rephrased slightly in view of the different emphases of the centuries. Whereas the main Puritan dilemma in Massachusetts was "the problem of doing right in a world that does wrong," the Georgia dilemma rested on the question of how to do well in an economy gone wrong. For no adequate groundwork was ever laid by Oglethorpe or the Trustees to create an operational economic system oriented either toward the agrarian ideal, about which Oglethorpe spoke, or toward a system based on trade with the Indians. Without an effective economic foundation the southern Zion became bogged down in rhetoric. By 1742 another Carolina was in the making.[33]

Unlike Puritan New England, Georgia's dilemma was not that of a second or third generation with young turks, who, as a result of the debilitating effects of prosperity, either did not live up to or rejected the principles that bonded the early leaders of their colonial society together. Indeed in Oglethorpe's province, the extraordinarily high rate of desertion and death meant that there was hardly a second or third generation of Georgians who came over with Oglethorpe to become disaffected. In addition, the outlines and aims for the colony had changed so radically when the Trustees gave over their power in 1752 that there were very few legacies to react against in the royal period. Noble Wimberly Jones and Joseph Habersham, however, sons of two of the most prominent officials who had come to Georgia during the early trusteeship and survived, joined the revolutionary cause in the 1770s while their fathers preferred the loyalist position.

In retrospect it seems hard to believe that the province of Georgia could ever have developed along the lines envisioned by James Oglethorpe. Even early in the movement he had been advised by Governor Jonathan Belcher of Massachusetts to scrap the various restrictions on landownership. The reversionary features and the tail male inheritance were all well and good, but they would cause Georgians to leave in search of a colony that gave lands on more satisfactory terms. Although inheritance restrictions had been handled in similar fashion in England in the past, Oglethorpe should bear in mind that lands in the old country had been cultivated in some cases for "thousands of years." For America to become accustomed to such a procedure would take centuries.[34] But Oglethorpe thought he could overcome this obstacle, and Belcher's advice went unheeded. William Byrd, among others, advised against the rum prohibition, and from Pennsylvania Thomas Penn "assured" Oglethorpe that "the moderate use of it [rum] mixed with Water in the very hottest Weather is very necessary." A chorus of voices, including Byrd's, counseled against the Negro Act. All other considerations aside, Byrd predicted that "the Saints of New England . . . will find out some trick to evade your Act."[35] But Oglethorpe, with unbounded self-confidence and riding the crest of a wave of popular adulation brought on by his roles in the gaols investigation and the Georgia movement, pushed ahead.

The importunings of those who thought differently made Oglethorpe all the more self-righteous in his defense of the colony. Early in 1739, shortly after the first of the important petitions had gone to England urging the Trustees to alter Georgia's makeup, he wrote: "If We allow Slaves, we act against the very Principles by which we as-

73

sociated together, which was to relieve the distressed." Slavery in Georgia would weaken—not strengthen—the southern frontier and would "glut the Markets" with crops grown in other of the southern continental colonies.[36] Six months later he pleaded with the Trustees not to change the landholding pattern. All appeared to be going well at that time, but an alteration in the ownership and inheritance provisions would lead to incredible complications, "tend to uniting of Lotts and destroying the Agrarian Equality, one of the first Principles on which you set out."[37] The outbreak of war with Spain all but destroyed any chance the Trustees' Zion might have had, and yet in May 1742 Oglethorpe again strongly defended the three laws. Slaves in Georgia, he wrote, would be either "Recruits to an Enemy or Plunder for them." To change the land laws in favor of fee simple ownership "would bring the stock jobbing temper, the Devill take the Hindmost." Rum "would destroy the Troops and labouring people . . . and would give a reputation of unhealthiness to the Province."[38] In other words, the southern Zion would be no more. By that time, however, Oglethorpe's influence with the Trustees had run its course. Wheels were in motion to alter or abandon all of the major premises upon which Georgia was founded. And Oglethorpe himself—although on the brink of a remarkable victory over the Spanish—was about to be stripped of the few administrative powers he still retained.[39]

Even so, in 1742 this crusty and cantankerous bachelor still attempted to instruct his Westminster counterparts on their proper role as Trustees. First, they must promote religion and "encourage Marriage and the rearing up of Children." As a result of an excess of men in the colony—most of them soldiers from Oglethorpe's regiment—it would be desirable for the permanency of the province to send women over to become their spouses. The importation of women, however, "might be attended with Indecencys" unless properly handled. It was a necessary function of the Trust to back up the magistrates but more particularly to protect "the people from . . . litigiousness and extortion in the shape of Fees." Finally, the Georgia backers must continue "persevering and encouraging the Europe kind of agriculture as Vines, Silk, Olives &c. all which by experience we know thrive in the Country."[40] Oglethorpe did not give up on his idea for Georgia easily. But this letter was his last full defense of what he had been trying to do in America; five months later he boarded ship in Charles Town and returned to England for the third and last time.[41] Zion had lost its spokesman.

Why did the Georgia plan fail? Certainly it was not from lack of effort on Oglethorpe's part. Perhaps the idea never came into full flower because it was grounded upon principles and standards that were too idealistic, self-sacrificing, and visionary for the cynical and pragmatic 1730s. When Oglethorpe said in 1732 that the British Empire was fortunate not to have the gold and silver mines that the Spanish possessed, his readers probably did not take him seriously. "By a *Lucky Kind of Poverty*," he wrote, the British had to deal in other products, all of which came from the sea or from hard work in the cultivated soil.[42] This brand of "luck" belonged more to the seventeenth century than the eighteenth.

Although they were promised only a modest subsistence, the colonists—once in America—expected far more. The sacrifices Oglethorpe anticipated his settlers to make in their expectations were too great to ask of human nature. That they meant no hardships to him who was accustomed to a spartan life had little meaning to the average settler. He was respected, disliked, or feared as a colonial leader but rarely emulated. The structure of the colony as envisioned by Oglethorpe expected much of the Trustees, but it required cognizance and sacrifice from the settlers as well. If the Trustees and Oglethorpe were unwilling to share power in a partnership arrangement in the political and administrative areas, the colonists refused to sacrifice their material aspirations to bring this Zion on the southern frontier to full life.

That Oglethorpe and the other Trustees wanted to establish a lasting legacy just as clearly as did the Puritans one hundred years before is perfectly obvious. Georgia was a province characterized by self-conscious philanthropy dominated by men who were accustomed to receiving credit for their accomplishments. As in Massachusetts Bay, many of the key figures wrote about what they wanted to do and how they planned to do it. Percival's *Diary* and *Journal* are the most obvious examples of this self-awareness, but perhaps a dozen other firsthand accounts patently written for posterity survive. William Stephens was hired by the Trustees as their secretary to keep the Georgia Board in England informed minutely of the situation in their southern Zion. Only Oglethorpe, from whom a journal would have been most enlightening, failed to keep one. This lack was not owing to oversight or laziness; he simply did not have the time in addition to his administrative, military, and other responsibilities. Even the divines who came to the colony, although not among the inner circle, kept journals that logged not only their personal relationships with the Almighty but their reactions to Georgia and the powerful Protestant effort being forged in old Guale.[43] Stephens's elaborate papers sent back to London for the Trustees and the exhaustive reports written by Boltzius rival one another in detail and minutiae. As in Massachusetts Bay, it was as though each moment or each individual contact or observation might provide the important insight that would lay bare the key to the colony's success. Boltzius's *Detailed Reports* were not intended for the eyes of the Trustees, but Stephens's *Journal* was. In the witty, perceptive, and occasionally introspective pages of this work is found the colony's raison d'être. The *Journal* is, in short, Georgia's version of Cotton Mather's *Magnalia Christi Americana*.[44]

Oglethorpe was an Independent in an age that did not respect Independency; he was a moralist in a time that paid little more than lip service to moralists. How to project his vision of England in the form of Georgia, then, to an era that delighted in hearing the message but ignored the implementation was his own personal dilemma. Oglethorpe had his idea and was strong enough to inspire his fellow Trustees with it, but bringing the dream to reality was beyond even his remarkable determination.

He adhered to political, social, and economic concepts that were largely seventeenth-century in nature, but his dialectic was an amalgam. His public letters dating from the 1770s and early 1780s reflect attitudes that he held even as a young man: a strong anti-French prejudice, an independence that defied categorizing, a deep respect for the gentry, a suspicion of luxury and the theater, and a powerful regard for the society and modes of life in England before the Glorious Revolution.[45] His thinking was something of a pastiche, but he made no claims to be either a political or a moral philosopher. But that he looked upon Georgia as an experiment in high-minded service and as a new Zion that might preach to the world the virtues of a purer, earlier England seems undeniable.

NOTES

1. For an excellent general account of the early Hanoverian years see William A. Speck, *Stability and Strife: England, 1714–1760* (Cambridge, Mass., 1977). See also Amos Aschbach Ettinger, *James Edward Oglethorpe: Imperial Idealist* (Oxford, 1936), 88, 89–95, 97–99, for brief and perceptive synopses of many of these social movements. The best primary source that reflects the times and also bears on the Georgia movement is *Diary of Per-*

cival. For a sweeping interpretation of Walpole's motivations during this entire period see J. H. Plumb, *Sir Robert Walpole,* 2 vols. (Cambridge, Mass., 1956, 1961.) On the question of slavery in the sermons delivered before the Trustees, see conflicting articles by James R. Hertzler, "Slavery in the Yearly Sermons before the Georgia Trustees," *GHQ* 59 (1975):118–26, and Phinizy Spalding, "Some Sermons before the Trustees of Colonial Georgia," ibid. 57 (1973):332–46.

2. See particularly Speck, *Stability and Strife,* 4. As the author aptly wrote concerning this era, "men became politicians more to advance themselves than a cause." See ibid., 203–38, for a thoughtful discussion of Walpole's rise and fall.

3. Ettinger, *Oglethorpe,* 116–18; *Diary of Percival,* 1:157, 226, 227, 235, 240, 254, 264, 273. Egmont became suspicious of Walpole's intentions as the charter procedure dragged on. Ettinger sees Walpole's reluctance to hurry the charter as a means of keeping the Georgia movement under control.

4. J. H. Plumb, "The Walpoles: Father and Son," in Plumb, ed., *Studies in Social History* (London, 1955), 205–6.

5. Patricia Kneas Hill, *The Oglethorpe Ladies and the Jacobite Conspiracies* (Atlanta, 1977). For Theophilus's loyal support of the Stuarts see Ettinger, *Oglethorpe,* 19–28.

6. Horace Maybray King, *James Edward Oglethorpe's Parliamentary Career* (Milledgeville, 1968), 2–12 and passim.

7. Milton Sidney Heath, *Constructive Liberalism: The Role of the State in Economic Development in Georgia to 1860* (Cambridge, Mass., 1954), 15.

8. Verner W. Crane, *The Southern Frontier, 1670–1732* (1929; reprint, Ann Arbor, 1956), 312–13. See also Crane, "The Philanthropists and the Genesis of Georgia," *AHR* 27 (1921):63–69; *Diary of Percival,* 1:90; and Leslie F. Church, *Oglethorpe: A Study of Philanthropy in England and Georgia* (London, 1932).

9. Boswell Papers, M 208:2, Yale University; cited with permission.

10. Henry Newman to Josiah Burchet (secretary to the Admiralty), June 1732, in Henry Newman, Private Letters, vol. 5, April 1732–November 1734, CN 4/5, SPCK Archives, Marlebone Road, London.

11. *Diary of Percival,* 1:293, 304; *Gentleman's Magazine* 2 (October, November 1732):1029, 1079–80.

12. [James Edward Oglethorpe], *A New and Accurate Account of the Provinces of South Carolina and Georgia . . .* (London, 1732), 26.

13. *London Magazine* 1 (June 1732):198.

14. *CRG,* 2:3.

15. Charles M. Andrews, *The Colonial Period of American History,* 4 vol. (New Haven, 1934–38), 4:99–102; see esp. the information in note 1, 101–2.

16. *Diary of Percival,* 1:244.

17. Phinizy Spalding, "Profile of an Old Independent: Oglethorpe as Seen in the Papers of James Boswell," *Yale University Library Gazette* 53 (1979):140–49.

18. John W. Croker, ed., *The Life of Samuel Johnson, LL.D, including A Tour to the Hebrides, by James Boswell,* 2 vols. (New York, 1859), 2: 327–28.

19. Albert B. Saye, *New Viewpoints in Georgia History* (Athens, 1943), 76.

20. Oglethorpe to the Trustees, February 12, 1743, *Coll. GHS,* 3:144.

21. *CRG,* 2:21; James Ross McCain, *Georgia as a Proprietary Province* (Boston, 1917), 213–14. The restriction on attorneys was not expressed as an official policy of the Trustees, probably because it would have caused a storm in Parliament and in London's administrative circles.

22. Oglethorpe to the Trustees, July 4, 1739, *CRG* 22, pt. 2:173. In spite of his attitude toward attorneys, Oglethorpe studied at Gray's Inn in 1729 and "Took a Master & read law there." See Boswell Papers, M 208:2. See also Joseph Foster, *The Register of Admissions to Gray's Inn, 1521–1889* (London, 1889), 369. Francis Moore, *A Voyage to Georgia; Begun in the Year 1735* (London, 1744), 26, reported that lawyers could not "plead for Hire" in Georgia. Oglethorpe wished everyone in the colony to espouse "his own Cause" in court as had been customary "in old times in *England.*"

23. Heath, *Constructive Liberalism,* 20.

24. Ms. CRG, 32:406–7; *CRG,* 2:120, 123.

25. For the full text of the Rum Act see *CRG,* 1:44–48. The Indian Act is found in ibid., 31–42.

26. See esp. Verner W. Crane, "Dr. Thomas Bray and the Charitable Colony Project, 1730," *WMQ* 3d ser., 29 (1962):49–63; Crane, "The Philanthropists and the Genesis of Georgia"; and Edgar Legare Pennington, "Anglican Influences in the Establishment of Georgia," *GHQ* 16 (1932):292–97. See also Church, *Oglethorpe.*

27. *CRG,* 1:50–52, for the text of the Negro Act.

28. For important aspects of the Puritan motivation see Perry Miller, *The New England Mind: From Colony to Province* (Cambridge, Mass., 1953), 25 and passim; Miller, *Errand into the Wilderness* (Cambridge, Mass., 1956), 3–8, and passim; Miller, *Orthodoxy in Massachusetts, 1630–1650* (Boston, 1959), 23, 52, 172–73; and Richard S. Dunn, *Puritans and Yankees: The Winthrop Dynasty of New England, 1630–1717* (Princeton, 1962), 9–11, 12, 14. For the best accounts of Oglethorpe on board the *Anne,* see E. Merton Coulter, ed., *The Journal of Peter Gordon, 1732–1735* (Athens, 1963), and Thomas Christie, "The Voyage of the *Anne*—A Daily Record," ed. Robert G. McPherson, *GHQ* 44 (June 1960):220–30.

29. Oglethorpe to the Trustees, May 28, 1742, *Coll. GHS,* 3:122.

30. Perry Miller, *The New England Mind* (Cambridge, Mass., 1953), 49;

Betty Wood, "Thomas Stephens and the Introduction of Black Slavery in Georgia," *GHQ* 58 (1974):24–40. See also the various pro-slave petitions, particularly the one of December 1738, *CRG*, 3:422–26.

31. That Boltzius was not as enthusiastic about Oglethorpe as would appear from the Trustees' correspondence becomes abundantly clear from material in Samuel Urlsperger, comp., *Detailed Reports on the Salzburger Emigrants Who Settled in America . . .* , ed. George Fenwick Jones et al., 7 vols. to date (Athens, 1968–).

32. Patrick Tailfer et al., *A True and Historical Narrative of the Colony of Georgia in America,* ed. by Clarence L. Ver Steeg (Charleston, 1742; reprint, Athens, 1960), 4.

33. Edmund S. Morgan, *The Puritan Dilemma* (Boston, 1958), 203; Paul S. Taylor, *Georgia Plan, 1732–1752* (Berkeley, 1972), and Milton L. Ready, *The Castle Builders: Georgia's Economy under the Trustees, 1732–1754* (New York, 1978).

34. Jonathan Belcher to Oglethorpe, May 25, 1734, *Collections of the Massachusetts Historical Society* 6th ser., 7 (1894):70.

35. Thomas Penn to Oglethorpe, August 4, 1734, Egmont Papers, 14200, pt. 1, p. 91; William Byrd to Egmont, July 12, 1736, "Documents," *AHR* 1 (1895):88. Byrd thought "that Diabolical Liquor Rum . . . dos more mischeif to Peoples Industry and morals than any thing except Gin and the Pope" (ibid., 89).

36. Oglethorpe to the Trustees, January 17, 1739, Egmont Papers, 14203, pt. 2, p. 380.

37. Oglethorpe to the Trustees, July 4, 1739, *CRG* 22, pt. 2:172–73.

38. Oglethorpe to the Trustees, May 28, 1742, *Coll. GHS,* 3:121.

39. Kenneth Coleman, *Colonial Georgia* (New York, 1976), 102.

40. Oglethorpe to the Trustees, February 12, 1743, *Coll. GHS,* 3:144.

41. *S.C. Gaz.,* July 25, 1743.

42. Oglethorpe, *A New and Accurate Account,* 68.

43. Benjamin Ingham, John and Charles Wesley, and George Whitefield are the most important of those who kept journals chronicling their experiences associated with the colony.

44. See *CRG,* vols. 4 and 4, Supplement, and E. Merton Coulter, ed., *The Journal of William Stephens, 1741–1745,* 2 vols. (Athens, 1958–59). The latter publication also contains the journal kept by Stephens in 1736, when he was on a mission in South Carolina for Samuel Horsey.

45. Several of these important later letters were preserved by James Boswell and are located in the Boswell Papers at Yale. In addition, the Granville Sharp Papers in Gloucestershire contain some fragments of Oglethorpe's later leanings.

BETTY WOOD

The Earl of Egmont
and the Georgia Colony

 N VIEW of all that has been written about him and of his enduring reputation on both sides of the Atlantic, one could be forgiven for thinking that James Edward Oglethorpe was solely responsible for the founding of Georgia. All too often scholars have neglected the significance of the fact that twenty-one men were named as Trustees in the Georgia Charter of June 1732 and that altogether seventy-two men served in that capacity.[1] Many, indeed the majority, of the Trustees were little more than ciphers: they seldom attended meetings of the Georgia Board, and their greatest contribution (which soon proved a mixed blessing) was their reputation and sometimes their money.

A handful of the Trustees shared Oglethorpe's commitment to the Georgia project, and none more so than Sir John Percival, afterward first Earl of Egmont. Although Egmont's diaries and journals of the Trustees' proceedings have long been recognized as being among the most valuable records for the study of Georgia's founding and early history, surprisingly little attention has been paid to their author.[2] Indeed, it is remarkable that there is no full-length biography of a man who was such a prominent figure in the political and social life of early eighteenth-century England and whose contribution to the Georgia project bears close comparison with that of Oglethorpe.[3]

Egmont was born in County Cork, Ireland, in 1683, the second son of Sir John Percival and his wife Catherine. His father died while he was still a child, and when his mother remarried in 1689 he was placed in the custody of his great-uncle, Sir Robert Southwell. Two years later, upon the death of his elder brother, John inherited his father's Irish title and estates. His education, which was wholly in England, was conventional for one of his social class. After being tutored at home he was placed in De Mouer's French School in London and, when he was fifteen, spent a year at Westminster School before going up to Magdalen College, Oxford, where by all accounts he was a serious but not an outstanding student of mathematics, logic, and history. After leaving Oxford Egmont embarked on two "Grand Tours"—the first of England and Scotland, the second an extended trip to the Continent. He visited Ireland briefly in 1708 and, together with his wife Catherine, the daughter of Sir Philip Parker à Morley, whom he married in 1711, he lived in that country from 1711 until 1714.

In 1714 Egmont and his family returned to England, and thereafter, although his Irish estates provided the bulk of his income, his career was based in London. As was the case with many Irish peers, the comparative provincialism of Dublin held little appeal for him. Recognition in and by English society, which was important to Egmont, was not long in coming. In 1714 he was made a Privy councillor and a year later created Baron Percival. Although he was elevated to the title of Viscount Percival in 1722 it was not until 1733 that he received the earldom, but not the English title, he had craved for most of his adult life.[4]

Egmont's diaries reveal only too clearly his deep consciousness of his Irish connections, his determination to make his mark in the upper echelons of English society, and his concern for his reputation. For all of these reasons Egmont trod carefully and self-consciously in the London of the 1710s and 1720s. He took care to cultivate but not to offend those in a position to advance his career. As the controversy surrounding the precedence accorded Irish peers at the English court and his aggressive defense of the Georgia plan reveal, however, Egmont did not hold his tongue if either his rank or his integrity was called into question.[5]

His parliamentary career involved Egmont with the Georgia project at a relatively early stage in its inception. In 1727 he was elected member of Parliament for Harwich, a rotten borough, which his marriage into the Parker family enabled him to control for the next six years. Both his winning and in 1734 losing of this seat were to play important parts in determining the fate of the Georgia plan.

Although the date and circumstances of their first meeting are uncertain, Egmont and Oglethorpe were both Associates of the Late Reverend Dr. Thomas Bray, and it is likely that they encountered one another in that capacity, if not socially, in London.[6] But it was probably in February 1729, when Percival was appointed to the Parliamentary Gaols Committee chaired by Oglethorpe, that the two men became well acquainted. Despite their association on the gaols committee and subsequently on the Georgia Board, they never became close friends, probably less because of differences in their backgrounds or the social circles in which they moved than as a reflection of their different political persuasions. Egmont, an independent-minded Whig, was convinced that Oglethorpe was "a very obstinate Tory."[7] Ironically, their "party" differences were what made the Irish peer such a valuable ally in Oglethorpe's endeavor to found a new colony.

The Georgia project sprang out of their mutual interest in "good works." But Egmont was not the first to hear of Oglethorpe's proposal "to procure a quantity of acres either from the Government or by gift or purchase in the West Indies, and to plant thereon a hundred miserable wretches who being let out of gaol by last year's Act, are now starving about the town for want of employment." Oglethorpe had already divulged his intentions to "other considerable persons" before consulting Egmont on February 13, 1730.[8]

Because of their collaboration on the gaols committee, Oglethorpe felt reasonably certain of enlisting Egmont's support for a project that could be construed as the logical extension of the committee's work. Initially, however, the support he sought was financial rather than political. Egmont's immediate usefulness to Oglethorpe was as a trustee of the D'Allone legacy of "about one thousand pounds" that had been bequeathed "to convert negroes."[9]

Although by no means an insignificant sum, the D'Allone legacy was not critical to the funding of Georgia. It was important because it provided Oglethorpe with the means of securing effective control of the £15,000 King legacy. After considerable wrangling, the executors of that fund agreed to release money for Oglethorpe's scheme provided that "the trusteeship be annexed to a trusteeship already in being." Mainly because of Egmont's reputation, it was decided to approach the trustees of the D'Allone legacy. Egmont was delighted when Oglethorpe consulted him because he felt that the D'Allone legacy was being wasted. Two of his co-trustees "were rendered incapable of serving and the third" he "never saw."[10] He instantly approved Oglethorpe's proposal to complete the "imperfect charity" begun by the gaols committee and intimated that he would not be a silent partner. The Georgia project had gained an influential and, as time was to prove, a most loyal supporter.

During the next few months Egmont and Oglethorpe met frequently, sometimes alone and sometimes with other of the original Georgia Trustees, to clarify their "scheme of settling poor debtors in Carolina."[11] Unfortunately, the record of these meetings (usually entries in Egmont's diary) is so scant as to preclude a detailed assessment of precisely what each man present contributed to the Georgia plan. That the original proposal to establish an American colony was Oglethorpe's is indisputable; that he was the sole architect of the Georgia plan is debatable.

Most of the original Trustees, including Egmont, were as conversant and as involved as Oglethorpe with the charitable and imperial impulses that converged during the late 1720s to bring the Georgia project into being. Thus Egmont's political career reveals that his interests encompassed more than the precedence ordinarily accorded Irish peers. He took a keen interest in every aspect of England's overseas commerce, especially as it pertained to Ireland, and brought to the Trustees' deliberation an intimate knowledge of the workings of the Old Colonial System, but that expertise was shared by many of the original Trustees.[12] Probably more distinctive were Egmont's thoughts about the nature of the society to be established in Georgia and, more pragmatically, the most appropriate way of proceeding in order to secure the necessary official support for the proposed new colony. Many of his ideas on both subjects stemmed from his friendship with George Berkeley and, more specifically, from his close familiarity with Berkeley's ill-fated Bermuda project.

Egmont met Berkeley in Dublin in 1708, and for the next forty years they remained firm friends.[13] Not surprisingly, Egmont was one of the first to hear of Berkeley's plan to establish a theological college in Bermuda.[14] Although all of the original Georgia Trustees must have known the broad outlines of Berkeley's proposal, which was published in 1725 and widely discussed in London, none was as conversant with the details as Egmont.[15] Indeed, several of the Trustees' more optimistic assertions concerning the potential of America as an arena for the achievement of moral and social regeneration, as well as the critique of contemporary colonial society implicit in the Georgia plan, probably owed much to Egmont's friendship with the future bishop of Cloyne.

Although they anticipated that Georgia would soon become of enormous economic value to Britain, Oglethorpe, Egmont, and their associates were perhaps more concerned with the society that would characterize their colony. This preoccupation, the very essence of their plan, reflected the deep disquiet felt by a number of Britons during the

1720s about the condition of their society and by a few, including Berkeley, about that of the New World as well. By 1730 the consequent desire to reform British and, by Berkeley, American manners and morals had found an important expression in the charitable endeavors that deeply involved most of the original Georgia Trustees.[16] In many respects the social blueprint they devised for Georgia was the culmination of this zealous concern to reform, if not to redeem, British society. But the Georgia plan, like Berkeley's Bermuda project, reflected in addition the continuing importance of the New World in the British imagination, the persistence of the belief that the redemption of the Old World could be achieved in the New.

Of course, Berkeley was not the only contemporary thinker or writer to influence the Trustees: their scheme also owed much to the work of those such as Sir Robert Montgomery who had previously sought to promote the British settlement of the southern borderlands.[17] But Berkeley's ideas assumed a particular significance by virtue of his friendship with Egmont. For both men North America presented the irresistible prospect of an environment in which a new social order could be created, a society from which could be excluded the moral and social ills that polluted contemporary Britain.[18]

There were some important points of difference between the Bermuda and Georgia projects. Although appreciative of the possible social consequences of his scheme, Berkeley had as his main objective the spiritual rather than the secular redemption of Americans, red, white, and black, through the traditional device of missionary work. The Georgia Trustees, on the other hand, were concerned primarily with the salvation of British society, which they hoped to achieve by removing those whom they regarded as both the symptom and a main cause of Britain's social and moral, rather than purely spiritual, malaise: the poor, the unemployed, and the unemployable. These "miserable wretches" and "drones" would be taken from a society that "offered such temptations to vice as . . . they are scarce able to resist" and placed in "a Christian, moral and industrious way of life, and [instructed] how by labour to gain a comfortable subsistence."[19] But the society they left behind would also benefit: it would be purified of this corrupt and corrupting element and gain materially from the useful employment proposed in America.

The Trustees believed that the plight of those who would settle Georgia stemmed from "idleness and necessity," and they determined to exclude both traits from their colony. The settlers would secure their redemption through work. But the Trustees' perception of contemporary American society, and particularly that of the plantation colonies, suggested that strict limits must be placed upon the material gains from that labor. As Berkeley pointed out to Egmont, one of the reasons why he had selected Bermuda for the site of his college was that it produced "no one enriching commodity . . . which may tempt men from their studies to turn traders."[20] Neither man disputed the economic significance of the plantation colonies for Britain, but each regarded the rampant materialism of those societies as a potent threat to their American design.

For Egmont and the other Trustees the "luxury" of the plantation colonies and the "idleness" of many of their white inhabitants were as damaging to manners and morals as the "idleness and necessity" of the unfortunates who would people Georgia. The latter would enjoy a "comfortable subsistence" (more than most of them could hope to achieve in Britain), but the Trustees were determined to prevent the emergence of equally dangerous extremes of unbridled wealth and abject poverty. This goal they hoped to achieve by imposing rigid controls on the distribution of land, labor, and capital.[21] But they went a vital step further than Berkeley by linking the "idleness" and concomitant vices of the plantation societies with the employment of black slaves. Slavery must at all costs be avoided in Georgia because it would inevitably "result not only in the corruption of the colonists . . . but also in the repudiation of the basic principle of the colony that independent men could gain a decent living by their own labor."[22] Slavery could have no place in the virtuous society envisaged by the Trustees.

Unlike the founders of any other American colony, the Trustees outlawed slavery, but none of them, including Egmont, could be described as an abolitionist. Egmont never questioned the morality of enslaving the African and never considered that there was any inconsistency between Christian teaching and slaveholding. His thinking closely followed that of the Anglican bishop of London, who in 1727 had explained that the freedom implicit in Christianity was freedom from the "bondage of sin" and that conversion to Christianity was unrelated to an individual's secular condition or status.[23] The duty of the Christian extended no further than attending to the spiritual welfare of the African—a duty Egmont accepted in his capacity as a trustee of the D'Allone legacy. The Georgia Trustees banned slavery not out of any deep regard for the natural rights of the African or because they perceived an inherent inconsistency between Christian teaching and chattel slavery, but because, like many later critics of the institution, they felt a compelling concern for the manners and morals of white society. In this respect they anticipated many of the antislavery arguments employed on both sides of the Atlantic after the mid-eighteenth century.

The Trustees appreciated that there were two other, more pragmatic reasons for prohibiting slavery which would have an infinitely greater appeal to British officialdom than a concern for the moral welfare of the unfortunates to be sent to Georgia. They argued that Spain would foment black unrest in Georgia as part of a campaign to dislodge this British intrusion into the borderlands and that Africans would jeopardize the physical as well as the moral well-being of the settlers. Moreover, the Trustees claimed that Georgia's main export crops, silk and wine, would not necessitate black labor. The moral, military, and economic arguments marshaled against the introduction of slavery dovetailed perfectly—at least in the minds of the Trustees.[24]

Although we cannot be entirely certain of Egmont's precise contribution to the Georgia plan, it may be said without fear of contradiction that he was totally committed to that plan, including the decision to outlaw slavery, and that had it not been for his sound political judgment and influential connections the Georgia project might never have got off the ground. The attachment of Egmont's name to the scheme was of the utmost importance in rallying support for it.

In 1730 Oglethorpe's and Egmont's top priority was to secure a royal charter and government backing for their colony. Berkeley's recent failure to do likewise provided ample evidence of how difficult this might prove.[25] Egmont was well aware of the problems likely to be encountered and of the importance of proceeding prudently through the often convoluted corridors of power in Whitehall. Unfortunately, not all of the Trustees realized how easy it was to offend those in a position to thwart them.[26]

Egmont, who, unlike the impetuous and often outspoken Oglethorpe, was on friendly terms with the Walpole ministry and a frequent visitor at court, made the most of his contacts but, even so, it was not until June 1732, after seemingly endless and often inexplicable delays, that the Trustees secured their charter.[27] There was by no means universal or unequivocal support in London for their scheme. But given the Trustees' financial needs, the attitude of Parliament, and in particular of the Walpole ministry, was crucial. Eventually, the

House of Commons agreed to appropriate money for Georgia but refused to give a cast-iron guarantee of continuing support. As early as May 1733, it was evident that the Georgia project would stand or fall according to the Trustees' skill as lobbyists.[28] Their critics would seek to exploit this financial vulnerability.

In part, the Trustees' vulnerability was of their own making. By 1734 they were disagreeing among themselves about their priorities and policies, a development that did not bode well for the future. In March of that year James Vernon, a Trustee loyal to Egmont, complained, with some justification, that Oglethorpe was a poor correspondent and that the Trustees must receive better information from Georgia. More seriously, he alleged that Oglethorpe's practice of "drawing bills upon us without advice is a dangerous negligence" and that he must be made more accountable to the Georgia Board.[29] The first difficulty was largely resolved in 1737 by William Stephens's appointment as the Trustees' secretary for Georgia, but checking Oglethorpe's often rash and arbitrary behavior was to prove more problematical for Egmont and Vernon.

Equally alarming to the two men were the factions that were developing on the Georgia Board. Vernon claimed that some Trustees, including George Heathcote and Thomas Tower, had "too little regard for the religious part of our design, leaning to the new opinions that are unorthodox." By the mid-1730s a potentially dangerous split had developed in the Anglican impulse that had been so important in inspiring the Georgia project. Egmont concurred with Vernon's analysis and confided to his diary that he "must labour to stifle" these differences "or our affairs will go on very heavily."[30] He appreciated the necessity of the Georgia Board presenting a united front to the world outside. But despite his efforts to smooth things over, these divisions erupted into a bitter conflict that resulted in several resignations.[31]

This internal strife had a dual significance. First and obviously, its outcome would decide the character of the Georgia plan to be persevered with, and, second, it cast doubt upon the Trustees' credibility. The factionalism on the Georgia Board could not be kept confidential. Indeed, much to Egmont's dismay and disgust, Thomas Coram continued to snipe at the Trustees after his resignation from the board.[32] This infighting, when combined with an incipient parliamentary opposition, which by the mid-1730s was being fanned by complaints from Georgia, spelled potential disaster for Egmont and his allies.

Shortly after the founding of Georgia the Trustees began to receive complaints about the colony's local government, but by 1735 a group of Lowland Scots settlers, headed by Patrick Tailfer, who had paid their own way to America, were making far more serious allegations. They claimed that Georgia's economy was languishing and that not even the "comfortable subsistence" promised by the Trustees, let alone the profits they craved, had materialized. In their view this sad state of affairs was the result of Europeans' inability to work productively in the unhealthy and unpleasant Georgia climate. They concluded that the colony could not survive, let alone prosper, without the employment of black slaves.[33]

Before 1739 the Trustees paid little heed to complaints from Georgia. When they bothered to reply, it was simply to say that they would not modify their scheme and that under no circumstances would they permit slavery. Egmont was not alone among the Trustees in believing that the growing clamor for slaves came from ungrateful and idle men who were unwilling to engage in the hard but morally uplifting work involved in implementing the Georgia plan and who deliberately falsified conditions in the colony in order to get their way.[34] This impression was confirmed by a steady flow of more favorable accounts penned by Oglethorpe or by those such as William Stephens who were in the Trustees' employ and who perhaps told the Georgia Board what they thought it wished to hear.[35] Although rumors began to circulate in London that all was not well in Georgia, before 1739 members of Parliament had little firm evidence of trouble. The danger was that they would be primed by the malcontents and, thanks to Thomas Stephens, this is precisely what happened.

Stephens, the son of the Trustees' secretary for Georgia, had gone to the colony in 1737 but soon became disillusioned with life there and by 1739 was sympathizing with the malcontents.[36] When he returned to England late in 1739 he broached his and the malcontents' complaints to Egmont. Although Egmont listened patiently on several occasions to Stephens's criticisms of the Georgia plan and his tirades against Oglethorpe, he disputed his account of both. Egmont might have suspected that there was a grain of truth in what Stephens was saying, especially about Oglethorpe's behavior, but he would not admit this to a man he considered guilty of the unpardonable sins of disloyalty and ingratitude. Egmont saw Stephens as an unscrupulous schemer bent on the destruction of the Trustees' project and, in the process, Oglethorpe's downfall.[37]

Thomas Stephens refused to be persuaded or placated by Egmont's counterarguments and decided that his only hope of securing changes in the Trustees' policies lay with the House of Commons. Through no fault of his own, except perhaps his unswerving loyalty to the integrity of the Georgia plan and to Oglethorpe as well as a concern for his own reputation, Egmont failed to head off this most determined opponent.

Stephens's campaign was simple in its intent: to persuade Parliament to make its financial support for Georgia conditional upon changes in the Trustees' policies and, in particular, upon the introduction of black slavery. Between 1739 and 1743 he lobbied vigorously to ensure that no member of Parliament could be in any doubt as to the real condition of the colony he was being asked to support.[38] The fate of the Georgia project would be decided by the House of Commons, but neither Oglethorpe, away in America, nor Egmont would be able to participate in the debates on the financing, and thereby the future, of their colony.

Egmont's amicable relations with the Walpole ministry had been vital in smoothing the path for the implementation of the Georgia plan, but in 1734 he fell out with Walpole. In that year Egmont stood down from his Harwich constituency in favor of his son John and, given his influence in the borough, could scarcely believe it when his son was defeated. He was firmly convinced that this result was caused by the intrigues of the ministry, and despite suggestions that it reflected an antagonism toward his son rather than himself (which in Egmont's eyes was the same thing) he refused to be mollified.[39] Thereafter every ministerial action that impinged however indirectly upon Georgia was interpreted by Egmont as an overt attack not only upon the Trustees' scheme but also upon himself. His reaction was to become even more resolute in his defense of the Georgia plan and, as he saw it, his own reputation. Against this stiffened resolve, however, must be set the fact that at a time of mounting opposition the Georgia Board lacked a committed and influential spokesman in the House of Commons. Moreover, Egmont had made it difficult for himself to exercise a less formal influence on the Walpole ministry.

Although excluded from the relevant parliamentary debates, Egmont played the key part in organizing the Trustees' defense against an increasingly vitriolic attack. More specifically, he briefed the parliamentary Trustees as to how they might best refute the charges likely to be leveled against them. In a series of unpublished papers, which included a point-by-point refutation of the allegations made by

Patrick Tailfer and his coauthors in their *A True and Historical Narrative of the Colony of Georgia in America*, Egmont produced a comprehensive and cogently argued defense of the Georgia plan.[40] Indeed, it is probable that Benjamin Martyn relied heavily on Egmont's comments when preparing his published defenses of the Trustees' scheme.[41]

Egmont's briefing papers for the parliamentary Trustees indicate that although still wholly committed to the Georgia plan in its original form, he now realized that in some respects the Trustees had erred, perhaps most seriously by promising both Parliament and the early settlers too much too soon. For obvious reasons, their promotional literature had emphasized that Georgia would soon become a valuable addition to the old colonial system, but by 1740 this was patently not the case. Egmont conceded that Georgia had not proved an instant economic success, but he argued that because the colony was less than ten years old this was scarcely surprising: Georgia was simply repeating the experience of all the other American colonies.

Egmont did not feel that the Trustees had erred on the question of slavery. Although he ultimately conceded that the malcontents were probably right about the comparative profitability of slave labor, he did not believe that this was the main point at issue. For Egmont the social and moral considerations that had prompted the prohibition of slavery were as strong and as valid as they had ever been: slavery might indeed enrich the few but would inevitably lead to the social and moral decline of Georgia's white society. But as in the early days of the Georgia project he thought it advisable for the parliamentary Trustees to emphasize the pragmatic reasons for maintaining the ban. Slaves would jeopardize Georgia's military function; that had been true in 1732 and with the outbreak of hostilities between Spain and England was now an even more potent consideration. If Parliament wished to override the Trustees, so be it; they would never accept the responsibility for putting Georgia, and thereby the Carolinas, at risk.[42]

Egmont was enough of a realist and a politician to appreciate that by making, or by appearing to make, some concessions, for example by tinkering with their land policy and even by going so far as to contemplate the employment of free blacks in Georgia, the Trustees might placate both their parliamentary critics and the malcontents.[43] But from first to last he, like Oglethorpe, refused to budge on the question of slavery. To have done so would have been to deny and thereby to destroy their hopes for Georgia.

The parliamentary Trustees could not have been better briefed. But as Egmont had long realized, few of them could be relied upon to support the Georgia Board in the face of concerted opposition. Initially the Georgia project had been well served by the fact that half the original Trustees sat in Parliament. But the differing "party" affiliations of the parliamentary Trustees had always threatened to work to the Georgia Board's disadvantage. For only a handful of these men did "loyalty to Georgia" come before "loyalty to party."[44] The remainder simply could not be depended upon by Egmont, and, in all probability, his presence in Parliament would not have altered that fact.

Although Egmont was scathing in his criticism of the parliamentary Trustees, he pinned the blame for the growing opposition to Georgia on Thomas Stephens and the Walpole ministry. He was correct in his assessment of the part played by Stephens in welding the Trustees' critics into a formidable pressure group, although some might disagree with his opinion that Stephens was nothing more than an unprincipled opportunist. But probably because of the Harwich election Egmont misjudged the Walpole ministry: it was not implacably opposed to the Georgia project. The ministerial attitude toward the Trustees' scheme, indeed to the continuation of Georgia in any form, depended upon an often shifting balance of fiscal, military, diplomatic, and purely political considerations. The fact of the matter was that Georgia could not be easily disentangled from the broader context of Anglo-Spanish relations in both the Old World and the New; neither could it be placed in a special category when it came to Britain's relations with the other mainland colonies. As Egmont finally realized, the fall of Walpole made little difference. For reasons he never fully accepted, no British ministry was prepared to give the Trustees the financial independence and thereby the political autonomy they had sought since 1730.[45]

The intrigues and intricacies of the successive parliamentary debates on the financing of the Georgia project have been examined in considerable detail elsewhere. Each attempt to secure funds met with more opposition than the last until in 1742, for the first time, the House of Commons summarily rejected the Trustees' money petition.[46] Egmont derived little satisfaction from the fact that although it had proposed some alterations in the Georgia plan the House had voted decisively against the introduction of black slavery and for the censure of Thomas Stephens on the grounds that he had made "false Scandalous and Malicious Charges, tending to Asperse the Characters of the Trustees."[47] Benjamin Martyn believed that these two decisions represented something of a triumph for the Trustees, but Egmont knew better. Without financial aid the Georgia project stood little chance of surviving in its original form. Moreover, even though Stephens had been severely reprimanded by the Speaker of the House of Commons, the Trustees had not been allowed to vindicate their reputations further by publishing details of "the manner or terms in which this fellow was reproved."[48]

For Egmont this "slight punishment" of Stephens was the last straw. He resigned his seat on the Common Council of the Trustees and advised his colleagues that if they valued their reputations they would surrender their charter because if they did not "the World will believe [we] receive some private advantage [from Georgia] which makes [us] cling so close to it."[49]

It has been suggested that Egmont advised the Trustees to resign en masse because he believed that "a series of refusals to serve . . . would bring the Ministry and Parliament to a more sensible position regarding Georgia."[50] The truth of the matter, however, or at least of Egmont's own resignation, was probably less devious. Egmont was almost sixty years old and, as he emphasized in his letter of resignation, he suffered increasingly bad health.[51] For almost ten years he had been one of the few Trustees in London willing to shoulder the emotionally taxing burden of upholding the integrity of the Georgia plan against a mounting tide of criticism. In part, his willingness to take on this responsibility reflected a concern for his reputation, which like Oglethorpe's was inextricably bound up with the Georgia project. But it also owed much to his unswerving belief in the fundamental tenets of the Trustees' social vision for Georgia.

By 1742 Egmont was thoroughly demoralized. As the events of the past few years, and especially of the past few months, had demonstrated, he could not even rely on the support of all his colleagues on the Georgia Board. Moreover, he believed, albeit incorrectly, that he was faced with the implacable opposition of the ministry. Despite Oglethorpe's presence in Georgia, neither he nor the other Trustees in London exercised the authority in America or in England necessary to persist with their design. Even if Parliament renewed its financial support (which it did in 1743), it seemed unlikely that the Georgia Board would be able to turn back the clock.

Although Egmont resigned from the Common Council of the Trustees, he did not completely sever his connection with the Georgia

Board. He remained a Trustee and attended a declining number of meetings until shortly before his death in 1748. As he had anticipated, these years witnessed the final collapse of the Georgia plan. By 1748, despite an often bold but ultimately irrelevant rhetoric, the Trustees had virtually abandoned their attempt to exclude black slavery from Georgia.[52] Egmont, whose bitter disappointment can be easily imagined, played little part in this final phase of the Georgia experiment.

By the time of Egmont's death, Georgia was already linked in the public imagination with the name of Oglethorpe, and that has remained the case down to the present day. Egmont never set foot in Georgia, and his name has not been commemorated by Georgians. Yet his contribution to the definition, promotion, and subsequent defense of the Georgia plan was of the utmost significance. Egmont's efforts on the domestic front in London were as unstinting and as unselfish as those undertaken in Georgia by his more illustrious associate, James Edward Oglethorpe.

NOTES

1. For a list of the Trustees see William Bacon Stevens, *History of Georgia*, 2 vols. (1847, 1859; reprint, Savannah, 1972), 463–75.

2. *Diary of Percival; Egmont's Journal; CRG 5: Journal of the Earl of Egmont, 1738–1744*. See also Egmont Papers. I am grateful to Charles Bourne, formerly an undergraduate at St. John's College, Cambridge, and now a graduate student at Columbia University, for his help in compiling a checklist of Egmont materials.

3. As McPherson, who edited *Egmont's Journal*, wrote: "no man other than Oglethorpe himself had a greater interest in the colony, or worked harder for its establishment and promotion" (p. xi).

4. This account is based on McPherson, ed., *Egmont's Journal;* Benjamin Rand, ed., *Berkeley and Percival: The Correspondence of George Berkeley, afterwards Bishop of Cloyne, and Sir John Percival, afterwards First Earl of Egmont* (Cambridge, 1914); and Ruth Saye and Albert Saye, "John Percival, First Earl of Egmont," in Horace Montgomery, ed., *Georgians in Profile: Historical Essays in Honor of Ellis Merton Coulter* (Athens, 1958).

5. For Egmont's account of this controversy see *Diary of Percival*, 1:405ff.

6. Leslie F. Church, *Oglethorpe: A Study of Philanthropy in England and Georgia* (London, 1932); Verner W. Crane, "Dr. Thomas Bray and the Charitable Colony Project," *WMQ* 3d ser., 19 (1962):49–63.

7. *Diary of Percival*, 1:12.

8. Ibid., 44–45.

9. Ibid.

10. Ibid., 45.

11. See, for example, ibid., 90, 98, 99, 120, 127–29, 157.

12. Geraldine Meroney, "The London Entrepôt Merchants and the Georgia Colony," *WMQ* 3d ser., 25 (1968):230–44.

13. Rand, ed., *Berkeley and Percival*, 3.

14. Ibid., 203–6.

15. A. A. Luce, ed., *The Works of George Berkeley, Bishop of Cloyne*, 9 vols. (London, 1948–57), 7:345–61, 363–66.

16. A. A. Luce, *The Life of George Berkeley, Bishop of Cloyne* (London, 1949), 94–152; J. E. Crowley, *This Sheba, Self* (Baltimore, 1974); and Crane, "Dr. Thomas Bray and the Charitable Colony Project," 49–63.

17. Sir Robert Montgomery, *A Discourse Concerning the design'd Establishment of a New Colony to the South of Carolina, in the Most delightful Country of the Universe* (London, 1717), reprinted together with other contemporary tracts in Trevor Reese, ed., *The Most Delightful Country of the Universe: Promotional Literature of the Colony of Georgia, 1717–1734* (Savannah, 1972).

18. This was the theme of Berkeley's "America, or the Muse's Refuge, A Prophecy," a poem Egmont read with considerable interest (Luce, *Life of Berkeley*, 95–96, and Luce, ed., *Works of Berkeley*, 7:369–71). Although Berkeley met Oglethorpe, whom he described as an "ingenious English gentleman," in France in 1713, there is no evidence that they remained in close touch (Rand, ed., *Berkeley and Percival*, 130–31).

19. Rand, ed., *Berkeley and Percival*, 276–77; [Benjamin Martyn], *Reasons for Establishing the Colony of Georgia* (London, 1733), reprinted in *Coll. GHS*, 1:204, 216–22.

20. Rand, ed., *Berkeley and Percival*, 203–6.

21. Many of the secondary works on the Trustee period discuss the Trustees' land and labor policies. For the most recent see Paul S. Taylor, *Georgia Plan, 1732–1752* (Berkeley, 1972); Milton L. Ready, *The Castle Builders: Georgia's Economy under the Trustees, 1732–1754* (New York, 1978); and Betty Wood, *Slavery in Colonial Georgia* (Athens, 1984).

22. Crowley, *This Sheba, Self*, 30, 32.

23. For the relevant portion of Bishop Gibson's statement, see Lorenzo J. Greene, *The Negro in Colonial New England, 1620–1775* (New York, 1942), 261.

24. Taylor, *Georgia Plan*, Ready, *Castle Builders*, and Wood, *Slavery in Colonial Georgia*, all provide detailed discussions of the decision to prohibit black slavery.

25. Luce, *Life of Berkeley*, 94–152.

26. Rand, ed., *Berkeley and Percival*, 209–10. For an excellent example see

Diary of Percival, 2:23. Egmont was appalled to discover that Benjamin Martyn had "officiously" invited "Dr. Rundell, whose preferment to the Bishopric of Gloucester is so much contested" to preach the Trustees' Anniversary Sermon. He believed that this was "a very indiscreet step," which would "draw on ourselves the ill-will of numbers of people, and particularly of the clergy."

27. *Diary of Percival*, 1:90–261.

28. Ibid., 1:226–27, 274, 373–74; 2:155–56, 199–200.

29. Ibid., 2:41–43.

30. Ibid., 43.

31. Ibid., 230–33, 286, 291.

32. Ibid., 199–200.

33. Taylor, *Georgia Plan*, passim; Betty Wood, "A Note on the Georgia Malcontents," *GHQ* 63 (1979):264–78; Ralph Gray and Betty Wood, "The Transition from Indentured to Involuntary Servitude in Colonial Georgia," *Explorations in Economic History* 13 (1976):353–70; Wood, *Slavery in Colonial Georgia*, chaps. 2–5.

34. For Egmont's opinion of the malcontents see *Diary of Percival*, vol. 3, passim; Egmont, "Character of the Persons who Sign'd the Representation for Negroes Dec. 9, 1738. A List of the Persons who Sign'd the Memorial to be allow'd Negroes," Egmont Papers, 14203, 181a–181t; and his critique of Patrick Tailfer, et al., *A True and Historical Narrative of the Colony of Georgia in America*, ed. Clarence L. Ver Steeg (1741; reprint, Athens, 1960).

35. See, for example, Egmont Papers, 14203, 185–88; E. Merton Coulter, ed., *The Journal of William Stephens, 1741–1745*, 2 vols. (Athens, 1958–59); and William Stephens, *A State of the Province of Georgia* (London, 1742). The Salzburgers and the Highland Scots at Darien remained loyal to the Trustees (Wood, *Slavery in Colonial Georgia*, chap. 4; Harvey H. Jackson, "The Darien Anti-Slavery Petition of 1739 and the Georgia Plan," *WMQ* 3d ser., 34 [1977]:618–31).

36. For a discussion of Stephens's campaign see Wood, *Slavery in Colonial Georgia*, chaps. 2 and 3, and Betty Wood, "Thomas Stephens and the Introduction of Black Slavery in Georgia," *GHQ* 58 (1974):24–40.

37. *Diary of Percival*, 3:84, 98–105; Egmont Papers, 14210, 95–110, 138–46, 148–54.

38. Stephens's written critiques of the Trustees' scheme included the following items: "Mr. Stephens the Son. His Thoughts on ye Colony of Georgia and the Trustees Measures, 24 Nov. 1739"; "Observations on the present State of Georgia"; both in Egmont Papers, 14210, 62–63, 95–110; *The Hard Case of the Distressed People of Georgia* (London, 1742); *An Account Showing What Money has been Receiv'd by the Trustees for the Use of Georgia. And How They Discharge Themselves Thereof. With*

Observations Thereon (London, 1742); and *A Brief Account of the Causes that have Retarded the Progress of the Colony of Georgia* (London, 1743).

39. *Diary of Percival*, vol. 2, passim.

40. See especially his "Paper for the use of the Trustees, December 11, 1739"; "Proofs of the Importance and Advantage of Georgia to Great Britain, if duly Encouraged"; and "Answers to Queries or Objections that might arise in the Committee of Supply," Egmont Papers, 14210, 138–46.

41. Benjamin Martyn, *An Impartial Inquiry into the State and Utility of Georgia* (London, 1741), and *An Account Showing the Progress of the Colony of Georgia* (London, 1741).

42. *CRG*, 5:583–86.

43. Ibid., 378–79; Egmont Papers, 14212, 38–39.

44. Richard S. Dunn, "The Georgia Trustees and the House of Commons, 1732–1752," *WMQ* 3d ser., 11 (1954):551–65; Taylor, *Georgia Plan*, 44–70, 153–57.

45. *CRG*, 5:643–45.

46. Taylor, *Georgia Plan*, passim; Dunn, "The Georgia Trustees and the House of Commons"; and Wood, *Slavery in Colonial Georgia*, chaps. 2 and 3.

47. *CRG*, 5:635–42.

48. Ibid., 643–44; Egmont Papers, 14213, 36–40.

49. *CRG*, 5:643–44.

50. Taylor, *Georgia Plan*, 212.

51. *CRG*, 5:642–45.

52. Taylor, *Georgia Plan*, chap. 8; Wood, *Slavery in Colonial Georgia*, chap. 5.

The
Settlements
and
Settlers

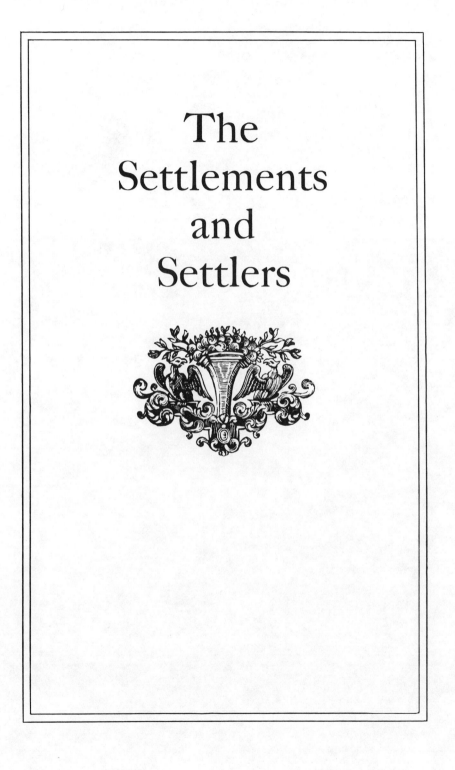

Innovative town planning was not high on the list of legacies Georgia's Trustees hoped to leave behind them, yet ironically the plan for Savannah remains the most visible remnant of the rational design those who sponsored the colony hoped to impress upon the American wilderness. Considering the remarkable condition in which that plan has survived and how it has been expanded by later generations, it is hardly surprising that the origins of its orderly streets and squares have been the subject of considerable study and speculation. In spite of this attention, the roots of the concept and who, if anyone, besides Oglethorpe was responsible for it have remained obscure. John Reps accepted the challenge of unraveling the twisted threads of evidence that lead to the answer and in his essay presents a clear, satisfying explanation of the sources that shaped the ideas of the man, or men, who designed this unique American City.

If town planning was not a high priority among those supporting the Georgia experiment, the defense of the southern frontier clearly was so important that it is impossible to grasp the full significance of settlements below the Savannah unless one understands the military motives behind the venture. Larry E. Ivers's essay on this aspect of the Georgia plan examines precolonization efforts to defend the region, the systems of defense that were used to that end, and the way Georgia's organization was shaped by the perceived need to occupy the "debatable land" militarily. Focusing on the rangers and scouts who formed Carolina's and later Georgia's first line of defense, Ivers evaluates relations between the new colony and her neighbor to the north. He explains what Georgians and their English sponsors wanted the colony to be and also assesses South Carolina's hopes for the Trustees' venture. The essay is revealing, both in its evaluation of frontier defense and in its analysis of the successes and failures of attempts at intercolonial cooperation.

The Settlements and Settlers

Following the first settlement of Georgia, colonists began to come into the province in relatively large, homogeneous groups. The Salzburgers, the Highland and Lowland Scots, the Palatines, the Moravians, and others dared the ocean voyage to challenge the unknown and make their homes on the southern frontier. The Spanish to the south, seeing Georgia burgeon and fearing the pressures that would ultimately be felt in old St. Augustine, commenced a diplomatic maneuver through traditional channels to have the Walpole ministry retract its position supporting Oglethorpe and his colonial mission. In America the Spaniards made threatening noises intended to crack the esprit that they perceived developing in Georgia. Many of the residents of outposts in remote areas of the colony set their jaws and prepared for the worst.

Of the various groups that came to Georgia none had more to lose than the group of Jews who began arriving in Savannah shortly after it was settled. Their presence was noteworthy first because they were allowed to enter at all, yet beyond that their accomplishments broaden our understanding not only of the Jewish experience in America, but also of the nature of the colony in which they chose to live. In spite of obstacles—legal and otherwise—which might have been put in their way, Georgia Jews were able to take active roles in the province's life. This they accomplished without forfeiting their identity, without compromising their beliefs, and, for the most part, without alienating the Christian-oriented majority. B. H. Levy's essay traces Georgia's Jews from Europe, through their initially uneasy acceptance in Georgia, to the ultimate recognition of them as significant members of provincial society. The result is a fascinating study of a small group's adaptation to life on the colonial frontier, and of the practical toleration which made their existence there possible.

JOHN W. REPS

$C^2 + L^2 = S^2$?
Another Look at the Origins
of Savannah's Town Plan

 AVANNAH occupies a unique position in the history of city planning. No complete precedents exist for its pattern of multiple open spaces, and it differs from other settlements in the details of its outlying land system. Many planned towns flourished in colonial America, but none possessed the distinctive character of Savannah. Nor did any other American city rival its record of carefully planned expansion during the first half of the nineteenth century.

Like the New England township and the Spanish pueblo, colonial Savannah combined town and country in a regional development plan. Contemporary surveys and illustrations record its main features. One early engraving shows the town as six tiny rectangles at a bend in the river (Figure 1). Two intervening grids representing gardens and farms separate the town from five-hundred-acre estates beyond. Highgate and Hampstead, two outlying villages each cut into wedge-shaped parcels by radial property lines, appear near the center.

A survey made about 1800 shows the peculiar and unexplained division of ten-acre squares by diagonals to create triangular, five-acre gardens (Figure 2). The forty-five-acre farms were arranged in groups of ten, corresponding to tythings of ten house lots in the town. A common surrounded Savannah on three sides, and it was on this land that the community expanded.

A Moravian drawing of ca. 1740 (Figure 3) and William De Brahm's survey of ca. 1770 (Figure 4) reveal the structure of urban Savannah. It consisted of six identical wards, each composed of forty house lots sixty by ninety feet and arranged in four tythings of ten lots. Flanking

1. *A Map of the County of Savannah.* Detail of map published in 1735 showing the land system of Savannah, Georgia. (Geography and Map Division, Library of Congress.)

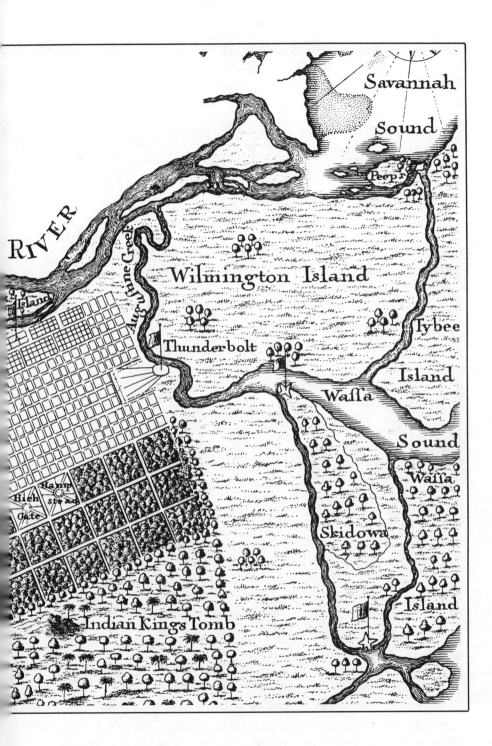

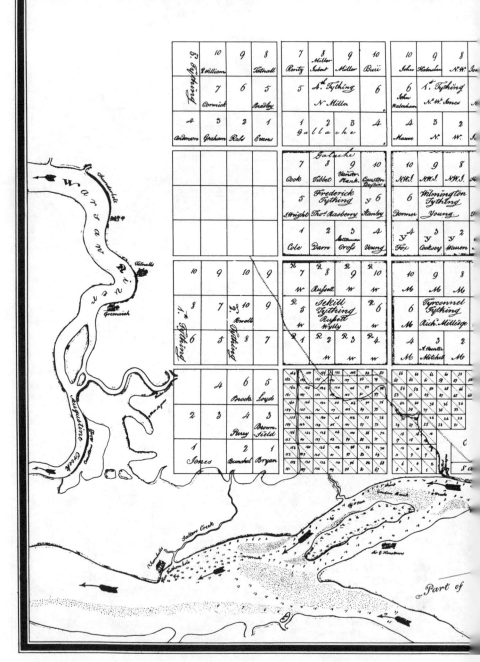

2. Untitled map of Savannah, Georgia, with its common, garden, and farms, drawn ca. 1800 by John McKinnon and published in 1904. (Geography and Map Division, Library of Congress.)

Map of wards and lots

Grid — upper left block

7	8 Rhett	9 Adams	10 Richard
5 S. Tything Minis Robᵗ Bolton	6 Oakman Almon		
1 Spencer	2 Minis	3 Minis	4

7 Brown John	8 Turner Minis	9 Milledge Minis	10
5 Slucks Tything Tetard	6 Minis		
1 Mivell	2 Grahm Tetard	3 Mercer Woodhouse	4

8 olland thing J. Lewden	9 Barbo Bulloch	10 Wilson Morel	
5 Morel	6 Ewen	7 Doveaux	8
1	2 Morel	3 Ewen	4 Ewen

Upper middle block

10 Cross C.W.	9 McSmith	8 Minis	7
6 Johnson	T. Tything Charles Watson	C.W. 5 McDonald Ross	
4 Walker Minis	3 Kitchman Richardson	2 Spang enburg	1 Windrope

10 Milledge Minis	9 Mollen	8 Potter Houston	7 Desbow
6 Hainks	Moores Tything T. Bailley	5 Millen	
4 Kelly	3 Egerton Sheftall	2 Desbow Sheftall	1 Blithi man

10 Greedy Bulloch	9 Papot	8 Papot	7 Wattman
6 H Parker Dews	Sloper Tything Jasᵗ Parker	5 W. Parker	
4 Cuny	3 Breton	2 Delgress	1 Breton

Third block (Belitka / Laroache)

7 Loyer	8 Baillou	D 9	10 Rone
5 Sheftall Aspten	Belitka Tything Dean David Trosan	6 Scott	
1 Bush	D 2 Loyer Gibbins	D 3 Becue	4 Peters

7 Mc	8 Mc	Dobit 9 Vickory	10 MC J. Wickenham
5 Mc	Laroache Tything Millen	6 Mc	
1 Mc	2 Gauet	3 Clark	4 Bailley

9 Grahm Baillou	10 Hanman	Dobyn Mc Mhason Bardman	10
Tyth by 7 Mises	S.F. Jenkins Green	S.F. Demsby Jatler	S.F. Nunes Molina
Dig by 5 Francis	S.F. 6 Mears	S.F. Tendee	S.F. Sheftall
Dig 3 Elphinson	S.F. 4 McKay	S.F. Heathcote Carleton	S.F. 4 Ball
Hall	2 Hall	2 Lever	2 Lever
Cuthbert	Zubly	Lever	Lever

Fourth block (Vernon / Eyl)

7 J. Gibbons	8 E. Minis Williston	9 Tailleu	10 Bowler
5 Barnett	Vernon Tything Thomas Tripp	W 6 Drobler Tripp	
D 1 Carleton	2 Vall	3 mer	W 4 Drobler

7 Mc	8 Mc	9 Kent	10 Mc
5 Mc	Eyl Tything Millen	6 Mc	
1 Tallapid Lyd Dean	2 Chaʳ Mc	3 Snooks	4 Tallapid

9 Oliver Unsell	10 Sale	9 Love	10 P. Inas
over Tyth 7 Dacosta	8 Green	7	8
S.F. 5 Dobyn	2 Emoy	ter 5	6
For 3 Foster	S.F. 4 Green	2 Love	4 Nunes Fabie
1 Zn	2 Zn	1 Zn	2
Duckie	Calvert	Gilbert	Nunes

Lower map (river / island area)

Bridge — Newington Road

Vale Royal

...sons Island

Docᵗ Beacroft

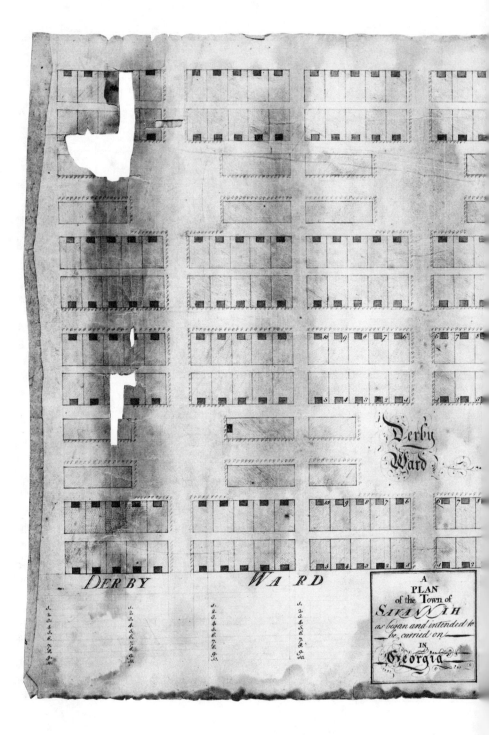

DERBY WARD

Derby Ward

A
PLAN
of the Town of
SAVANNAH
as began and intended to
be carried on
IN
Georgia

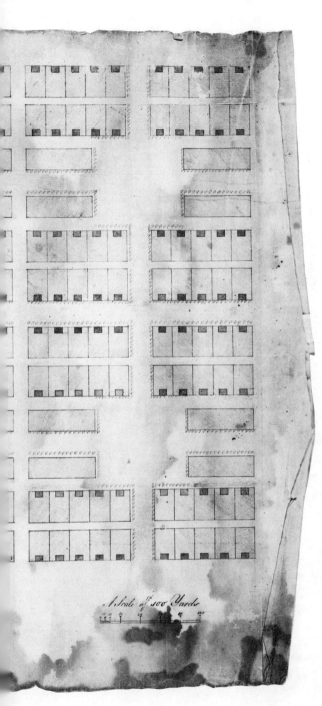

3. "A Plan of the Town of Savannah as began and intended to be carried on in Georgia." Unsigned manuscript plan of Savannah, Georgia, drawn ca. 1740. (Moravian Archives, Bethlehem, Pennsylvania.)

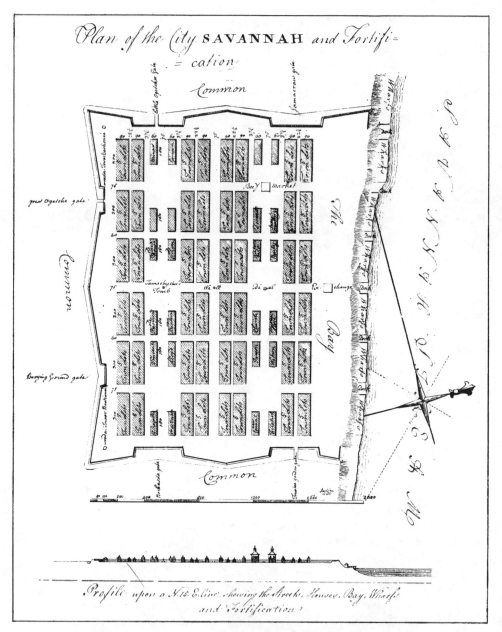

4. "Plan of the City Savannah and Fortification." Manuscript plan of
Savannah, Georgia, drawn ca. 1770 by William Gerard De Brahm.
(Harvard University Library.)

the open square in the center of each ward were four small blocks called trust lots intended for civic, religious, and institutional buildings.[1]

The open space created by the placement of blocks and the location of streets took an unusual and intricate pattern. On the north and south sides only a single street enters the square. On the east and west sides streets also enter on the axis of the square but are paralleled by two others at the corners.

It is no surprise to learn that such a distinctive urban design attracted the attention of persons curious about its origins. Not quite a century ago William Harden addressed the Georgia Historical Society on this subject. He introduced the now discredited theory that one or more garden layouts in Robert Castell's *Villas of the Ancients* provided a prototype for the Savannah plan.[2]

Harden's explanation remained unchallenged for many years, but in 1936 Amos A. Ettinger, a biographer of Oglethorpe, referred to Sir Robert Montgomery's abortive settlement scheme of 1717 and pointed out that Savannah had been surveyed "in rigidly regular blocks, relieved only by squares, much on the old Margravate of Azilia plan" (Figure 5) devised by Montgomery.[3]

Two other theories assume that Oglethorpe knew of engraved plates in two dissimilar works, remembered them, and relied on them in part as models for the design of Savannah. One was Robert Barret's *Theorike and Practike of Modern Warres* published in London in 1598 and put forward by Turpin Bannister in 1961 as a possible prototype for Savannah's system of multiple squares.[4]

In 1964 Laura Palmer Bell offered a new explanation: that Oglethorpe drew his inspiration from a design for an extension of Peking published in 1705 as a plate in John Harris's *Complete Collection of Voyages and Travels*. She noted that Oglethorpe's older brother returned from China in the year of publication and that the book would thus surely have been known to the Oglethorpe family.[5]

More recently Anthony Morris in his *History of Urban Form* advanced the notion that William Newcourt's plan for rebuilding London after the Great Fire in 1666 could have offered an example for the repeating squares of Savannah.[6] Newcourt proposed a modular pattern based on blocks 570 feet by 855 feet, each constituting a parish and with a parish church occupying a square at the center. Newcourt's parishes and Savannah's wards are thus almost exactly the same size. But because Newcourt's plan existed only in manuscript and was not

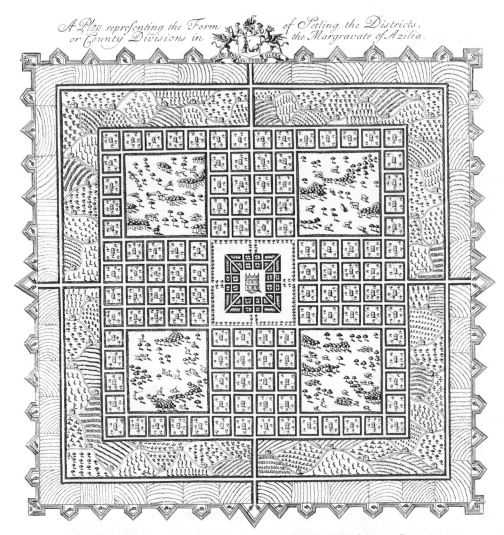

5. "A Plan Representing the Form of Settling the Districts, or County Divisions in the Margravate of Azilia." Plan of the Settlement in Georgia proposed by Sir Robert Montgomery in 1717. (Olin Library, Cornell University.)

reproduced until 1939 it seems unlikely it could have been known to Oglethorpe or any of his associates.[7]

The distinctive pattern of the Savannah squares formed by the open space and the streets entering it has also been the subject of speculation. In his *Design of Cities* Edmund Bacon suggested that an ideal town illustrated in a book by Pietro di Giacomo Cataneo in 1567 may have inspired the planner of Savannah.[8] The central square in this design and those of Savannah are essentially identical, whereas the four others resembled the squares at New Ebenezer (Figure 6), where the two trust lots on each side are combined into one. This argument assumes, as does Bannister's, that Oglethorpe devised the plan of Savannah and was familiar with the works of Cataneo and Barret. Oglethorpe had served as aide-de-camp to Prince Eugene of Savoy and doubtless would have had access to books on various aspects of military science used by this most modern of European generals.[9]

Tracing the origins of design concepts can rarely be done with certainty. As one scholar of London's planning history observed, "It is foolhardy to pretend to know the real motives either of individuals or of groups. The agents and stewards and surveyors of the great London estates were not given to putting down on paper the innermost secrets of their hearts for the instruction of future historians."[10] The Earl of Egmont and James Oglethorpe were no more obliging.

Simpler explanations are more likely to be nearer the truth than those requiring multiple assumptions, and examples from the recent past seem more plausible as prototypes than those of much earlier eras. For city planners, executed projects offer more persuasive models than those with only a paper existence. Finally, a planner more often looks for inspiration to other town plans than to designs for gardens, whether those illustrated by Robert Castell in 1728 or prepared by Dominique Girard in 1717 for the Belvedere palaces in Vienna of Prince Eugene.[11]

Using these criteria as guides to a renewed inquiry helps to narrow the range of possibilities. We can start with what seems to be Oglethorpe's only statement concerning town planning before the founding of Savannah. In a promotional tract issued in 1732, unsigned but attributed to Oglethorpe, the author defended the proposed settlement of Georgia by referring to "a Precedent of our own for planting Colonies, which . . . may be worthy of our Imitation." He then described the systematic settlement of Northern Ireland early in the seventeenth century by the London companies in Ulster. Each company, like the

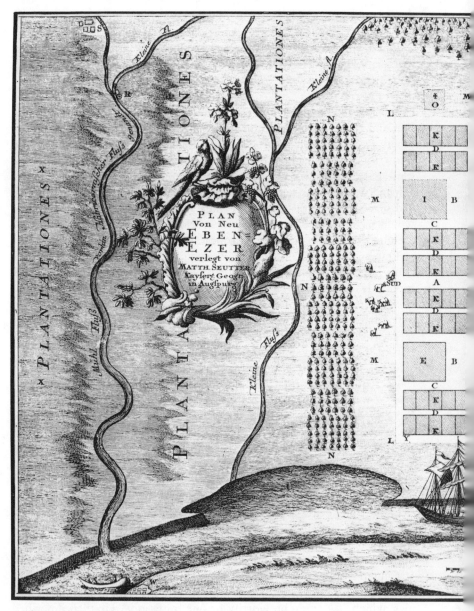

6. *Plan Von Neu Ebenezer*. Plan of New Ebenezer, Georgia, drawn and published by Matthaus Seutter in 1747. (John W. Reps.)

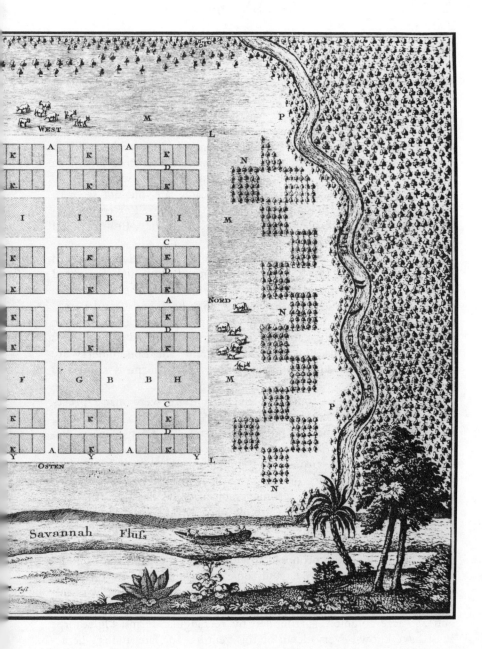

WEST

M

L

P

N

K

A

K

A

K

D

K

K

K

K

D

K

I

I

B

B

I

M

N

K

K

K

D

K

K

K

K

D

K

A

NORD

K

K

K

D

N

K

K

K

D

K

M

F

G

B

B

H

P

C

K

K

K

D

K

K

K

K

D

K

Y

A

Y

A

Y

L

OSTEN

N

Savannah Fluss

Drapers at Moneymore, built one or more towns in its own domain. Together, as Oglethorpe noted, they founded Londonderry and Coleraine.[12]

In my first published study of Savannah in 1960 I called attention to this significant passage and used it again in 1965 in *The Making of Urban America*. It took another four years and one book later before it dawned on me that the square at Coleraine (Figure 7) resembled the distinctive patterns used at Savannah, lacking only the streets on either side that would have created the equivalent of the trust lots. The square at Londonderry—the classic Renaissance type with a single street entering on axis at the midpoint of each side—did not seem to be related to Savannah (Figure 7), although it was used extensively in South Carolina in such places as Charleston, Childbury, Beaufort, and Orangeburg.[13]

Combine the two squares, however, and the Savannah pattern emerges (Figure 8). The formula in the title is explained if restated in a way now fallen into disuse: The square of C plus the square of L equals the square of S, where S stands for Savannah and C and L represent Coleraine and Londonderry. The question mark in the title suggests some scholarly caution, for more straightforward solutions exist. The fact remains, however, that Coleraine and Londonderry are the only two places whose planning history Oglethorpe is known to have considered.

For the common surrounding Savannah there were many precedents. Montgomery incorporated this feature in his Azilia plan, placing it between the city and the mile-square estates and larger parks beyond. Montgomery described it as "a large void space, which will be useful for a thousand purposes and among the rest, as being airy and affording a fine prospect of the town in drawing near it."[14] Town commons were also used in planning such places as Bath, North Carolina, and Georgetown, South Carolina. The latter town, laid out not long before Savannah, had one hundred acres set aside for this purpose.

Immediately before the settlement of Georgia the Trustees learned at first hand about the proposed town of Purrysburg on the opposite bank of the Savannah River and some miles upstream. In July 1732 they entertained Jean Pierre Purry shortly before he led his Swiss colonists to the site.[15] Purry probably showed them his plan for a town and 260-acre common, surrounded by rectangular farms. Oglethorpe must have known every detail of this venture, for late in 1731 he acquired a one-fourth interest in the project.[16]

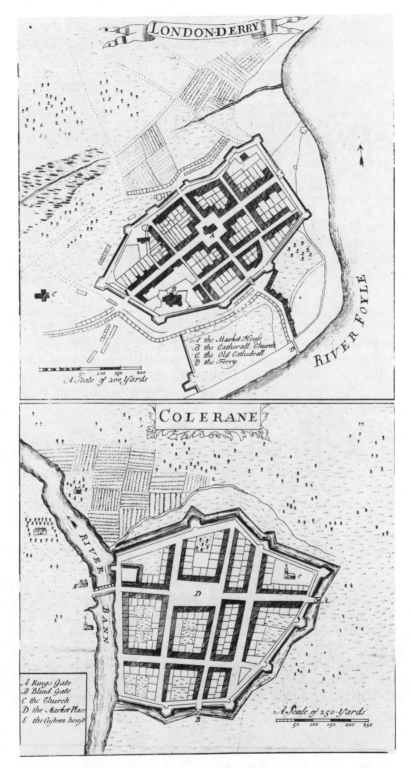

7. *London-Derry. Colerane.* Plans of Londonderry and Coleraine, Northern
Ireland, published in 1683 in William Petty, *Hiberniae Delineatio.*
(Newberry Library.)

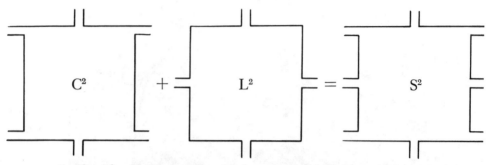

8. $C^2 + L^2 = S^2$. Diagram showing how the plans of squares used at Coleraine and Londonderry can be combined to produce a square like those of Savannah. (John W. Reps.)

Purrysburg was the first of several new townships resulting from Governor Robert Johnson's policy to revitalize South Carolina. The instructions from the crown handed to him in 1730 culminated many years of abortive settlement attempts. Kenneth Coleman has pointed out the similarities between Trustee policies and regulations and several of these earlier proposals, indicating close scrutiny of Carolina precedents by the Trustees.[17]

Clearly, then, they would have examined carefully Johnson's land system calling for townships of twenty-thousand acres "to be laid out in square plats of ground, one side thereof to front ye respective rivers." Each township was to have "a town contiguous to the river." There "each inhabitant" was to be granted a town lot in addition to fifty acres elsewhere for cultivation. Finally, "a quantity of land not exceeding 300 acres contiguous to ye sd. town shall be set apart for a common."[18]

Before proceeding further we need to consider three related questions: when was Savannah's plan prepared, where was it done, and who determined its design? The unusual pattern of Savannah's squares, its unique combination of streets and open spaces, and the intricate land system of the surrounding region argue strongly against the notion of its design as an inspiration of the moment. Oglethorpe's military background and orderly mind also suggest that he would not have left such an important matter to be determined so casually. In writing to the Trustees that he had founded the town he neither described it nor mentioned sending them a plat. A not unreasonable inference is that such information would have been unnecessary because the Trustees knew the plan's details.[19]

A more persuasive clue is the engraved frontispiece (Figure 9) used by the secretary to the Trustees, Benjamin Martyn, in his promotional tract published shortly before Oglethorpe's report arrived from Georgia. This view shows the outline of the common, the farm area with the tything parcels, and—beyond—radial field divisions of villages corresponding to the locations used for the outlying hamlets of Highgate and Hampstead. Moreover, Martyn described the land system as consisting of "one lot for a house and yard in the town, another for a garden near the town, and a third for a farm at a little distance from the town."[20]

A conclusion that the plan of Savannah was prepared in England leads inevitably to the issue of its authorship. It seems almost certain that Oglethorpe was involved, but the only evidence that links him with city planning is his general references to the towns of the Ulster Plantation and his statement to the Trustees that he "laid out the town" and "marked out the town and common" of Savannah. Are these the words of a planner who has created a novel urban design or of a surveyor who is applying a preconceived plan to a vacant site?

If not Oglethorpe, who might have filled the role of city planner? Benjamin Martyn emerges as the strongest candidate. As secretary to the Trustees and responsible for a host of administrative details he may have been asked to plan or help plan the town, but that is mere conjecture. That he was preoccupied with towns and town planning, however, is amply documented by page after page in a draft of his tract, *Reasons for Establishing the Colony of Georgia*. The published version omitted these many passages.

They include statements on the importance of towns, references to town founding in history, a lengthy extract from Vitruvius concerning site selection for new towns, and the following prescription for how the first town of Georgia should be laid out in which one can note the possible genesis of the trust lots: "The streets should be spacious & laid out by line & a large Square reserved for a Market place & for exercising the Inhabitants, on the sides of which may be the Church, infirmary for the Sick, and House for new Comers, Town House & other publick Buildings." Martyn also proposed grouping the colonists into hundreds, laths, and tythings and arranging ownership patterns so that those living as neighbors in town would also have adjoining farms. Further, he advocated creating satellite villages and

9. Untitled prospective view of Savannah, Georgia, and vicinity in 1732, drawn and engraved by John Pine for [Benjamin Martyn], *Reasons for Establishing the Colony of Georgia* (London, 1733). (Olin Library, Cornell University.)

specified that "Without the Town a Mile square which amounts to 640 Acres might be reserved as a Common for the pasturing of the Cattle." Finally, his manuscript recommended the procedure that Oglethorpe followed almost to the letter on July 7, 1733, when he assembled the colonists at dawn, led them in prayer, named the wards and tythings, and assigned house lots to each family.[21]

As the author of this document, it seems almost inconceivable that Martyn did not play a major, perhaps dominant, role in devising the city plan. Nevertheless, the Savannah that Oglethorpe laid out differed in several ways from Martyn's vision. The common was smaller, and the names and sizes of the groups into which Martyn proposed dividing the colonists were modified. Far more important, Savannah in 1733 consisted of four wards and squares, not one, and there is every reason to believe that its early expansion by two additional wards was envisaged from the day of its founding.

We can only speculate about the process by which Martyn's first city planning proposals may have been reviewed by the Trustees, modified, and refined, so they emerged as the basis for Oglethorpe's surveys. The records of the Trustees contain no clues, nor do Egmont's journals. It is possible that in their deliberations or in informal discussions Oglethorpe or others pointed out the multiple square city plans in the works of Robert Barret or John Harris. Martyn, who regarded Vitruvius highly, might have owned a copy of Cataneo's book. Perhaps Lord Percival, soon to be the Earl of Egmont in the Irish peerage, remembered the squares at Londonderry and Coleraine and thought of combining their features.[22]

There is no evidence that *any* of this took place, nor does one need to believe that it did. For a few minutes' walk from their Westminster office in Old Palace Yard Martyn and the Trustees could find prototypes of the city planning elements they so ingeniously combined in their plan of urban Savannah. By 1732 the creation of defined neighborhoods, each focusing on an open square, had become the prevailing and accepted method for developing London real estate (Figure 10). To understand the significance of this development in tracing the pedigree of Savannah's urban form we need to look briefly at how London grew in the century before the colonization of Georgia.

The process began a century before the Georgia colony, when Inigo Jones designed Covent Garden for the Earl of Bedford in 1631 (Figure 11). This first London residential square proved so popular and profitable that the earl soon subdivided other parts of his estate. His pioneering venture set the stage for designs that were to follow as growth took place in this area west of the ancient bounds of the city.[23]

The Civil War halted two other projects of similar character—Leicester Square and the completion of buildings facing Lincoln's Inn fields—but these were carried out shortly after the Restoration. Several entirely new squares and neighborhoods then joined these older projects, starting with the Earl of Southampton's Bloomsbury Square in 1661 and St. James's Square, begun a year later by Henry Jermyn, the Earl of St. Albans (Figure 12).

The Great Fire of 1666 stimulated further construction in this area, and several new squares provided centers for fashionable neighborhoods. Golden Square in 1674, Soho Square in 1681, Red Lion Square in 1684, and Queen Square in 1705 brought their number to nine. Early in the eighteenth century what was to become Berkeley Square began to take its present form although it was not fully enclosed by buildings for many years.

At the beginning of the Georgian period modern London thus consisted of a series of neighborhoods, each centered on an open square. No overall plan governed their locations, however, nor were the squares connected to one another by clear and direct links. Donald Olsen explained why: "Each landlord's power was confined to his own estate, and no centralized authority existed to coordinate the individual plans. Each estate was dealt with as if it were an autonomous village."[24]

One can understand the seemingly whimsical location of London's squares and the alignment of the streets around them only by tracing the outlines of the major landholdings that their owners gradually converted to neighborhoods (Figure 13). These varied and irregular boundaries reflect ancient field lines, manorial assignments, ecclesiastical patents, grants to royal favorites, and more recent purchases by speculative builders.[25]

Shortly before the colonization of Georgia, owners of three adjacent estates lying at London's northwestern fringe created, almost simultaneously, new neighborhoods centering around Grosvenor Square, Cavendish Square, and Hanover Square (Figure 14). Taken together the three developments departed from previous practice in their fairly consistent use of a grid street system and, of greater significance, in their coordinated linkages that tied the three squares together so that visually and functionally each gained something from the other. This relationship was not unlike that of the Savannah squares.[26]

10. *A Plan of the Cities of London and Westminster* . . . Detail of a plan of London drawn by John Rocque and published in 1746 by John Pine and John Tinney. (John W. Reps.)

COVENT GARDEN

11. *Covent Garden.* View of Covent Garden, London, engraved by Sutton Nicholls and published by John Bowles ca. 1731. (Print Room, British Library.)

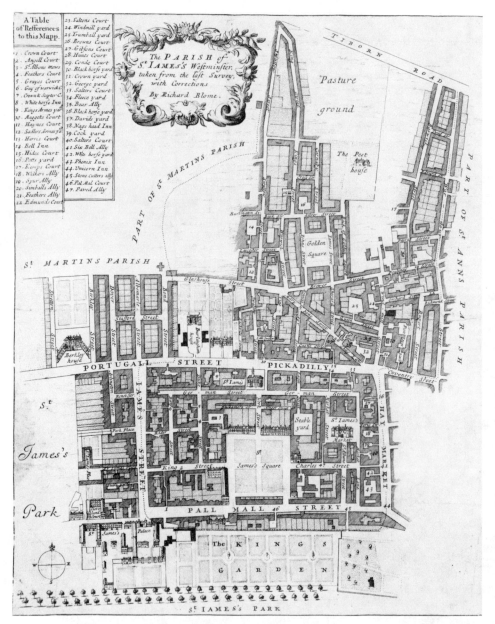

12. "The Parish of St. James's Westminster." Plan of St. James's Square and vicinity, London, drawn by Richard Blome in 1689. (Map Room, British Library.)

Other features of this portion of London suggest a connection with the planning of Savannah. Note the distinctive design of Hanover Square, entered on axis by single streets from north and south and by two streets on each side at the corners.[27] In this respect it closely resembles the Savannah pattern and is almost identical to that used at New Ebenezer (Figure 6). Reinforcing the case for Hanover Square as a model for those of Savannah is the fact that one of the first residents of Lord Scarborough's development in 1717 was General George Carpenter, later Lord Carpenter, a charter member of the Council of the Georgia Trustees.[28]

At this point let me indulge in a bit of historical fantasy. Suppose that in the years these three squares were begun the entire area had been in single rather than divided ownership and the suppositious landowner had controlled adjacent property as well. Might he not have planned his vast estate much as John Gwynn proposed be done for this area forty years later? Gwynn's plan (Figure 15) exhibits the same regularity of standardized open squares, all carefully coordinated in a grid street system, that one finds at Savannah. What Gwynn articulated in 1766 merely expressed the principles of estate development that were fully accepted decades earlier but could not be carried out in London because of the limited size of estates and the irregularities of their borders.[29]

Or—to depart even more from the conventions of historical investigation—consider the plan the Earl of Scarborough might have proposed for a town in Georgia if he and not Robert Montgomery had received the Azilia grant in 1717. Unfettered by ancient property limits that confined his London neighborhood to a single square and a few streets, Scarborough might have produced a plan for half a dozen such squares so arranged as to recall the relationships between Hanover Square and its two neighbors to the west and north (Figure 16).

Far less speculative is the argument that these new additions to London were regarded as something more than mere residential appendages and could have been looked on as prototypes for an entirely new community. George Rudé points out in his *Hanoverian London* that these projects "firmly established . . . the principle of a complete unit of development, comprising square, secondary streets, markets and even a church." In turn these created demand "not only [for] shops, inns and markets but also the erection of smaller houses and dwellings for the nobleman's retainers or others."[30]

In short, each of these estates resembled a complete town or small

13. *Plan of the Cities of London and Westminster and Borough of Southwark, with the Contiguous Buildings*. Detail of a plan of London drawn by M. Folkes and P. Davall from an earlier plan by John Rocque,

published in 1742 by John Pine and John Tinney. Boundaries of the major
London estates are added. (John W. Reps.)

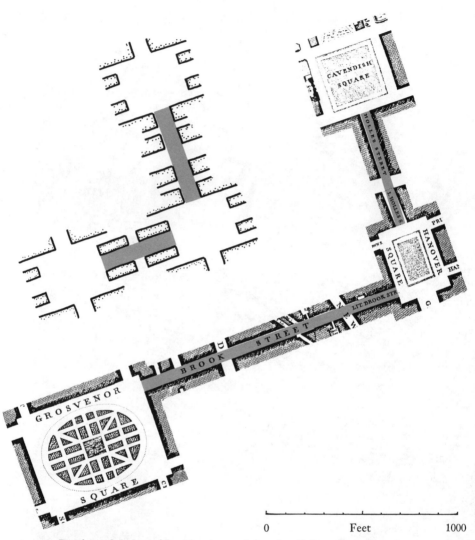

CAVENDISH SQUARE

HANOVER SQUARE

GROSVENOR SQUARE

BROOK STREET

LIT BROOK STR

0   Feet   1000

14. Portion of a plan of London in 1746 showing linkages between Grosvenor, Hanover, and Cavendish Squares and part of the plan of Savannah at the same scale. (John W. Reps.)

city, as many contemporary observers noted. John Evelyn in 1665 called Bloomsbury Square "a little towne," and Daniel Defoe in 1724 referred to Cavendish Square as "that new City on the *North* Side of *Tyburn* Road." A writer for the London *Weekly Medley* visited Hanover Square when building began in 1717 and found "so many . . . edifices that a whole magnificent city seems to be risen out of the ground."[31]

In 1731, on the eve of Georgia colonization, John Bowles, an enterprising print dealer and publisher, issued a fine set of engravings by Sutton Nicholls showing all of the London squares. The view of Grosvenor Square in Figure 17 is a typical example. Bowles must have sold thousands of these prints as wall decorations. They would have called attention—if any such reminder were necessary—to how prevalent and widely accepted this form of development had become as a means of converting vacant land to productive urban uses.[32]

Several Trustees and members of the Common Council would have needed no such prompting, for—like Lord Carpenter—they, too, lived on or near one of the squares. George Heathcote then resided on Soho Square, as had James Vernon in earlier years. The Earl of Egmont and John Laroche lived on Pall Mall and William Sloper on St. James's Place, all three within a stone's throw of St. James's Square.[33] We do not know where every Trustee lived, but it would have been virtually impossible for a Londoner to move about the city in middle- and upper-class society and remain for long unfamiliar with the appearance of these squares and at least some knowledge of their place in the history of real estate development.

London influenced the plans of other colonial towns. In 1683 Thomas Holme described the plan for Philadelphia that he and William Penn devised a year earlier and referred to the four squares "in each Quarter of the City . . . to be for the like Uses, as the Moore-fields in London."[34] In South Carolina the town of Willtown was renamed New London when it was replatted, apparently in 1714. London place names abound: Chelsey Road, Fleet Ditch, Cornhill, Limehouse, Piccadilly, and others. Almost every block or "square" bears a name: Golden Square, St. James's Square, Berkley Square, Leicester Field, Red Lyon Square, and many more.[35]

Look at the nomenclature in Savannah. What is now Telfair Square in Heathcote Ward received in 1733 the name of St. James's Square. Remember also the two suburban villages south of the city shown in Figure 2: Highgate and Hampstead. In London if one looked north

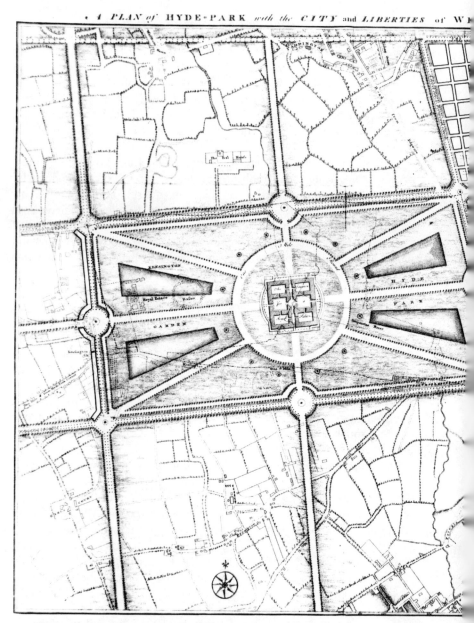

15. *A Plan of Hyde-Park with the City and Liberties of Westminster &C.
Shewing the several Improvements propos'd.* Plan by John Gwynn for the
West End of London in 1766, from his *London and Westminster Improved.*
(Olin Library, Cornell University.)

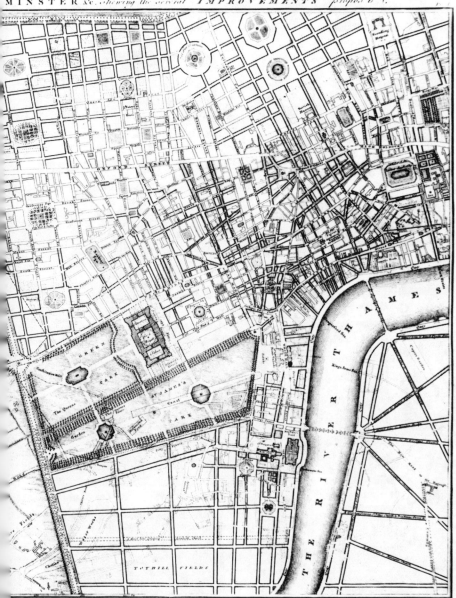

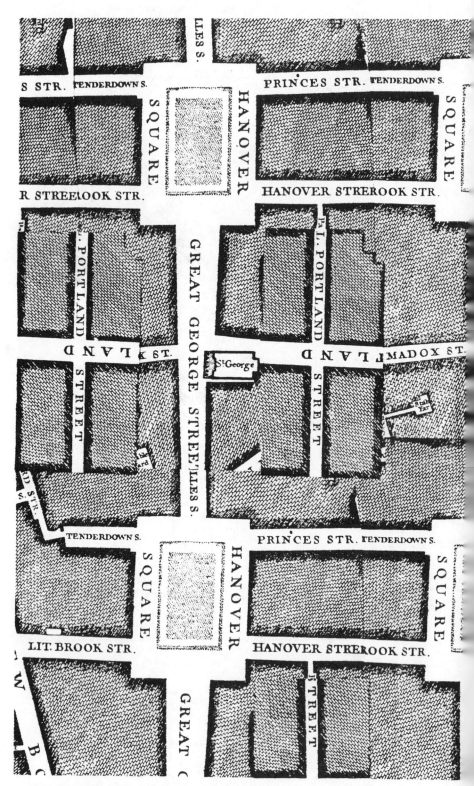

16. Imaginary plan for a town created by repeating the design for Hanover Square in London as drawn by John Rocque in 1746. (John W. Reps.)

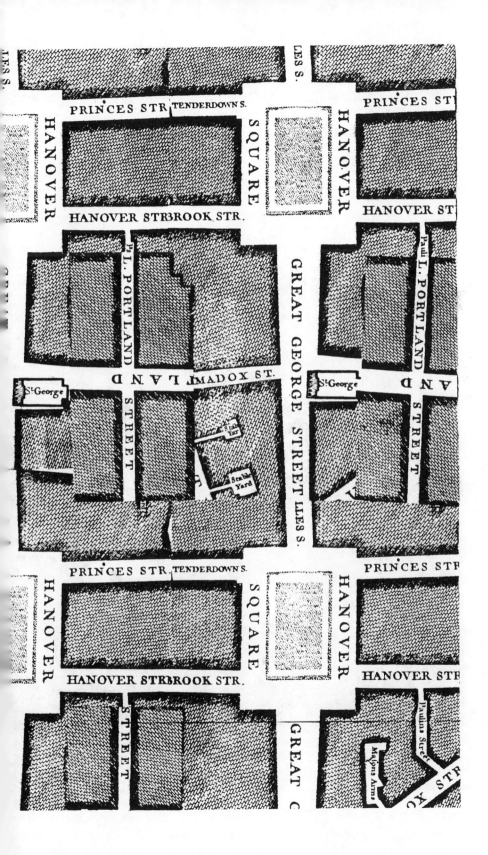

17. *Grovenor Square*. View of Grosvenor Square, London, probably engraved by Sutton Nicholls and published by John Bowles, ca. 1731. (Print Room, British Library.)

from Hanover Square, Highgate would be on the right, Hampstead on the left. The Savannah planner maintained this relationship although the compass directions were reversed.

The case for London's squares as a major influence in the planning of Savannah also rests on similarity of scale (Figure 18). Although Golden Square is smaller than Savannah's open spaces and Grosvenor and St. James's Squares and Lincoln's Inn Fields are somewhat larger, the others are about the same size. For example, the Savannah squares measure 270 by 315 feet, while Hanover Square is 275 by 375 feet.

It thus requires no great stretch of the imagination to believe that the Georgia Trustees derived their orderly and symmetrical city plan from the pattern of London's West End. At Savannah, laid out on a virgin site previously unviolated by land surveyors, neatly rectangular wards precisely centered on squares of uniform area replaced London's irregularly bounded and variously sized private estates and squares.

The modular nature of the original town is clearly revealed in Peter Gordon's engraving of 1734 (Figure 19), suggesting that the persons responsible for its design also envisaged expansion by the addition of one or more units when the need arose. Creation of two new wards in 1735 thus echoed the manner in which London grew during the previous century.

Savannah followed that tradition after the Revolution but used the power gained through municipal ownership of the common to shape growth in the public interest. The decisions to do so and, in the process, to replicate the original, spatially nonhierarchical system of uniform open spaces produced America's most unusual city plan.

At the end of this unparalleled era of phased and controlled urban growth John William Hill depicted Savannah looking north on Bull Street from a point above Monterey Square (Figure 20). The close resemblance of his lithograph to the Sutton Nicholls engraving illustrated in Figure 21 showing Hanover Square and its Cavendish Square neighbor to the north rests on more than mere coincidence or shared artistic convention. Instead, it reflects a genetic relationship, for Monterey Square is one of eighteen clones derived from the six laid out in the colonial era. Like the seedlings for the Trustees' Garden, those original squares came as transplants from the London estates whose first English rootstock was put down in the soil of Covent Garden. Ignored for a time, allowed to wither and decay, the squares of Savannah's incomparable city plan now flourish under a new generation of urban caretakers.

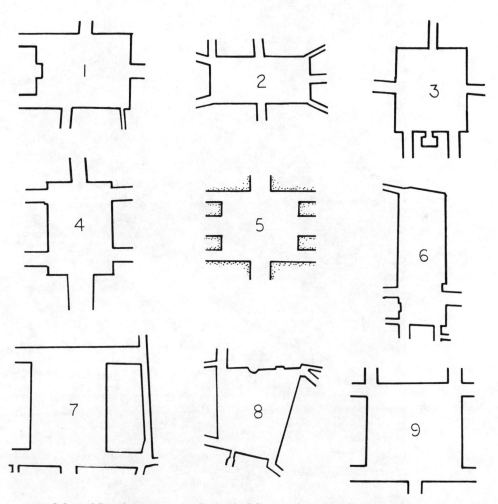

18. Selected London squares and a typical Savannah square drawn to the same scale: (1) Covent Garden; (2) Red Lion Square; (3) Soho Square; (4) Hanover Square; (5) Savannah; (6) Queen's Square; (7) Bloomsbury Square; (8) Leicester Square; (9) Cavendish Square. (John W. Reps.)

1. The Stairs going up.
2. M.r Oglethorpe's Tent.
3. The Crane & Bell.
4. The Tabernacle & Court House.
5. The publick Mill.
6. The House for Strangers.
7. The publick Oven.
8. The draw Well.

To the Hon.ble the Trustees for establis.

This View of the Town of Savanah

vüe de Savanah

19. *A View of Savannah as it stood the 29th of March, 1734.* View of Savannah, Georgia, in 1734, drawn by Peter Gordon and engraved by P. Fourdrinier. (Prints and Photographs Division, Library of Congress.)

e Colony of Georgia in America

dedicated by their Honours

Obliged and most Obedient Servant.

Georgie. Peter Gordon.

P. Fourdrinier Sculp.

9. The Lott for the Church.
10. The publick Stores.
11. The Fort.
12. The Parsonage House.
13. The Pallisadoes.
14. The Guard House and
     Battery of Cannon.
15. Hutchinsons Island.

20. *Savannah, Ga. 1855.* View of Savannah, Georgia, in 1855, drawn by
J. W. Hill. (Georgia Historical Society.)

21. *Hanover Square*. View of Hanover Square, London, drawn and engraved by Sutton Nicholls, ca. 1731, as reissued in 1754. (John W. Reps.)

QUARE.

gh gate

Princess Str:

Hannover Street

NOTES

1. Except for De Brahm's survey, all of the maps mentioned are reproduced at large page size in John W. Reps, *The Making of Urban America* (Princeton, 1965), 188–91. De Brahm's plan of the city was reproduced from his manuscript "History of the Province of Georgia," Harvard University Library. These and other early surveys and plans of Savannah have been frequently reproduced elsewhere.

2. William Harden, *A Suggestion as to the Origin of the Plan of Savannah. Remarks by Wm. Harden, before the Georgia Historical Society, Monday, Sept. 7th, 1885.* A copy of this printed address is in the collection of the Georgia Historical Society. Harden stated that Castell's plight as a debtor awakened Oglethorpe's interest in prison reform and led to the Georgia Trustees' policy of bringing such persons to America to begin a new life. Harden's title promised more than he delivered, for he had to admit that he could "not . . . point out the particular features wherein the plan of Savannah as originally laid out resembles the descriptions given in the book," although he maintained that "to my mind, unskilled as it is in the knowledge of architecture, there are points of resemblance."

3. Amos Aschbach Ettinger, *James Edward Oglethorpe: Imperial Idealist* (Oxford, 1936), 132. The plan for the Margravate of Azilia is an engraving in Sir Robert Montgomery, *A Discourse Concerning the design'd Establishment of a New Colony to the South of Carolina, in the Most delightful Country of the Universe* (London, 1717).

4. Turpin C. Bannister, "Oglethorpe's Sources for the Savannah Plan," *Journal of the Society of Architectural Historians* 20 (1961):47–62. In an earlier work I noted that "Bannister's argument fails to explain why Oglethorpe used a quite different pattern for the very towns where one would expect castrametation theories to be applied—at the fortress communities of Frederica and Augusta" (Reps, *Making of Urban America*, 199, n. 24).

5. Laura Palmer Bell, "A New Theory of the Plan of Savannah," *GHQ* 48 (1964):146–65.

6. A. E. J. Morris, *History of Urban Form* (London, 1972), 230.

7. Newcourt's plan was first published in T. F. Reddaway, "The Rebuilding of London after the Great Fire: A Rediscovered Plan," *Town Planning Review* 18 (1939):155–61. It is reproduced in Reps, *Making of Urban America*, 164, in which I pointed out the similarity in the location of Newcourt's five great open spaces to the design of Philadelphia. Because Thomas Holme (who, with William Penn, laid out Philadelphia) was a surveyor, he might have known Newcourt, the co-cartographer of a detailed survey of London published in 1658. Penn's father was close to Charles II, and through him the young Penn might also have been familiar with Newcourt's plan for rebuilding London, which doubtless came to the attention of the

king as did those of Evelyn and Wren. It seems far less likely that any of those responsible for the Georgia colony would have known about the Newcourt plan. Nevertheless, although not noted by Morris, the area of Newcourt's parishes and the Savannah wards is nearly identical—a feature I had not realized until preparing this paper.

8. Edmund N. Bacon, *The Design of Cities* (New York, 1967), 292–93. Cataneo's work is *I Quattro Primi Libri de Architettura*, available in a facsimile reprint (Ridgewood, N.J., 1964).

9. Prince Eugene's military career was first recorded in English in George Bruce Malleson, *Prince Eugene of Savoy* (London, 1888). It is not known if Eugene owned books authored by Barret or Cataneo.

10. Donald J. Olsen, *Town Planning in London: The Eighteenth and Nineteenth Centuries* (New Haven, 1964), 13.

11. Nicholas Henderson, *Prince Eugen of Savoy: A Biography* (London, 1964), 253. Henderson reproduces plates showing the design of the garden at the Belvedere palaces. Like all others of the period, they are divided into parterres of geometrical designs, and it is likely that an imaginative person could find some elements of the Savannah plan incorporated in the pattern of paths and planting beds.

12. [James Edward Oglethorpe], *A New and Accurate Account of the Provinces of South Carolina and Georgia* (London, 1732), iv–v. For the authorship of this tract see Ettinger, *Oglethorpe*, 121, 121 n. 8. Ettinger cites Verner W. Crane, "The Promotion Literature of Georgia," in *Bibliographical Essays: A Tribute to Wilberforce Eames* (Cambridge, Mass., 1924), as "the only opponent of the view that Oglethorpe wrote this prospectus." Crane believes that it was the work of Benjamin Martyn. If so, this strengthens my own argument that Martyn played a vital role in the planning of Savannah.

13. My initial study of Savannah was John W. Reps, "Town Planning in Colonial Georgia," *Town Planning Review* 30 (1960):273–85. The reference to Coleraine appears in Reps, *Town Planning in Colonial America* (Princeton, 1969), 25. It was there also that I pointed out the similarity of Hanover Square in London to the squares of Savannah, a point developed later in this paper at much greater length.

14. Montgomery, *Discourse*.

15. Letter in *S.C. Gaz.*, December 2–9, 1732, as quoted in Henry A. M. Smith, "Purrysburgh," *SCHM* 10 (1909):192.

16. Kenneth Coleman, "The Southern Frontier: Georgia's Founding and the Expansion of South Carolina," *GHQ* 56 (1972):171, citing "An Agreement between John Pierre Purry and James Edward Oglethorpe, December 4, 1731," translated copy in Georgia Miscellaneous Collection, University of Georgia Library, Athens.

17. Ibid., 163–74. Johnson's township plan and its results are described in

greatest detail in Robert L. Meriwether, *The Expansion of South Carolina, 1729–1765* (Kingsport, Tenn., 1940). See also Verner W. Crane, *The Southern Frontier, 1670–1732* (1929); and Richard P. Sherman, *Robert Johnson: Proprietary and Royal Governor of South Carolina* (Columbia, 1966).

18. The instructions are in *Calendar of State Papers, Colonial Series, America and West Indies, 1730,* (London, 1937), 136–44, and are dated June 10, 1730.

19. One other bit of evidence supports this conclusion. Just before Oglethorpe's departure from England in November 1732, certain colonists received appointments as local officials. These included "tythingmen." I think this designation indicates that the peculiar division of each Savannah ward into four tythings had been already decided. See the entry for November 1, 1732, *Egmont's Journal*, 7. Nowhere does the *Journal* indicate that a town plan was considered by the Trustees, and at this meeting Oglethorpe was given "Powers under the Corporation Seal . . . To Set out limit and devide the 500 acres." Egmont is similarly silent on the authorship of the town plan in his *Diary*.

20. [Benjamin Martyn], *Reasons for Establishing the Colony of Georgia* (London, 1733), reprinted (without the frontispiece) in *Coll. GHS*, vol. 1. Although the title page is dated 1733, it was published before Oglethorpe's first letter to the Trustees from Georgia dated February 10, 1732–33. Martyn prefaces the text of the letter with the statement that it was received "since the publishing [of] this book." Evidently there were two editions of the work, the earlier lacking the text of the letter.

21. The manuscript, "Some Account of the Design of the Trustees for Establishing Colonys in America," is in the collection of the Tampa, Florida, Public Library. It consists of ninety-two closely written pages and is undated. I am grateful to Mills Bee Lane IV for calling this manuscript to my attention and providing me with a copy. Possibly it is identical to or a variant of the Martyn manuscript cited by Ettinger, *Oglethorpe*, 121, n. 4, as Sloane MSS. (British Museum), 3986, ff. 38–39. Martyn's first sentence in the preface indicates the importance he placed on urban communities as the basis for successful colonization: "The first Honours of the ancient World were paid to the Founders of Citys [and] they were esteemed as the Parents from whose Wisdom whole Nations had their being & were preserved." The quotation used in the text first appeared in print in Mills Lane, *Savannah Revisited*, 3d ed. (Savannah, 1977), 43. Lane's treatment of the origins of the Savannah plan can be found on pp. 43–47. Martyn's manuscript includes a long passage suggesting a ceremony that took place on July 7, 1733, under Oglethorpe's direction and almost exactly as Martyn proposed: "After the Land is divided into Farms & the Town into Alotments and a House built upon each Alotment & an Acre sowed upon each Farm, it may not be improper that a Thanksgiving Day be appointed on

which the people should in their cleanest & best Apparel assemble themselves in the great Square by break of Day, & begin the Day by Prayers &
Thanksgiving to God for his delivering them from misery & establishing
them in a happy State of life. After prayers . . . the Town & the Colony
may be publickly named. After the naming the Town & Province the
articles or Laws under which they are to be Governed should be read & it
would be proper to give . . . Names to each Lath. Then the . . . Men of
each Lath . . . should draw Lots for the Lands. . . . After this the Cannon
& small Shot may be fired & the rest of the Day spent in Manly Exercises &
in decent joy & gladness a comfortable Meal being provided for the whole
People at the expense of the Society" (pp. 64–65). For what actually occurred see *S.C. Gaz*, August 25, 1733. A small portion is quoted in Reps,
Making of Urban America, 186, and it can be found in many other sources.

22. Percival's firsthand knowledge of Londonderry and Coleraine cannot
be documented, but it seems likely that he visited Ulster at one time or
another. He certainly knew the history of this area, and less than a decade
before he became involved in the Georgia project his attention was called
to the plan of Londonderry by his friend, the philosopher George Berkeley.
Berkeley and Percival maintained a long correspondence that began in 1709,
when both were in their twenties. On May 5, 1724, Berkeley wrote to Percival announcing that he had "received my patent for the best Deanery in
this kingdom, that of Derry." A month later Berkeley described for Percival
his new residence: "The city of Londonderry is the most compact, regular,
well built town, that I have seen in the King's Dominions, the town house
(no mean structure) stands in the midst of a square piazza from which
there are four principal streets leading to as many gates. It is a walled town,
and has walks all round on the walls planted with trees, as in Padua" (Berkeley to Percival, June 8, 1724, in Benjamin Rand, ed., *Berkeley and Percival:
The Correspondence of George Berkeley, afterwards Bishop of Cloyne, and
Sir John Percival, afterwards Earl of Egmont* (Cambridge, 1914), 220. At
that time Berkeley was pursuing his plan to establish a college on the island
of Bermuda, and in 1729 he came to Rhode Island to further this project.
He did not succeed, and in October 1731 he returned to England. During
his stay in America he and Percival exchanged several letters. In one of
them, written December 23, 1730, Percival outlined "a project on foot for
settling a colony of a hundred English families on the river Savannah"
(ibid., 270). Berkeley also received a long letter from Oglethorpe in May
1731 describing the settlement plans and the intended "division of the people . . . into hundreds and tithings under constables and tithing men" (ibid.,
277–78). Almost immediately after Berkeley's return to England he met
with Percival and Oglethorpe, as Percival records in his Journal for January
12, 1732: "Mr. Oglethorpe met Dean Berkeley at my house, and we sat
from dinner to ten o'clock discoursing of our Carolina project" (ibid., 279).

If Oglethorpe and Percival were unacquainted before then with the history of Ulster settlement and its planned towns, they may have been informed about it at that time by Berkeley. It is thus possible that Oglethorpe's reference to Ulster as a precedent for the Georgia colony originated at this meeting. Rand's introduction to the Percival-Berkeley correspondence provides much useful information about the two men, their extensive travels in Europe, their shared interest in art and architecture, and their Irish backgrounds.

23. Works dealing with the development of London during this and subsequent periods of growth are numerous. I have relied on the following: Gillian Bebbington, *London Street Names* (London, 1972); Norman Brett-James, *The Growth of Stuart London* (London, 1935); E. Beresford Chancellor, *The History of the Squares of London, Topographical and Historical* (London, 1907); Arthur Irwin Dasent, *The History of St. James's Square* (London, 1895); Simon Jenkins, *Landlords to London: The Story of a Capital and Its Growth* (London, 1975); Olsen, *Town Planning in London;* Hugh Phillips, *Mid-Georgian London* (London, 1964); George Rudé, *Hanoverian London, 1714–1808* (Berkeley, 1971); and John Summerson, *Georgian London* (London, 1945). Appropriate volumes of the *Survey of London* have also been consulted.

24. See Olsen, *Town Planning in London,* 201.

25. The best known of the speculative builders was Nicholas Barbon, a physician by training but a land developer by choice. He reluctantly laid out Red Lion Square as the price he had to pay for permission to build on land adjoining Gray's Inn. See Jenkins, *Landlords to London,* 38–42.

26. Sir Richard Grosvenor retained Robert Andrews to lay out the Grosvenor Square development. John Prince prepared the plan of Cavendish Square and its environs for Edward, Baron Harley of Wigmore. The Earl of Scarborough developed the smaller Hanover Square area. I have not been able to identify his designer.

27. Summerson, *Georgian London,* 11, uses the word "unique" to characterize the layout of Hanover Square, noting that it "is a rectangle, with two streets entering on the long (east and west) sides and one street in the middle of each of the short (north and south) sides."

28. Scarborough was a general. Three other generals in addition to Carpenter were among Hanover Square's first residents. As Summerson notes in his *Georgian London,* 82, "This little gang of military Whigs . . . can hardly have come together . . . by chance. Building developments of the period were very apt to take on a political character and the whole atmosphere of Hanover Square is as Whig as it can be." Bebbington, *London Street Names,* 161, makes the same point: "The year 1714 was a time of triumph for the Whig party, as it saw the Hanoverian George I, whose favour the party had prudently been cultivating, safely installed on the

throne of England. Lord Scarborough, a retired Whig general, went one better than his contemporaries in welcoming the king by building Hanover Square. . . . Many of the early residents of Hanover Square were eminent Whigs." Cavendish Square, by contrast, was as Tory in character as Hanover Square was Whig. Oglethorpe, a Tory of independent persuasion, may well have had friends in both of these neighboring camps. The point is, of course, that Georgia was regarded as a Whig enterprise, and the case for Hanover Square as a possible model for those of Savannah is thus strengthened.

29. Gwynn's engraving appeared in his *London and Westminster Improved* (London, 1766).

30. Rudé, *Hanoverian London*, 13.

31. Evelyn's comments are quoted in Douglas Newton, *London West of the Bars* (London, 1951), 181. Defoe's reference is in his *A Tour Thro' the Whole Island of Great Britain* . . . , 2 vols. (1724; reprint, London, 1927), 1:331. Edward Walford quotes the *Weekly Medley* in *Old and New London*, 6 vols. (London, 1873), 4:315. Another observer in 1725 visited the new western additions to London and reported that "in the tour I passed an amazing scene of new foundations, not of houses only, but as I might say of new cities, new towns, new squares, and fine buildings, the like of which no city, no town, nay, no place in the world can show; nor is it possible to judge where or when they will make an end or stop building" (*Applebee's Journal*, as quoted in Chancellor, *History of the Squares of London*, 61.

32. A complete set, bound in a volume titled *London Described* and dated 1731, is in the Guildhall Library, London. As Phillips, *Mid-Georgian London*, 6, observes, "It proves that all Sutton Nicholls's engravings described by Strype as 'Published by Act of Parliament for Stowe's Survey 1754' (and hitherto accepted by historians without question) were mere reprints, showing the scene of twenty-four years earlier. Strype acquired Bowles's old worn plates, re-engraved the diagonal paths across the gardens in the squares, altered one solitary house (in Soho Square) and published them all as his own." Although the Guildhall Library seems to have the only bound set, individual impressions of these views abound. In the Print Room of the British Library they have been assigned various dates, and it is clear that most of the engravings were sold individually.

33. The addresses that I have been able to find come from *The Court Kalendar* (London, 1733).

34. *A Short Advertisement upon the Situation and Extent of the City of Philadelphia . . . by the Surveyor General* (London, 1683).

35. The plat of Willtown or New London is reproduced in Henry A. M. Smith, "Willtown or New London," *SCHM*, 10 (1909):20–32.

LARRY E. IVERS

Rangers, Scouts, and Tythingmen

 HE COLONIZATION of Georgia was advertised as an extension of English benevolence; the actual result, however, was a planned military occupation of the uninhabited land between Spanish Florida and British South Carolina. With a relatively small effort the British government provided a large amount of military protection to the established southern colonies in North America.

The southern frontier had long been a bloody tract of real estate. Before the settlement of Georgia, the colony of South Carolina provided the principal defense of the British southern frontier. Initially, South Carolina relied upon friendly Indians for protection. For almost a decade at the beginning of the eighteenth century, South Carolinians led Indian war parties on raids against enemy Indian villages and Spanish settlements. In addition, Indians defended against a Spanish and French invasion in 1706 and helped North Carolina survive a major Indian war in 1712 and 1713. The powerful nations of Chickasaw, Creek, and Cherokee Indians secured the far frontier against overland invasion from French Louisiana. The frontier areas close to the settlements were secured against invasion from Spanish Florida by small, friendly Indian nations such as the Yamasee, whose towns sat astride the principal entrances to the colony. In April 1715, however, almost all of the once-friendly Indians made war upon South Carolina. During the resulting Yamasee War most of the unfortified plantations were depopulated and left in ruins. South Carolina was rendered unable to defend the southern frontier without assistance from Britain.[1]

The British government began receiving proposed plans for the strategic defense of the frontier soon after the Yamasee War. The first practical plan was recommended by John Barnwell, a South Carolina planter and experienced frontier soldier. Noting that the French were securing their American frontier by placing forts with garrisons at strategic places, he recommended that the British government do the same and place forts, garrisoned by British regular soldiers, at half a dozen key locations on its frontier. Token concern was shown, and in 1721 Barnwell and a detail of South Carolina scouts, proceeding according to instructions from the British government, built the only one of his proposed forts—Fort King George on the Altamaha River near modern Darien, Georgia.[2]

Yamasee war parties from Spanish Florida easily bypassed Fort King George and raided South Carolina's southern frontier plantations. In late 1727, the fort's small garrison of invalid British soldiers was withdrawn to Beaufort, South Carolina, to help protect that portion of the frontier. Barnwell had intended that communities of settlers be established at Fort King George and the other strategic locations so as to provide a local militia to support the forts' garrisons and extend the frontier. But the British government was not willing to spend the necessary funds and energy to build additional forts, raise troops for America, and recruit bands of immigrants. In addition, most of the empty land on the southern frontier was owned by the Carolina Lords Proprietors, a corporation that had refused to grant or sell land after the South Carolinians revolted against its governmental authority in 1719. Thus the frontier lay exposed to Spaniards, French, and enemy Indians. The vast land that would be Georgia lay nearly devoid of inhabitants. To the south were the Spaniards and their Yamasee Indian allies. To the west lay the two Creek Indian nations, most of whose villages were now friendly to the British. To the southwest of the Creeks lay the French at New Orleans and their nearby Choctaw Indian allies. To the northwest were the three nations of friendly Cherokee Indians. To the northeast were the South Carolinians.[3]

After South Carolina became a royal colony in 1729, strategic settlement plans were soon placed into operation. During the following year Robert Johnson, the newly appointed royal governor, presented his proposal for establishing frontier townships. The British government ordered him to carry out his plan without the assistance of regular troops. Two of the projected townships were soon settled as part of the new colony of Georgia: Savannah became the township on the lower Savannah River, and the later Frederica-Darien settlements became the township on the lower Altamaha River. Thus the Georgia project activated a major portion of a well-formulated, strategic plan for the defense of the southern frontier.[4]

The Georgia Trustees, meeting in London, also adopted certain pol-

icies for strategic military purposes. One such policy was a law limiting the ownership of land. No one individual could be granted more
than fifty acres unless he emigrated at his own expense with at least
four indentured white servants, in which case, the limitation was five
hundred acres. Grantees were required to farm their lands. A practice
taken from early Norman England was the requirement that ownership of land be in tail male; only males could inherit the lands of deceased grantees. The obvious purpose of the restrictions was to assure
the presence of a large number of men for a strong militia. The landownership restrictions were disliked by the colonists, however, and
proved to be impractical. Opportunities for economic advancement
were restricted, widows and daughters might be left destitute, and
fifty acres were often insufficient if a large portion of the tract proved
unsuitable for farming. The Trustees soon began easing the landownership restrictions until by 1750 most of them were removed.[5]

The Trustees also passed a law prohibiting slavery in Georgia. The
primary reason for the prohibition was military. South Carolina's
black slaves outnumbered the free white population, and the number
of free whites available for militia duty was thus reduced. Moreover,
one of the chief concerns of the white population of South Carolina
was the possibility of a slave rebellion. Slaves had given good service
as soldiers during the Yamasee War, but afterward the fear of a slave
revolt grew stronger year by year. The fear was fanned by the action
of Spanish Florida in welcoming runaway slaves. Whether real or
imagined, that fear effectively neutralized the South Carolina militia
as a viable military force for use at any distance from the companies'
home parishes; they were retained close at hand to counter potential
trouble with slaves. But Georgia's available labor force was so small
that the slave prohibition was sometimes ignored and proved difficult
to enforce.[6]

One of the few tactical military issues undertaken directly by the
Georgia Trustees was the establishment of a militia system. The adult
male settlers were to be organized into tythings,[7] a system that had
developed during the early Middle Ages in England. The members of
a tything, usually about ten adult males, were responsible to the lord
of the manor for one another's whereabouts and good conduct. In the
Georgia wilderness, members of tythings lived as neighbors and served
as militia squads of about ten men each, commanded by a tythingman.
Larger units composed of four tythings each were placed under the
command of constables. Initially, Savannah had four tythings. Each

night a different tything served as the military guard and police watch for the town. The system allowed authorities to observe the welfare of the settlers, especially during times of sickness. Service in the militia was a new experience for most of the first settlers because England's militia system had fallen into a sharp decline.[8] Nevertheless, the militia provided Georgia's chief defense for the first five years.

A large amount of tactical military advice and assistance was provided to Georgia by the government and people of South Carolina. Having engaged in frontier warfare for more than thirty years, South Carolinians were well qualified to give advice. They instructed the new Georgians in the use of the military techniques that they had developed on their own and those they had learned from the experiences of the older colonies. A short time after the Georgians' arrival at the site where they were to build the town of Savannah, the governor of South Carolina sent Colonel William Bull to advise Trustee James Oglethorpe and his people on fortifications and other matters. With Colonel Bull's help, Savannah's initial fortifications were soon constructed.[9] Almost any palisade or stockade structure would suffice in defense against Indians because they lacked artillery, a knowledge of siegecraft, and a stockpile of supplies for the investment of a fort. Once the settlers began living and farming beyond the confines of Savannah, however, they were exposed to attack. The abundance of forest and swamp provided cover for the movements of war parties and assisted them in their method of warfare—raiding and ambushing. The same problem had previously plagued the other southern colonies.

Using trial-and-error planning, the older colonies had first placed small, immobile garrisons in forts astride the major entrances to the settlements. The Indian war parties easily bypassed the widely spaced forts, raided and ambushed among the settlements, and withdrew before the garrisons and militia could react.[10] The governments of the tiny colonies needed "a runninge armye continually a foote" to provide early warning of impending attacks, to delay war parties until the militia had time to assemble and march, and to serve as a show of force to discourage minor depredations.[11] A specialized military unit evolved to satisfy those needs. In seventeenth-century British America, the word "range" was a verb commonly used to explain the movement of soldiers in patrolling an area, and "rangers" was the noun that named them. The terms had apparently gained general usage by the fourteenth century, when rangers, called "rangiatorem" in the Norman French dialect, acted as a constabulary for certain English forest dis-

tricts. In the southern American colonies military rangers were horsemen who rode along the paths beyond the settlements looking for hostile Indians. As early as 1634 Edward Backler was hired as a "rainger"
for the Virginia settlement on Kent Island in the upper Chesapeake
Bay when both hostile Indians and Marylanders were raiding the
island.[12]

By March 1648, Maryland was maintaining a force of "raingers" to
patrol its frontier, and it used small units of rangers from time to time
throughout the remainder of the seventeenth century. Between 1693
and 1701 two parties of full-time rangers patrolled seventy-five miles
of frontier from two stockade forts located near the modern cities of
Washington, D.C., and Baltimore, Maryland. Each party was divided
into two sections; one patrolled for a week and then returned to its
fort while the other patrolled for a like period.[13]

Virginia used rangers to patrol its frontier during the period 1676–
1718. Initially, forts were used as bases of operations but were abandoned in 1683 because of the high cost of maintenance. Thereafter, the
members of the small ranger troops and parties worked as laborers on
frontier plantations until required to muster for bimonthly or weekly
ranging duties.[14]

North Carolina asked for and received instructions from Virginia
regarding the method of employing rangers but apparently used them
little until the period 1712–18, following the Tuscarora War and
during the Yamasee War, when enemy Indians caused frequent problems in the outermost settlements.[15]

South Carolina was the most exposed of any of the southern colonies to the mercy of powerful Indian nations. In 1715, when the Indians of the sentry towns revolted, a screen of garrisoned forts was
placed on outlying plantations. It soon became evident that immobile
garrisons could not prevent Indian war parties from raiding the settlements. In late 1716, after the system of garrisons had been reorganized
twice, the harassed government adopted the ranging system. The
Northward, Westward, and Southward divisions, or companies, of
rangers began scouting the frontier from forts near the Santee, Edisto,
and Ashepoo rivers, respectively. Men were drafted from militia companies to serve as rangers because of a lack of volunteers, and after
June 1717 indentured servants were also drafted. Although money was
appropriated for a hundred men, less than half that number apparently
served because many who were drafted never reported for duty. The
Indian raids were frequent and deadly, making ranging a very danger-

ous occupation. Raising men was so difficult that no ship was allowed to sail from Charles Town while men were being sought for the units.[16]

Following a December 1717 reorganization, the Company of Southern Rangers was transferred to the Savannah River. All three companies were disbanded in June 1718, but a single company was apparently raised in July and served for five months as a mobile defense force at Congaree near the modern city of Columbia, South Carolina.[17]

A unit of rangers called the Palachacola Garrison built and occupied Fort Prince George at Palachacola near the lower Savannah River in the spring of 1723. Two years later a detachment from the garrison was given scout dogs and stationed west of the Edisto River for a short time. In the fall of 1726 a new Company of Southern Rangers was organized and placed first near the Edisto River and later near the Combahee River to combat an increasing number of raids by Yamasee Indians based in Spanish Florida.[18]

Compared with smartly dressed British dragoons, the rangers of the southern colonies would have looked more like outlaws than soldiers. Rangers were normally required to outfit themselves with horses, saddles, bridles, weapons, clothing, and food. Their horses were small but rugged, bred in the colonies. The primary weapon was a flintlock carbine or a musket with the barrel sawed off short for easier handling on horseback. Two flintlock pistols were holstered in front of the saddle. Initially, only a sword was required to complement the three slow-loading firearms, but by the end of the seventeenth century, rangers had begun to carry hatchets, which served as both weapons and tools on the forest trails. Clothing was usually the same civilian apparel worn by the English workingmen of the period. Rangers usually received good wages, paid in tobacco in Virginia and Maryland, in inflated paper currency in South Carolina, and later in bills of exchange in Georgia.[19]

By 1732 each southern colony had experimented with and adopted when necessary the system of ranging horsemen as the most convenient and reliable early warning system for frontier defense. The small, regular units provided economy of force in both men and money by releasing the militia from having to conduct frequent patrol musters. Usually little administrative or logistical difficulty was encountered in organizing small units, for they equipped and maintained themselves with only casual attention from the colonial governments.

Fifteen men of South Carolina's Company of Southern Rangers were put at the disposal of the new Georgia colonists upon their arrival in early 1733. The company, under the command of Captain James Mc-Pherson, soon built First Fort and Fort Argyle in Georgia and garrisoned those sites until 1737, when the company was disbanded by South Carolina.[20]

Oglethorpe, as commander of Georgia's defenses, adopted the system of rangers with little change. He stationed small garrisons of rangers in tiny forts "upon the passes of the River[s] and the Roads to the Indian Countrey. . . . Those men having horses patroll about the Countrey, and thereby give alarms of Indian Enemies, intercept Spies &c."[21] By 1739 Oglethorpe was also using rangers as mobile scouting and raiding forces, operating on horseback and in their scout boats.[22] They were organized into troops that varied in strength from about twelve to twenty-five "men acquainted with Woods mounted on horseback[;] they not only carry advices through these vast Forests & swim Rivers, but in Action, by taking an Enemy in Flank or Rear, do great Service. . . . They also are of great service in watching the Sea Coasts, since they can swiftly move from one Place to another, and engage to advantage Men with wet arms & Accoutrements, before they can be able to form themselves after landing."[23]

Georgia, like South Carolina, had an additional early warning defense problem. By following the Inland Passage (presently known as the Intracoastal Waterway) of rivers and streams between the coastal islands and the mainland, enemy Indians and Spaniards in shallow-draft boats could quickly and silently approach exposed settlements. Over a period of about twenty years, South Carolina perfected a special military service of scouts to detect an enemy's approach up the Inland Passage, and by 1702 their use was well established.[24]

Scouts were combination seamen-marines. They patrolled along the Inland Passage in their boats on the lookout for waterborne raiders, but they were also armed with muskets and other hand weapons to fight on land. During and after the Yamasee War they participated in several successful amphibious operations against hostile Indians.[25]

Scout boats were usually giant dugout canoes or piraguas constructed from cypress or cedar logs. Strakes, or sideboards, were added to create more depth. One or more swivel guns were mounted on each scout boat for offensive use. Although scout boats usually carried two gaff-rigged or schooner-rigged sails, the principal power was provided by the scouts, who manned the oars.[26]

At the time of the settlement of Savannah, one scout boat, the *Caro-*

lina, was in service in South Carolina. It was commanded by Captain William Ferguson and was crewed by ten men known as the Southern Scouts. Ferguson and his scouts were loaned to the new Georgia settlers to patrol the Inland Passage below Savannah. In England, the rivers and streams had been used for transportation for centuries, so the new Georgians were probably familiar with using small boats. The South Carolina canoes were such a novelty, however, that Oglethorpe purchased one and gave it to the Georgia Trustees, who then presented it as a gift to the British queen. In 1737 the *Carolina* and its crew were ordered deactivated by South Carolina, but Oglethorpe immediately took them into Georgia's service. He adopted the scout boat system of early warning on the Inland Passage, and by 1740 ten scout boats and crews were patrolling from the Savannah River in the north to the St. John's River in the south.[27]

South Carolina's early assistance proved invaluable in enabling Georgia to avoid much of the trial-and-error tactical planning used by the other southern colonies. When Oglethorpe inspected the nearby frontier with Captain McPherson and his rangers and explored the Inland Passage with Captain Ferguson and his scouts, he learned to appreciate and use these groups as systems of defense. Relations between the two colonies would sour after 1736 because of competition over the Indian trade.[28] Nevertheless, the South Carolinians were adequately reimbursed for their early assistance; Georgia served as a successful protective buffer between South Carolina and its enemies in Florida and Louisiana for thirty years.

The soundness of the strategic and tactical military planning for the colonization of Georgia was severely tested during the first decade of settlement. In some respects planning was necessarily modified: key points of the frontier were garrisoned with regular British soldiers, the restrictions on landownership were eased, and slavery was authorized. But the basic strategic plan was proved successful. A major Spanish invasion of the southern colonies was repelled, and numerous minor incursions were absorbed. Tactical methods of operation also proved sound. The system of ranging horsemen that Oglethorpe borrowed and perfected was copied by other governments, and a hundred years later mounted rangers were patrolling the new frontier from Texas to Wisconsin.[29]

NOTES

1. Verner W. Crane, *The Southern Frontier, 1670–1732* (1929; reprint, Ann Arbor, 1956), 11–33, 71–107, 162–86.

2. Ibid., 206–34; Joseph W. Barnwell, ed., "Fort King George—Journal of Col. John Barnwell," *SCHM* 27 (1926):189–203.

3. Crane, *Southern Frontier*, 231, 238, 246–49, 281, 282; M. Eugene Sirmans, *Colonial South Carolina: A Political History, 1663–1763* (Williamsburg, 1966), 103–28. John Barnwell, a map of Southeastern North America, ca. 1722, original in PRO, tracing in the South Carolina Department of Archives and History, Columbia.

4. Crane, *Southern Frontier*, 251, 282, 293, 294; Phinizy Spalding, "South Carolina and Georgia: The Early Days," *SCHM* 69 (1968):83–89.

5. Trevor R. Reese, *Colonial Georgia: A Study in British Imperial Policy in the Eighteenth Century* (Athens, 1963), 41–44.

6. Ibid., 47–50; Thomas Cooper and David J. McCord, eds., *The Statutes at Large of South Carolina*, 10 vols. (Columbia, 1836–41), 9:658; Crane, *Southern Frontier*, 33, n.3.

7. *Egmont's Journal*, pp. 8, 9, 44.

8. Doris Mary Stenton, *English Society in the Early Middle Ages, 1066–1307* (Baltimore, 1959), 146, 147; *Egmont's Journal*, 44, 46; E. Merton Coulter, ed., *The Journal of Peter Gordon, 1732–1735* (Athens, 1963), 38; Sarah B. Gober Temple and Kenneth Coleman, *Georgia Journeys* (Athens, 1961), 116, 117; Cecil C. P. Lawson, *A History of the Uniforms of the British Army*, 5 vols. (London, 1940–67), 2:212.

9. Coulter, ed., *Journal of Gordon*, 37.

10. Raphael Semmes, *Captains and Mariners of Early Maryland* (Baltimore, 1937), 196–98; Charles M. Andrews, ed., *Narratives of the Insurrections* (New York, 1915), 50, 51, 108, 112, 113; William H. Nelson and Frank E. Vandiver, *Fields of Glory* (New York, 1960), 88.

11. H. R. McIlwaine, ed., *Journals of the House of Burgesses of Virginia*, 13 vols. (Richmond, 1905–15), 1619–59, 1:38.

12. A. G. Bradley, ed., *Travels and Works of Captain John Smith*, 2 vols. (Edinburgh, 1910), 2:584, 585, 594; G. J. Turner, ed., *Select Pleas of the Forest*, vol. 13 of the Seldon Society Publications (London, 1901), 25, 26; "Clairborne vs. Clobery," *Maryland Historical Magazine* 28 (1933): 183–85.

13. William H. Browne et al., eds., *Archives of Maryland*, 65 vols. (Baltimore, 1883–1952), 1:228; 2:476, 501, 502, 560; 3:524–30; 7:23, 24, 155; 13:282, 283, 310; 15:56, 58, 92, 125, 181, 186, 362, 363, 373–75, 384–86; 18:87, 354, 398, 461, 469; 19:227, 383; 20:394–96, 487, 523; 22:509, 510; 23:111, 403, 404, 406, 416; 24:121, 122, 25:101, 184–86; *Calendar of State Papers, Colonial Series, America and the West Indies, 1701* (London, 1910), vol. for 1701, 246–48.

14. William H. Hening, ed., *The Statutes at Large; Being a Collection of all the Laws of Virginia*, 13 vols. (New York, 1809–23) 2:331, 433–40, 469–71, 498–501; 3:17–22, 38, 82–85, 115–17, 119–21, 126–28, 164; H. R. McIlwaine, ed., *Executive Journals of the Council of Colonial Virginia*, 5 vols. (Richmond, 1925–45), 1:129, 142, 202, 254, 272, 273, 312, 313, 375, 376; 2:113, 180; 3:296, 315, 342, 372; William P. Palmer, ed., *Calendar of Virginia State Papers*, 6 vols. (Richmond, 1875–86), 1:32, 38, 43, 44, 63, 71, 118, 152, 153, 164, 189; R. A. Brock, ed., *The Official Letters of Alexander Spotswood, Lieutenant Governor of the Colony of Virginia, 1710–1722*, 2 vols. (Richmond, 1882), 2:203–7.

15. McIlwaine, ed., *Virginia Council Journals*, 1:146; William L. Saunders, ed., *The Colonial Records of North Carolina*, 10 vols. (Raleigh, 1886–90), 2:158, 200, 275, 308, 309, 313, 316.

16. Crane, *Southern Frontier*, 162–83; *SCCHJ*, November 14, 20, 30, December 7, 13, 1716, June 13–15, November 1, 1717, Transcript Green Copy No. 5, South Carolina Archives, pp. 166, 173, 184, 194, 203, 316, 318, 324, 347, 348; Cooper and McCord, eds., *South Carolina Statutes*, 2:691, 3:9.

17. Ibid., 3:23–30, 39; W. L. McDowell, ed., *Journals of the Commissioners of the Indian Trade, 1710–1718* (Columbia, 1955), 309, 312.

18. Cooper and McCord, eds., *South Carolina Statutes*, 3:180, 181, 335, 359, 391; 9:61, 62, 65, 86; *SCCHJ*, January 19, February 16, May 15, 1723, Transcript Green Copy, Commons House Journals No. 6, S.C. Archives, pp. 136, 207, 245; South Carolina Upper House Journals, October 8, 1726, September 23, 1727, August 16, 1732, PRO, CO 5/429, pt. 1, p. 33, 5/434, pp. 1, 1a.

19. Hening, ed., *Virginia Statutes*, 2:435, 501; 3:17; Stephens's Journal, December 3, 1739, *CRG*, 4:(1906), 461; James Oglethorpe to Georgia Trustees, December 29, 1739, Ms. CRG, 35:234; Cooper and McCord, eds., *South Carolina Statutes*, 9:62; The Accompt of James Oglethorpe . . . for Extraordinary Services Incurr'd, Exchequer and Audit Office, June 25, 1740, PRO, 3/119; Browne, ed., *Archives of Maryland*, 2:559, 560; 10:224; 23:37; 29:244; 38:3, 4; *Collections of the South Carolina Historical Society*, 5 vols. (Charleston, 1857–97), 5:318.

20. South Carolina Council Journal, January 26, 1733, PRO, CO 5/434, p. 11; T. F. Lotter, *A Map of the County of Savannah* (London, 1740), copy in the University of Georgia Special Collections Library, Athens; James Oglethorpe to the Trustees, September 17, 1733, Egmont Papers, 14200, 113; James Oglethorpe, "State of the Colony of Georgia in America," March 1735, ibid., 513; *SCCHJ*, January 18, March 5, 1737, pp. 179–81, 321; Common Council, May 10, 1738, March 25, 1740, *CRG*, 2:234, 235, 318; *Egmont's Journal*, 354, 355; Oglethorpe to the Trustees, October 7, 1738, *CRG*, 22, pt. 1:274–81.

21. Oglethorpe's Extraordinarys of the War, January 22, 1743, Ms. CRG, 36:68.

22. Ibid., 67; A List of the Military Strength of Carolina & Georgia, June 7, 1742, ibid, 35:465.

23. Oglethorpe's Extraordinarys, January 22, 1743, p. 67.

24. Cooper and McCord, eds., *South Carolina Statutes*, 2:10, 24, 111, 278, 610; 3:32; 9:623, 624; Headlam, ed., *Calendar of State Papers, Colonial Series, America and the West Indies, 1702–1703* (London, 1913), 815; *SCCHJ*, August 15, 27, 1701, pp. 3–7, 21, August 21, 1702, p. 68, May 5, 7, September 14, 16, 1703, pp. 85, 89, 118, 124.

25. *Ibid.*, June 9, 1724, p. 17, February 8, 1727, p. 101; Cooper and McCord, eds., *South Carolina Statutes*, 2:11; 3:25; 9:625, 626; Larry E. Ivers, "Scouting the Inland Passages, 1685–1737," *SCHM* 73 (1972):123–26.

26. William Dampier, *A New Voyage Round the World*, 3 vols. (London, 1717), 1:29, 214, 215; Hugh Lefler, ed., *A New Voyage to Carolina by John Lawson* (Chapel Hill, 1967), 16, 17, 103; Trustees' Journal, July 2, 1735, *CRG*, 2:109; President and Assistants, June 25, 1735, ibid., 3:124; *S.C. Gaz.*, May 17, 1740; Peter Gordon, *A View of Savannah as it Stood the 29th of March 1734* (London, 1734), copy in the University of Georgia Special Collections Library, Athens.

27. Francis Moore, "A Voyage to Georgia Begun in the Year 1735," *Coll. GHS*, 1:91, 104, 106–52; Dorothy Hartley, *Lost Country Life* (New York, 1979), 303–5, 307, illustrations 51–57; President and Assistants, June 25, 1734, *CRG*, 3:124; *SCCHJ*, January 18, March 5, 1737, pp. 179–81, 321; Expense of the Southern Division, August 12, 1737, Ms. CRG, 39:435; Account of Boats, April 30, 1740, ibid., 35:258.

28. Reese, *Colonial Georgia*, 109–12.

29. Frank E. Stevens, *The Blackhawk War* (Chicago, 1903), 131, 141, 142, 159, 160; Otis E. Young, "The United States Mounted Ranger Battalion, 1832–1833," *Mississippi Valley Historical Review* 41 (1954):453–70; Walter Prescott Webb, *The Texas Rangers: A Century of Frontier Defense* (Boston, 1935), 21–48.

B. H. LEVY

The Early History of Georgia's Jews

URING the late seventeenth and early eighteenth centuries the large Jewish populations in Spain and Portugal were forced by the Inquisition to conform to Catholicism, leave the country, or suffer burning at the stake.[1] King William I of Prussia (1714–40), although despotic, generally meant well toward his conformist subjects, but to the Jews he was almost unbelievably harsh; upon the death of a father only the eldest son could inherit his right to remain in Prussia and then only if he possessed not less than 2,000 thaler.[2] The obvious result was large migrations of Jews. On the other hand, in England at about the same time Jewish ownership of land was permitted for the first time since 1290, and in 1740 Jews were granted full British citizenship.[3] Also during this period, Holland threw off the rule of Spain and its Inquisition and welcomed Jewish newcomers as citizens. Thus England and Holland became the favorite places of refuge for displaced Jews.[4]

Worldwide Jewry was then (and still is today) divided into two groups: Sephardic and Ashkenazic. Their methods and manner of worship, even their pronunciation of Hebrew, are distinctly different. The differentiation was originally geographic—Sephardic Jews were those residing in western Europe (Spain, Portugal, southern France, and so on) and Ashkenazic were those who had resided in eastern Europe (Russia, Poland, Prussia).[5]

Jewish refugees arriving in London gravitated to the Bevis Marks Synagogue, the citadel of English Sephardic Judaism. It adhered strictly to the Sephardic "Minhag" (order and type of religious services) familiar to Spanish and Portuguese Jews. The Prussian Jews were apparently Ashkenazic, so why many of them affiliated with Bevis Marks is a mystery, particularly because the London Ashkenazim "had, in 1690, established their own synagogue in Duke's Palace."[6] Perhaps the reason was that the most prominent and wealthy Jewish families of London were at that time affiliated with Bevis Marks.

Once George II signed the Georgia Charter, the Trustees immediately began to issue commissions to solicit and receive subscriptions to help finance the establishment of the new colony. Among the commissioners so appointed were three Jews: Anthony da Costa, Alvarez Lopez Suasso, and Francis Salvador. Each was a prominent, wealthy, and highly respected Londoner.

Anthony da Costa's family had been in London since 1680. He was a successful London merchant and a director of the Bank of England. In 1736 he was elected a member of the Royal Society, then as now the oldest and most highly regarded learned society in England. His wife, Catherine Mendes, was named for Queen Catherine, wife of Charles II, who was her godmother.[7] Alvarez (or Alvaro) Lopez Suasso was a member of a family of bankers originally from Spain who in the seventeenth and eighteenth centuries had branch banks in Holland and England. His grandfather was Baron Antonio Lopez Suasso, who had been made a hereditary baron by Charles II. Alvarez was one of the wealthiest residents of London, and in 1735 he, too, was elected to the Royal Society.[8] Francis Salvador was a nephew of Joseph Salvador, a very wealthy Londoner. His father had died when he was two years old, leaving him a sizable inheritance. He was educated suitably for his station in life and enjoyed the advantages of extensive travel. He married his first cousin, the daughter of Joseph Salvador, and his wealth was vastly increased by her dowry. Much of the Salvador family's wealth was later swept away by the failure of the Dutch East India Company in which members of this family were the largest shareholders.[9]

One should not be misled by the fact that the three commissioners were scions of prominent, wealthy Jewish families. The Jewish population of England was divided, just as was the Protestant population, into three strata: those in the upper class who were prominent, wealthy, and, to a limited extent, accepted into the influential British upper class; a larger middle class, mostly artisans and small shopkeepers; and the vast majority of poor, itinerant, penniless recent refugees, many of whom traveled from city to town seeking charity from the small Jewish communities.[10]

Commissions were issued to Salvador, da Costa, and Suasso less than four months after George II signed the Georgia Charter. They immediately began soliciting funds from the wealthier members of the London Jewish community—men who were aware of the plight of the refugees who made up the Jewish lower class in England. But it was obvious to Salvador, da Costa, and Suasso that the Trustees' desire to send English poor to Georgia was to be restricted to worthy Christians. With motives identical to those of Oglethorpe and the Trustees, the three commissioners had in mind poor, worthy Jews. Solicitations in behalf of this group were in keeping with both an age-old tradition of Jews helping Jews and a Sephardic practice of diversion rather than retention of poor immigrants. Sending immigrants abroad, where they would have a good chance of becoming self-supporting, seemed preferable to permitting them to remain in London, where they would be a burden on the Jewish communal charities. Jewish settlements had already been established in the Guianas and on Curaçao, and the three commissioners had similar hopes for Georgia.[11] Unencumbered by specific instructions as to how the money they collected was to be used, they set about organizing a Jewish group to settle in Georgia and began arranging for transportation. The manner in which they proceeded, however, suggests they had suspicions that once the Trustees learned of their intent, efforts would be made to stop the Jewish emigration.

Such suspicions were well founded. At a meeting of the Trustees held at Palace Court in December 1732, with only four Trustees in attendance, the vote on allowing Jews to settle in Georgia split two to two. But at a meeting of the full board held in January 1733, the Trustees resolved by an overwhelming majority that the Jewish commissioners be ordered to surrender their commissions.[12] The minutes of that meeting make their reasons for that demand very explicit: Thomas Coram, a Trustee who sometimes resided in Taunton, Massachusetts, argued that the very idea of Jews settling in Georgia was "shocking," that it would ruin the enterprise, that Georgia would "soon become a Jewish colony," and that all her Christian settlers would "fall off and desert it, as leaves from a tree in autumn."[13]

The Trustees were too late. Perhaps anticipating the board's action, the commissioners had already arranged for the transportation to Georgia of forty-two Jewish men, women, and children (plus an infant who died en route).[14] Early in January 1733, before the second vote of the Trustees, this group set sail from England aboard the *William and Sarah*, William Hanton, master, on their seven-month voyage to Georgia.

Mordecai Sheftall later published an account of the voyage as told him by his father, Benjamin Sheftall, one of the original Georgia Jewish settlers:

> When the ship first started, she sustained some serious injury in the river Thames, and was compelled to land her passengers and undergo repairs. After this was accomplished a reembarkation of the passengers took place, and the ship set sail for the "NEW WORLD." The passage was a disagreeable and boisterous one; gale succeeded gale, and the ship came near being wrecked off the coast of North Carolina, and was forced to seek safety in "New Inlet," where she was necessarily detained for some weeks.[15]

In the first part of July 1733, the ship dropped anchor in the Savannah River opposite the little settlement on Yamacraw Bluff. The trials and tribulations of the Jewish settlers, however, were just beginning. Obviously, the last thing Oglethorpe had expected to see on board the *William and Sarah* was a group of Jews. The Trustees established the colony for poor but respectable Protestants, and many of the colony's progenitors were Christian churchmen concerned with finding a home for co-religionists. The immigrants aboard the *William and Sarah* hardly fit those expectations.[16]

There are two theories regarding the reason Oglethorpe permitted the Jewish settlers to land; one is a family tradition, the other a historically documented fact. The traditional tale centers on the man who was known in Portugal as Dr. Diago Nunez-Ribiero and came to be known in North America as Dr. Samuel Nunes. At the time the *William and Sarah* dropped anchor, the settlers in Savannah were suffering a very serious epidemic of intestinal disease and "fever." Oglethorpe blamed the health problems on consumption of too much rum in hot weather. Dr. William Cox, the only physician in the colony, had succumbed, and there was no one to prescribe for the sick. More than twenty people had already died. When Oglethorpe learned that a distinguished physician was a member of the Jewish group aboard ship, he invited the doctor alone to land. Dr. Nunes refused, stating that he would remain on board unless his family and fellow religionists were permitted to settle permanently in Savannah. Oglethorpe agreed.[17]

When the *William and Sarah* dropped anchor opposite Savannah, Oglethorpe, knowing full well that the Trustees were vehemently opposed to permitting Jews to settle in Georgia, was faced with a dilemma. It was the fourth vessel since the *Anne* to arrive and the first since the arrival of Oglethorpe and his initial colonists to carry new settlers.[18] The little community on the bank of the muddy Savannah contained only about 120 colonists. Thus the 42 Jewish colonists would constitute more than 25 percent of the entire population of the settlement. This was the largest single group of Jews to land on North American soil in colonial days.[19]

Should he, or should he not, permit them to disembark? There was no English lawyer in the colony, so Oglethorpe referred the question to English attorneys in Charleston. Their answer was that the Jews should be permitted to land, an opinion obviously based on the wording of the Georgia Charter: "Forever, hereafter, there shall be a liberty of conscience allowed in the worship of God, to all persons [except Catholics]."[20]

Once on shore, Nunes quickly showed his medical capabilities. On August 12, 1733, Oglethorpe wrote the Trustees about this "doctor of physick who immediately undertook our people and refused to take any pay for it. He proceeded by cold baths, cooling drinks and other cooling applications. Since which the sick have wonderfully recovered, and we have not lost one who would follow his prescriptions."[21] The answer of the Trustees was short and to the point: allot no lands to the Jews, and pay Dr. Nunes for his services. The reaction of the man who, when only a young subordinate, had thrown a glass of wine in the face of the prince of Wurttemberg, was typical. He disregarded the instructions of the Trustees and welcomed his new settlers.[22]

Oglethorpe was no Judeophile. In addition to obtaining the services of Dr. Nunes, he had other good reasons for welcoming his newest settlers. The Trustees were determined that Georgia should produce wine. There was, however, no wine-growing expert among Oglethorpe's original settlers. But one of the Jewish group, Abraham De Lyon, born and raised in Portugal, was an experienced vigneron. Just as Nunes had done, De Lyon soon proved his worth: even the Earl of Egmont, who had precious few nice things to say about the Jews, noted that he was an "industrious man . . . on whom were all our expectations for cultivating vines and making wine." William Stephens, secretary for the affairs of the Trustees in Georgia, described De Lyon's success:

Nothing has given me so much pleasure, since my arrival, as what I found here; though it was yet (if I may say it properly) only in miniature; for he had cultivated only for two or three years past about half a score of them, which he received from Portugal for an experiment; and by his skill and management in pruning, &c., they all bore this year very plentifully, a most beautiful large grape, as big as a man's thumb, almost pellucid, and bunches exceeding big.[23]

Perhaps more important than Nunes or De Lyon to acceptance of the Jews was Oglethorpe's military orientation. Most of the Jews were young, able-bodied men. They were excellent potential soldiers, and not long after their arrival he appointed one of them, Benjamin Sheftall, the first lieutenant of his militia.

On July 7, 1733, four days before the Jewish contingent arrived, the colonists had met on the bluff before Oglethorpe's tent. He had named the wards and streets and assigned to the settlers their town and farm lots, although the deeds were not executed and delivered until several months later. Sometime between July and December of that year Oglethorpe assigned fourteen of the Jews similar lots of land. On December 27 all of the verbal assignments were confirmed by legal deeds.[24] But why did Oglethorpe grant land to only fourteen of the male Jews when there were then twenty-six in the colony?[25] And how did he select the particular fourteen? There is no specific documented evidence, but a number of the Jewish settlers were known to be men of means, some of them with sufficient funds to bring servants with them. Therefore, it seems likely that the fourteen Jews purchased their lands whereas the largely indigent Protestants had been given theirs. This theory was hinted at but never actually stated by William Stephens, who said the Jews "demand[ed] from the Trustees nothing but their freeholds which their money purchased."[26]

Even though Oglethorpe's plan to found the colony had been strongly backed and financed by the Anglican clergy, once established, Georgia was characterized in its early days by an amazing lack of interest in religion. Savannah had to wait almost twenty years before its first church of any denomination was built. The Jews seem to have led the way in religious observances. Johann Martin Boltzius, the Salzburger religious leader, was shocked that the English settlers mingled with the Jews on Sundays, disregarding the holiness of the day: "They [the English] drink, play, walk, and pursue all worldly amusements with them [the Jews]; indeed they desecrate Sunday with the Jews, which no Jew whatever would do on his Sabbath to please the Christians."[27]

The Jews early showed their devotion to their religious heritage.

The Hebrew group brought with them a "Safertora" with two "Cloaks" and a Circumcision "Box" given them by a Mr. Benjamin Lindo, a merchant of London.[28] Even before this group left England its members' determination to form a congregation in the New World was evidenced by Sheftall's statement that these religious articles were "for the use of the congregation that they intended to establish." During the first two years after the group landed in Georgia, services probably were held in the homes of members. In July 1735, their purpose was finally accomplished when the Georgia Jews "met together, and agreed to open a Synagogue. . . . which was done immediately . . . [and] named K.-K. Mikva Israel. [Hope of Israel]."[29] It is most likely that even for some years after 1735 services continued to be held in the homes of members. At an unknown date a house was rented on Market Square (now Ellis Square) from Aaron Champion and was altered for regular congregational services. Two years later the young congregation received another Torah, a Hanukkah menorah (a nine-branched candelabrum), and a collection of books, gifts from Benjamin Mendos of London.[30]

The house on Market Square must have been a very poor excuse for a synagogue. In 1738 Boltzius reported that the Jews were holding services in "an old miserable hut, men and women separated . . . a boy speaking several languages and especially good in Hebrew is their reader and is paid for his services."[31]

This small congregation faced problems from within. A schism between the Sephardic group from Iberia and the Ashkenazic group of Germanic background started almost immediately upon their landing. Eight of the original settlers were Ashkenazic; the remaining thirty-four were Sephardic. Ten more Ashkenazim had arrived in Savannah by 1738. But the differences between the Germanic and Portuguese groups already were evident to Christian churchmen. Under date of July 4, 1735, the Reverend Samuel Quincy of the Church of England wrote to his associates in London:

> We have here two sorts of Jews, Portuguese and Germans. The first having professed Christianity in Portugal or the Brazils, are more lax in their way, and dispense with a great many of their Jewish Rites. . . . The German Jews, who are thought the better sort of them [i.e., more religious], are a great deal more strict in their way and rigid observers of their Law. Their kindness shew'd to Mr. Bolzius and the Saltzburgers, was owing to the Good temper and humanity of the people, and not to any inclination to Change their Religion. . . . They all

in general behave themselves very well, and are industrious in their business.[32]

And on February 21, 1738, Reverend Boltzius wrote to a friend in Halle: "[The Jews] want to build a Synagogue, but the Spanish and German Jews cannot come to terms."[33] A year later, on July 3, 1739, Boltzius wrote to a friend in Germany: "Even the Jews, of whom several families are here already, enjoy all privileges the same as other colonists. . . . They have no Synagogue, which is their own fault; the one element hindering the other in this regard. The German Jews believe themselves entitled to build a Synagogue and are willing to allow the Spanish Jews to use it with them in common; the latter, however, reject any such arrangement and demand the preference for themselves."[34]

The "make do" synagogue on Market Square lasted only until the early 1740s, when the fortunes of the Jewish community waned with those of the entire infant colony. The laws and regulations forbidding rum, slavery, and ownership of land and strictly regulating commerce and trade nearly caused the disintegration of Georgia. As E. Merton Coulter phrased it: "So many left that the colony became almost extinct."[35]

For the Jews, however, there was a second, even more compelling, reason to leave the province. The European war between Spain and England had reached the New World, where it was known as the War of Jenkins' Ear. On July 5, 1742, Spanish General Manuel de Montiano with a large fleet and three thousand soldiers landed on St. Simons Island with plans to capture Georgia quickly and then move on against the more heavily defended Carolina.[36] Except for the Minis and Sheftall families most of the Jewish settlers in Savannah were Sephardic and had openly professed Catholicism in Spain and Portugal but had reverted to Judaism while in England before emigrating to Georgia. In Catholic eyes they were guilty of the crime of apostasy. The Inquisition's punishment for apostasy was death by burning at the stake. Most Jews fled to Charleston, a few even farther north. Only the Minis and Sheftall families remained in Savannah because, being of Germanic origin and never having professed Catholicism, they could not be accused of apostasy. The lease on the Market Square quarters was not renewed; such religious services as were held were informal and were apparently conducted in the home of Benjamin Sheftall.

The years 1742 and 1743 were the low points for all of Savannah, including the city's Jewish community. Slowly, however, the pendulum of fortune swung back. By 1746 thirteen Jewish families were reported to be residing in Savannah. Then, in 1774, the Sheftall Diaries report: "Having a sufficient number of Jews here to make a Congregation we came to a resolution to meet at the house of Mordecai Sheftall, which was done." This meeting was held on the eve of the Day of Atonement at Mordecai Sheftall's home in a room he had furnished as a chapel. But the unrest of the patriots was already stirring. War with England was imminent.[37]

From the outbreak of hostilities until the Treaty of Paris there was a virtual cessation of all formal organized religious activity in Savannah. The vast majority of Savannah Jews were Whigs. Many of them, notably Mordecai Sheftall, held high positions of honor and trust in both the provisional governments and the Continental army.

There are obvious reasons why Jews were among the leaders of the American revolutionary movement. As Rabbi Saul J. Rubin stated, "The Jeffersonian ideal—including a love of religious liberty, the recognition of the right of all to equal status under law . . . motivated American Jews to respond to the separatist movement."[38] A second reason, and perhaps just as important, was that most of Savannah's Gentiles were of English ancestry and felt a natural loyalty to the mother country. The Jews were almost entirely of Spanish, Portuguese, or German descent and felt no particular partiality toward England.

The end of the Revolution ushered in a period of optimism, as expressed in April 1783 in a letter from Mordecai Sheftall in Savannah to his son, Sheftall Sheftall, then in Charleston:

My dear Son:

Allthoe I wrote you on Friday last, yet so happy an event haveing taken place, [the declaration of suspension of hostilities between Great Britain and the United States] as the inclosed will communicate, since my writing, I could not help giving it to you and all my friends by the first and earliest opp[ortunit]y.

What my feelings are on the occasion is easier immagined than described. For it must be supposed that every real well wisher to his country must feel him self happy to have lived to see this longe and bloody contest brot to so happy an issue. More especially, as we have obtained our independence, instead of those threats of bringing us with submission to the foot of that throne whose greatest mercies to Americans has been nothing but one continued scene of cruelty, of which you as well as my self have experienced our shares.

But, thanks to the Almighty, it is now at an end. Of which happy event I sincerely congratulate you and all my friends. As an intier new scene will open it self, and we have the world to begin againe.[39]

Sheftall answered:

Honored Sir:
  Since writing this morning, a packett schooner is arrived from Phila-delphia in six days, with official accounts of peace. Inclosed is a hand bill; it will speak of it self. I sincerely congratulate you on the great and happy event. We are delivered from a cursed, proud nation, Britton [Britain].[40]

Although several Jews rose to prominence in the Georgia commu-nity during both the colonial and the revolutionary periods, I will mention only two of the families here. During the colonial period Dr. Samuel Nunes, who was the most prominent physician in the colony, remained in Georgia for only about six years. Following his departure, Abraham and Abigail Minis, two of the original 1733 Jewish colonists, became the outstanding Jew and Jewess in Georgia. Within three years after the founding of the colony Abraham became a merchant-shipper, one of the first Georgians to engage in commerce. During Oglethorpe's two attacks on Spanish Florida (1740–43), Minis operated boats shuttling supplies between Savannah and Oglethorpe's base at Fort Frederica. He died on January 15, 1757, leaving his wife, Abigail, with eight children. Abraham had willed most of his estate to his widow, and she immediately took over and continued his business as a rancher, farmer, storekeeper, and tavern owner, successfully operating and expanding these endeavors until the beginning of the Revolution in 1776. During the Revolution, without compensation or reimburse-ment, she and her eldest son, Philip (the first Caucasian male child conceived and born in Georgia) used their personal funds to help sup-ply and provision the Continental forces in and around Savannah. With the British attack on Savannah Mrs. Minis and her children joined most Savannah women with children in seeking refuge in Charleston, which was much more strongly defended. Upon the cessa-tion of hostilities, she immediately returned to Savannah and not only successfully resumed active management of the family enterprises, even including the operation of the tavern, but expanded the Minis interests and made them vastly more profitable than they had ever been during her husband's lifetime.[41]

During the prerevolutionary and revolutionary periods Mordecai

Sheftall, only son of the original 1733 Jewish colonists Benjamin and
Perla Sheftall, undoubtedly became the outstanding Jewish leader in
Georgia and one of the most prominent citizens of the colony.[42] When
Mordecai was only twenty-five he became the owner of a warehouse
and wharf lot "under the bluff" on the Savannah River and soon
branched out into ranching with his own cattle brand "5₈". At twenty-
six he owned five slaves—the then accepted index of a man's wealth.[43]
As reform fermented in Georgia, Mordecai became an early and enthusiastic member of the Whig group and was appointed the chairman of the rebel organization known as the Parochial Committee of
Christ Church Parish, which shortly became a de facto government of
Georgia.[44] With the beginning of hostilities against England, Sheftall
was named commissary general to the Georgia militia, and in 1777
Brigade General Samuel Elbert appointed him commissary to the Continental troops in Georgia as well. He must have discharged these
duties most creditably for a year later Major General Robert Howe,
the Continental commander for the Southern Department, added to
Sheftall's other duties that of deputy commissary general of issues (for
all Continental troops in Georgia and South Carolina) with the rank
of colonel, the highest rank attained by any Jewish officer in the
American Revolution.[45] Unfortunately, before that commission could
be made permanent by the Continental Congress, he was captured by
the British in the Battle of Savannah; he remained a prisoner of war
for a little more than a year until he was exchanged for a British officer captured by the Continentals.[46] He had advanced his own money
when no other funds were available to perform his military duty of
furnishing food and supplies to the Georgia and Continental troops
for whom, as commissary general, he felt responsible. As a leading
patriot he invested the remainder of his available monies in the currency issued by the state of Georgia and printed in Savannah between
1775 and 1782, which, at the end of the Revolution, was worthless.[47]
Mordecai found himself virtually penniless. Following the Revolution
he returned to Savannah and set out to prove that he was still an energetic businessman, dedicated family man, political activist, friend of
the poor, devotee of his religion, leader of the Jewish community, and
one of the most highly respected citizens of the state of Georgia. He
was successful in all of these endeavors.

It was not until 1786 that the Jewish community felt itself again
well enough established to reorganize the congregation, elect officers,
rent a house from Ann Morgan on Broughton Street Lane (between

Barnard and Whitaker streets), and furnish it for use as a synagogue.[48] Again all hopes were in vain. The small congregation was not financially strong enough to support itself. By 1793 the rent was in arrears, Miss Morgan became insistent, and Mordecai Sheftall came to the rescue. At the congregation's request, he paid the rent due by giving Miss Morgan merchandise from his general store.

For the next twenty-seven years the congregation met with various successes and failures in rented buildings. Finally in 1820 it raised sufficient funds to construct a wooden structure on a lot given it by the city of Savannah at the southeast corner of Perry Lane and Whitaker Street. This was the first synagogue built in Georgia, and the site is marked by a bronze marker in the Liberty Street sidewalk. It was destroyed by fire in 1829 and was replaced by a brick structure. With the arrival of the wave of German Jewish newcomers in the mid-1850s, that building became too small and the present Gothic revival synagogue on Monterey Square was constructed in 1876.[49]

The story of the Jews of Georgia in colonial times was perhaps best summed up some 150 years ago by the noted Georgia historian, William Bacon Stevens:

> Oglethorpe did not remove them [the Jews] from Georgia; for to have done so would have been to strip the colony of some of its most moral, worthy, and industrious citizens. One of their number was the principal physician of Savannah; as benevolent and kind as he was skilful and deserving [Dr. Samuel Nunes]. Another of them was the vigneron of the colony, who laboured assiduously to improve its horticulture, and extend its usefulness, by introducing and cultivating valuable foreign plants and drugs [Abraham De Lyon]; and the principal importer and merchant was an Israelite, with whom Oglethorpe and the Trustees had dealings to a large amount [Abraham Minis]. . . . The descendants of [these] have occupied many distinguished offices under the federal, state, and municipal governments; and though in the narrow views which then influenced the Trustees, they deplored their arrival into their infant colony, yet we, looking back through the vista of a hundred years, can aver that their settlement in Savannah was a benefit to Georgia; and while the Trustees were expending large sums in subsisting many slothful and discontented emigrants, whose idleness weakened, and whose factions almost ruined, their scheme of benevolence, these descendants of the "father of the faithful"—asking for no charity, clamourous for no peculiar privileges, demanding from the Trustees nothing but the freeholds which their money purchased—proved their worth by services of real value and by offices of tried devotion.[50]

NOTES

1. R. D. Barnett, *Migration and Settlement* (London, 1971), 65–66.

2. *Jewish Encyclopedia*, 12 vols. (New York, 1905), 10:237; *Encyclopedia Judaica*, 16 vols. (Jerusalem, 1972), 13:1290.

3. *Registers of Devon and Cornwall, 1538–1837* (Torquay, England, 1979), 1.

4. *Jewish Encyclopedia*, 10:237; *Encyclopedia Judaica*, 13:1290.

5. For a short and excellent history of Sephardism see Isaac J. Levy, "The Sephardim: End of an Odyssey," and Henry V. Resso, "Recent Theories on the Origins of the Sephardim," both in Sol Beton, ed., *Sephardim* (Atlanta, 1981), 1–18.

6. George Fenwick Jones, "The Lost Tribe of Georgia, or What Became of the Ashkenazim?," 11, unpublished paper of which Jones was kind enough to furnish me a copy. For this statement Jones cites Vivian D. Lipman, *Three Centuries of Anglo-Jewish History* (Cambridge, 1961), 54.

7. *Jewish Encyclopedia*, 4:289.

8. Ibid., 11:577; *Encyclopedia Judaica*, 15:467.

9. Jacob R. Marcus, *Early American Jewry*, 2 vols. (New York, 1975), 2:258–65.

10. Todd M. Endelman, *The Jews of Georgian England, 1714–1830* (Philadelphia, 1979), 23.

11. Jacob R. Marcus, *The Colonial American Jew*, 3 vols. (Detroit, 1970), 1:351–52.

12. *CRG*, 1:76; George White, *Historical Collections of Georgia* (New York, 1854), 328.

13. Marcus, *Colonial American Jew*, 1:352; *CRG*, 1:98; Marcus, *Early American Jewry*, 1:283. For an excellent discussion of the pros and cons of the Trustees' viewpoint and Oglethorpe's refusal to follow their instructions, see Charles C. Jones, Jr., *History of Georgia*, 2 vols. (Boston, 1883), 1:155.

14. This infant was the child of Isaac Nunes Henneriques and his wife. See Sheftall Diaries (a record kept by Benjamin Sheftall in German or Yiddish and translated and amplified by his son, Levi Sheftall), original in the Keith Reid Collection, University of Georgia Libraries, Athens; published in Malcolm H. Stern, "The Sheftall Diaries," *American Jewish Historical Quarterly* 54 (1965):243–77.

15. Marcus, *Colonial American Jew*, 1:354; Malcolm H. Stern, "New Light on the Jewish Settlement of Savannah," *American Jewish Historical Quarterly*, 52 (1963):174–75.

16. Marcus, *Colonial American Jew*, 1:355–56; Barnett, *Migration and Settlement*, 82–88.

17. Joseph I. Waring, "Colonial Medicine in Georgia and South Carolina," *GHQ* 59, Supplement (1975):145; Marcus, *Colonial American Jew*, 1:357.

18. Webb Garrison, *Oglethorpe's Folly* (Lakemont, Ga., 1982), 85.

19. Marcus, *Colonial American Jew*, 1:354.

20. *CRG*, 1:21.

21. Oglethorpe to Trustees, August 12, 1733; reprinted in Mills Lane, ed., *General Oglethorpe's Georgia: Colonial Letters, 1733–1743*, 2 vols. (Savannah, 1975), 1:19–23.

22. Leon Huhner, "The Jews of Georgia in Colonial Times," *American Jewish Historical Quarterly* 10 (1902):71–72, quoting *Boswell's Life of Johnson* (Murray's edition, 1851), 3:217–18; Garrison, *Oglethorpe's Folly*, 8.

23. William Bacon Stevens, *A History of Georgia*, 2 vols. (1847, 1859; reprint, Savannah, 1972), 1:103, n. 17; E. Merton Coulter and Albert B. Saye, eds., *A List of the Early Settlers of Georgia* (Athens, 1949), 71; Stevens, *History of Georgia*, 1:103.

24. Jones, *History of Georgia*, 1:155–62, Marcus, *Colonial American Jew*, 1:358. The original grant to Benjamin Sheftall under seal of George II is in the Levy Collection of Marion Abrahams (Mrs. B. H.) Levy, Savannah.

25. According to Stern, "Sheftall Diaries," 246, twenty-five male Jews arrived on the *William and Sarah* and one (David Mendoza) arrived on November 12, 1733.

26. Stevens, *History of Georgia*, 1:103.

27. James M. Hofer, "The Georgia Salzburgers," *GHQ* 18 (1934):99ff.; Abram Vossen Goodman, *American Overture* (Philadelphia, 1947), 190.

28. Stern, "Sheftall Diaries," 247.

29. Ibid., 247–48. In all early writings the word "Mickva" is spelled with an "a"; later an "e" was substituted for the "a." The original Torah is still a prized possession of Congregation Mickve Israel, Savannah, and is read from each year on the Day of Atonement.
   In 1909 Edmund H. Abrahams, a collateral descendant of Benjamin Sheftall, wrote: "The original Hechal (a wooden container for a torah) remained in possession of the Sheftall family until nine years ago. It was then tendered to the Congregation Mickve Israel, to be kept by it as a relic. The shortsightedness of latter-day 'commercialism,' however refused the tender, and this memorial was then destroyed, to prevent its desecration" ("Some Notes on the Early History of the Sheftalls of Georgia," *American Jewish Historical Quarterly* 9 [1909]:169, n. 3).

30. Stern, "Sheftall Diaries," 248.

31. Stern, "New Light," 186.

32. Ibid., 184.

33. Ibid., 185–86, quoting from W. Gunther Plaut, "Two Notes on the History of Jews in America," *Hebrew Union College Annual* 14:580–81 (in German).

34. Samuel Urlsperger, *Ausführliche Nachricht von den Saltzburgischen Emigranten*, 2277 translated in Goodman, *American Overture*, 191.

35. E. Merton Coulter, *Georgia: A Short History* (Chapel Hill, 1933; rev. ed. 1960), 78.

36. Garrison, *Oglethorpe's Folly*, 221. Saul J. Rubin, rabbi of Temple Mickve Israel, has been kind enough to furnish me with a typescript of his unfinished history of Mickve Israel, Savannah, "Third to None: A History of Savannah's Mickve Israel," which has been of considerable help to me in certain aspects of this period.

37. Marcus, *Early American Jewry*, 2:346; Stern, "Sheftall Diaries," 250.

38. Rubin, "Third to None."

39. Original letter is in the Levy Collection; published in Marcus, *Early American Jewry*, 2:372-73.

40. Original letter is in the Levy Collection; published in Jacob R. Marcus, *American Jewry—Documents* (Cincinnati, 1959), 40.

41. Stern, "Sheftall Diaries," 246, 249, 266; Coulter and Saye, eds., *List of Early Settlers*, 88 (No. 834), 89 (Nos. 835, 836, 838, and 840); Malcolm H. Stern, *Americans of Jewish Descent* (New York, 1971), 138, 227; Malcolm H. Stern, *First American Jewish Families* (Cincinnati, 1978); Joseph R. Rosenbloom, *A Biographical Dictionary of Early American Jews* (Lexington, 1960), 113; Marcus, *Early American Jewry*, 2:291ff., 354ff.; Marcus, *Colonial American Jews*, 2:535, 562-63, 569, 588, 593, 713, 823; *CRG*, 4:621, 6:66; *American Jewish Historical Quarterly* 52 (1962):188ff.; Samuel Rezneck, *Unrecognized Patriots* (London, 1975), 124; Harry Simonhoff, *Jewish Notables in America* (New York, 1956), 17-20; George White, *Statistics of the State of Georgia* (Savannah, 1849), 167; *Abstract of Colonial Wills of the State of Georgia* (Atlanta, 1962), 96; Will Book A, pp. 20-21, Georgia State Archives, Atlanta.

42. Sheftall Family Records maintained in front of a Hebrew prayer book, original in the Levy Collection.

43. Marcus, *Early American Jewry*, 2:342-45.

44. Marcus, *Colonial American Jew*, 3:1276; Ronald G. Killion and Charles T. Waller, *Georgia and the Revolution* (Atlanta, 1957), 34.

45. Jacob R. Marcus, *The Jew and the American Revolution* (Cincinnati, 1974), 5; Marcus, *Early American Jewry*, 2:348, 363; Reznick, *Unrecognized Patriots*, 41; Leon Huhner, "The Jews of Georgia from the Outbreak of the American Revolution to the Close of the 18th Century," *American Jewish Historical Quarterly* 17 (1909):94.

46. Mordecai's manuscript account of his and his son's capture and subsequent treatment as prisoners of war is in the Levy Collection; published in Jacob Radar Marcus, *Memoirs of American Jews*, 2 vols. (Philadelphia, 1955), 1:42-44, 113, and Killion and Waller, *Georgia and the Revolution*, 186-89. The original release is in the Levy Collection; see also Reznick, *Unrecognized Patriots*, 44; Marcus, *Early American Jewry*, 2:348; Simonhoff, *Jewish Notables*, 15.

47. More than forty of the original receipts given Mordecai by various Continental officers for food and supplies purchased with his own funds and furnished by him to their men are in the Levy Collection. The same collection contains several pieces of Georgia currency printed and issued in Savannah in various denominations, each authenticated by handwritten signatures of some of the leading local patriots. Many similar examples are in other collections (including the Georgia Historical Society, Savannah); still other examples are in the hands of antique currency dealers throughout the country.

48. Stern, "Sheftall Diaries," 254. Every officer elected in the reinstated congregation had fought with or assisted the American forces in the revolutionary war.

49. Minutes, Congregation Mickve Israel, in the possession of the congregation: B. H. Levy, *A Short History of Mickve Israel* (Savannah, 1950); copies are available without charge from Congregation Mickve Israel.

50. Stevens, *History of Georgia*, 1:103-4.

Socioeconomic Life

*I*n the past students of Georgia's colonial experience seemed to agree with James Oglethorpe that women in the province were "a dead charge" and of little real use beyond doing the washing and mending. The rules and regulations that governed the colony codified this attitude and left women with little role to play beyond the domestic one the Trustees felt them capable of handling. In time, however, those restrictions were changed, and Georgia women began to play a more important role in the life of the colony than ever envisioned by its founders. Lee Ann Caldwell carefully catalogs their emergence and assesses its impact on both the colony's socioeconomic system and on the women who were involved. This analysis of a long-neglected topic opens the door for future studies of the role of women not only in Georgia but in the southern colonies in general.

The forces that enabled Georgia women to assume a greater role in colonial affairs were felt even more strongly in other segments of colonial society. A socioeconomic system emerged south of the Savannah that was much like the one operating successfully in Carolina. This evolution and its effects can best be understood by examining the handful of leading merchant-planters in Georgia. As W. Calvin Smith shows, the Habersham family most clearly exemplifies the rise of the colonial businessman and the world he created. Georgia's few active and influential merchant-planters led the settlement through its transition from Trustee ward to royal province, from colony to state, and in so doing laid the foundation for the economic system based on slave labor that was to characterize Georgia and the South. Their careers clearly demonstrate how Georgians struggled to accommodate themselves to prevailing colonial commercial patterns.

Whereas the Habershams represent the rise of one segment of

Socioeconomic Life

Georgia society, John Adam Treutlen represents another. Treutlen, one of the immigrants who settled at Ebenezer, grew to manhood in the province, and his life illustrates how German refugees could not only survive but succeed in an English colony. Treutlen's story of hard work and prosperity, as told by George Fenwick Jones, is also an account of the Georgia experience from a perspective that is different from those already told, and it serves as yet another example of the complexity of society in colonial Georgia.

LEE ANN CALDWELL

Women Landholders of Colonial Georgia

S HISTORIANS explore the lives of less-noted people who settled the New World, the significance and role of women in that enterprise becomes better understood. In all the colonies, the presence of women and the family unit changed military garrisons and trading posts into permanent agricultural communities whose inhabitants were concerned about progress and posterity. Georgia followed this pattern of settlement. Women were included in the first embarkation in February 1733. The tasks of men and women within the family were complementary and equally necessary for survival and progress, and as wives, women contributed to the economic progress of the community. But in this frontier society women frequently were left as the sole providers for themselves and their often large families. Like their male counterparts, they helped create communities in the hostile environment of colonial Georgia.

In a society in which landed property provided the basis of subsistence, income, and mobility, the relationship of women and land was crucial. Because the Georgia colony was young, it lacked the extended families common to established communities. Thus real property was particularly significant to maintaining the self-sufficiency of women who outlived their husbands, a frequent occurrence in spite of the dangers of childbirth, and to women who never married. Married women, too, often attempted to maintain ownership and control of their own property.

Women landholders in colonial Georgia have not yet received adequate scholarly attention. Elizabeth Dexter in *Colonial Women of Affairs* states that "through the management of the land [women probably] shared more in building up this country than in any other way."[1] Although Dexter devotes an entire chapter to women land-holders, she does not discuss Georgia women. Helen Bartlett's dissertation, "Eighteenth Century Georgia Women," is the only work on women in the colony in this period, but it gives little attention to women as landowners.[2] "Landgranting in Colonial Georgia" by Robert Lipscomb gives a brief but illuminating discussion of women land-owners, particularly for the Trustee period.[3] But a study focusing on women and land is still lacking.

The current historiography of American women debates whether the status of women in the colonial period was better or worse than that of their postrevolutionary sisters. This argument seems premature, for much research still must be done to determine the status of women within their own society before valid comparisons can be made. A more productive scholarly approach for the present seems to be to examine these women in the context of their own time—how they lived, their relationships with others, and their roles within their communities. Therefore, this study examines the relationship of colonial Georgia women to the land they came by choice or chance to own and control, exploring the opportunity and ability of women to function economically in the agrarian society of the colonial Georgia community.

The colonial Georgia experience was unique in many ways, and the story of women and property is no exception, for while other English colonies used land to attract women, that policy was precluded by the reasons for Georgia's founding. The laws and regulations of Trustee Georgia reflected the philanthropic goals of the Trust as well as the military and economic aims of the English government. Nowhere were these objectives more evident than in land policy. To ensure a colony of hardworking yeoman farmers, no person could own slaves or acquire more than five hundred acres of land. Those coming at Trust expense got fifty-acre grants per family. To fulfill the economic purposes of the crown and Trust, landholders were required to cultivate specified crops, including mulberry trees for silkworms, and to remit quitrents. Finally, to secure a military buffer between Spanish Florida and English Carolina landholders had to be adult males capable of performing military duties. So, unlike other colonies, Georgia did not use land to entice female settlers. In fact, the Trustees made no provisions for Georgia women to own property, for they were also excluded from inheritance of land. Regulations called for inheritance in tail male, with land passing to the eldest son, or in failure of male issue, reverting to the Trust for regrant.[4] The passing of the entire estate to a sole male heir guaranteed a soldier on every fifty acres. It also promoted the Trustees' desire to prevent large accumulations of property through marriage, which might lead to the creation of a landed aristocracy such as had developed in South Carolina. Trust Secretary Benjamin Martyn explained that the Trustees objected to female inheritance "inasmuch as every Female Heir in Tail, who was unmarried, would have been entitled to one lot, and consequently have taken from the Garison the portion of one soldier; and by intermarriages several lots might be united into one."[5]

The prospective male colonist objected to this controversial policy because he resented sacrificing to the Trust land for which he had diligently worked and which he had substantially improved. The husband and father feared as well the fate of his widow and daughters left with little or no means of support. As one member of the first group of colonists explained to the Trust, he had only one child, a daughter as dear to him as a son, and "he could never enjoy any peace of mind, for the apprehension of dying there, and leaving his child, destitute and unprovided for, not having the right to inherit or possess any part of his real estate."[6] Objections were heard from others as well. Non-English settlers, particularly the Salzburgers, expressed grave concern "that the land that was given to them could be held only by a man and that the female sex was excluded from inheriting it after the death of the husband or father."[7] Even members of the Trust, including James Vernon and Lord Tyrconnel, agreed that the regulations were unjust to widows, daughters, and other relatives.[8] Although no words on this subject written by Georgia's female settlers have survived, they must have found the thought of embarking to a frontier under such conditions frightening.

The protests of the settlers on the first embarkation were vehement enough to persuade the Trust to indulge that particular group. At a meeting on October 24, 1732, the Common Council agreed that each man in the group could designate an heir in case he died without a son and that "widows shall have their thirds as in England."[9] But although this dispensation placated those first colonists, the uneasy knowledge remained that future colonists faced tail male inheritance.[10] To alleviate the settlers' fears, the Trustees, while retaining the regulation, demonstrated some laxness in enforcement. At times, upon petition, the Trust allowed women to inherit real property but with the provision that subsequent inheritance would be tail male. In the 1730s eight women requested and received such permission, and additional requests for female inheritance came from men.[11] Some men made inheritance by their wives or daughters a condition of their settlement in the colony,[12] and Oglethorpe himself recommended that land descend to daughters in several cases.[13] So, in spite of policy, women did inherit land during the Trustees' rule. Because few wills are extant from that period, it is impossible to determine how many women did inherit, but in 1755, when colonists were required by the royal government to enter claims of land obtained under the Trustees, thirty-two women registered holdings they had received, mainly through inheritance and deed of gift.[14] There is evidence throughout the *Colonial Records of Georgia* that women did inherit property. On his trips to Savannah Oglethorpe stayed on the property of the Widow Overend.[15] As early as 1735, Mrs. Mary Cooper was receiving rent for her house in Savannah.[16] There are numerous other references to the property of women.

The Trustees also deviated from their regulations by making several outright grants to women who, like Margaret Bovey, "proposed to go with all speed to settle and inhabit and clear and improve such lands as the Common Council would grant."[17] In 1735 Elizabeth West, who went to Georgia at her own expense, received a five-hundred-acre grant.[18] When Peter Gordon and his wife left the colony, they proposed Ann and Susannah Cook as successors to their property, and a fifty-acre grant was made jointly to these sisters.[19] Oglethorpe himself made some grants to women such as those to Ann Cuthbert for a fifty-acre town-garden-farm lot and five hundred acres in farmland at Joseph's Town.[20] The president and assistants recorded nineteen grants to women from 1741 to 1754.[21] There may have been others, for record-keeping throughout the Trustee period was incomplete. In 1737 John Brownfield wrote the Trustees that there had been "no Register kept nor even Remarks of the time when several material things happened; such as the granting and exchanging Lotts."[22] When John Reynolds assumed control of the colony as governor and asked for records of grants and allotments of land, he learned that "no person in this Country has taken any Register or Record thereof, except Mr. Jones, a member of the Council, who told me he had kept a sort of Account of those things for his own private use."[23] He also discovered that many colonists took possession of land with a warrant only, never taking out the grant itself. Women may have been among those who settled in this way.

Thus in the colony's infancy women were hampered by legal restrictions and impractical policy and only occasionally acquired property. Their precarious status, with no legal right to ownership and inheritance in the early years of the colony's existence, caused constant apprehension. In spite of the Trustees' assurance that any next of kin could inherit upon petition, colonists saw this "as a thing of courtesie only. And not such as they had a right to claim by the laws, and Constitution of the colony."[24] While respecting the good intentions and integrity of the current Trustees, the colonials feared the possibility that future unscrupulous Trustees might dispose of property without regard for widows and daughters. Landholders wanted the reassurance of written law.

The continuation of these land policies began to evoke attack on other grounds by the late 1730s, for they proved detrimental to the growth of the colony. Settlers left Georgia, and prospective colonists did not immigrate. Many Georgians argued that absolute inheritance would strengthen the colony numerically, economically, and militarily. Men would not fear their property reverting to the Trust, and the presence of landed women would attract new men to the colony. Many men also hoped to attract single women to the colony for "women, if they are sober and of good behavior, are generally in good esteem and very valuable all over our settlements."[25] The Salzburgers indicated to the Reverend Mr. Samuel Urlsperger that they hoped the next group coming to Georgia would include some "unmarried Christian Salzburger women or other honest members of the female sex who it is hoped would not regret to marry here and likewise to establish an orderly household."[26]

The colonists sent their first petition to the Trustees in December 1738 asking for a change in several policies, including the land regulations. They were refused.[27] In the next year, however, the Trustees enacted a resolution allowing a landholder to appoint an heir by deed or will if he had no sons, although subsequent inheritance was to be tail male.[28] In the summer of 1739 new provisions allowed a widow lifetime use of a house, garden, and one-half of any additional land. The eldest daughter, if a spinster, received land not inherited by her mother if the daughter owned no other land. If the widow was sole survivor, the entire estate descended to her for her lifetime.[29] Under these provisions women began to manage land and thus have an economic role in the colony's development even though they could not choose their own heirs. But in spite of these concessions, Georgians still clamored for absolute inheritance. That cause was taken up by the malcontents, a group of Georgians dissatisfied with Trustee rule, who vocally protested many restrictive regulations. Patrick Tailfer dramatically argued against an inheritance policy that excluded all but the eldest son: "Their younger children, however numerous, are left to be fed by Him who feeds the Ravens; and if they have no children, their Labor and Substance descends to Strangers. How . . . could . . . any free born Spirit brook such a Tenor?"[30]

Although the public pressure of the malcontents undoubtedly had an effect, the continuing decline of the colony finally brought the desired reforms because the regulations theoretically designed to promote the philanthropic, economic, and military purposes of the colony had proved unworkable.[31] On March 19, 1750, the Common Council of the Trustees adopted a resolution making all existing and future grants subject to absolute inheritance.[32] By the end of their rule, the Trustees had granted approximately 153,000 acres of land, most of it after the restrictive land regulations and the prohibition against slavery had been removed.[33] When the crown took over the Georgia government in 1754, women registered approximately 9,000 acres, but many colonists did not register their land, and women probably owned more than was recorded. Most of the women landholders in Trustee Georgia had town lots, but toward the end of this period a few women began to venture beyond the village security.[34] This trend would accelerate under royal government.

The experience of two women gives some insight into the lives of women in Georgia's early years and their attempts to obtain and manage their land. Penelope Fitzwalter lived in Georgia twenty-five years before receiving her first grant of land, but she managed land through inheritance much earlier. She came to Georgia on the *Anne* with her first husband, John Wright, and their two children. Wright owned a public house which his wife inherited after his death in 1737. She continued to manage it, at first alone and then with her second husband, Joseph Fitzwalter. At his death in 1742, Penelope succeeded her husband as wharfinger in order to support herself and her children. When the job of wharfinger ceased to exist, she was forced to accept aid from the Georgia government in 1748. She lived on her lot in Savannah until 1758, when she sold it to Lewis Johnson. But in July of that year she obtained a grant for another town-garden-farm lot in Savannah.[35] Her will indicated that she owned two such lots when she died at the age of eighty in August 1767.[36]

Elizabeth Bowling's husband, Timothy, a potash maker, left England with the first embarkation, with Elizabeth and their daughter Mary following on the *Susannah* in September. Timothy died in November and left Elizabeth and her daughter on the land.[37] They were allotted an Irish servant to aid in cultivating the land, but he died two months later. They evidently managed until 1741, when their house burned down and her poor health forced Elizabeth to petition the Trust for relief.[38] In January 1753 Elizabeth and Mary sold the farm lot portion of Timothy's original grant for £3.10. In 1755 Mary Bowling, identifying herself as daughter and heir of Timothy, registered her claim to the town-garden lot. In December 1759 she received a grant for this lot and in November 1761 a grant for another town-garden lot.[39] In 1774 Mary Bowling still owned her property for she mortgaged one lot for £40 currency of the province.[40] This land had remained in the Bowling family under the management of women throughout the colonial period.

The method of land distribution changed under royal rule, when under the headright system land was granted in fee simple with the head of the household, male or female, eligible for one hundred acres for himself and fifty acres for each dependent, including indentured servants and slaves. This system, used in many English colonies, was based on the idea that the grantee received the amount of land that one person could feasibly cultivate. If the grant applicant could demonstrate that he or she could productively use more land than he or she could claim under the headright system, the governor and council, upon petition, often allowed purchase of additional land for one shilling per ten acres.[41] After receiving headright grants, several of Georgia's women were permitted to purchase additional acreage, an indication that they had successfully cultivated their original grants. For example, Abigail Minis, one of Georgia's early Jewish settlers, became a very successful planter. She obtained her original land in headright in 1757, having eight children and one slave. Ten years later she received an additional 500 acres in headright for sixteen more slaves. In March of that year she received seven town lots in payment of a debt; one month later she got an additional headright grant for 350 acres and purchased 450 more.[42]

Under the laws of the royal period women could inherit land. As a royal colony Georgia was subject to English common law, which provided some protection for the surviving spouse. The widow's common law right was known as dower and gave her one-third interest for life in all lands owned by the husband at any time during the marriage. Upon marriage a woman became a feme covert whose legal existence was, according to Blackstone, "suspended during the marriage, or at least incorporated and consolidated into that of the husband." Under coverture the husband had the right of curtesy, which entitled him to all the wife's land during the marriage or for his life as well when she died.[43] But the feme covert was given protection from alienation of property to which she could later claim dower rights. As an April 1760 act of the Georgia assembly stated: "It has been customary in the conveyances of lands by husband and wife, to acknowledge her consent before a judge or justice, being first privately examined whether she acknowledged the same voluntarily and freely . . . without any compulsion or force."[44] Thus the feme covert had to renounce any title or claim of dower to the land before it could be sold or willed. The weakness in this protection lay in the fact that she still returned home with the husband even if she refused. The recording of land conveyances began under the Trustees in 1750 and continued throughout the royal period. These conveyances indicate that renunciation of dower was indeed practiced in the colony. Conveyances either have a separate codicil stating that the wife renounced her dower or a phrase within the conveyance indicating that her signature was evidence of her consent to the alienation of the land.[45]

Another method for women to protect themselves and maintain control of property was through marriage agreements, which in Georgia set a woman's property aside in a trust to which her husband had no access. She thus kept the management of the land, sole right to alienation, and choice of heirs. Fifty-two marriage agreements can be found in Georgia colonial records, and there are allusions to others.[46] For example, Lydia Saunders, as a feme sole (a widow), settled in Georgia with ten slaves in January 1758. She received a grant for 550 acres in headright, which she evidently managed successfully, for seven years later she purchased an additional 500 acres. When she consented to marry John Winn, she had an agreement drawn up making her estate distinct, including 1,150 acres of land, ten cattle, six hogs, three sheep, numerous household goods, some books, her pew in the chapel, and even her crop for the year of her marriage.[47] The widow Ann Harris of Frederica executed a marriage agreement which included a lot in Frederica, fifty acres on the Newport River, a town lot in Savannah owned jointly with her mother, seven slaves, eleven head of cattle, a mare, a schooner, a store in Frederica, timber, and a sawmill in partnership with her mother. The agreement gave her household goods to her mother.[48] She and her mother, both widows, had managed land and businesses successfully.

More than 400 extant wills reveal that men inherited most real property in Georgia. If a man had sons, land usually was left to them, with daughters receiving household goods, livestock, or slaves. In some cases, nephews or brothers were chosen over wives and daughters to inherit land. Widows were often left personal property "in lieu of their dower or thirds." Of the 386 wills written by men, however, 75 designate women as outright heirs to land. Some women received entire estates but most shared land with their children. Usually the widow received a town lot, and her sons got farm acreage. An additional seventy-five widows received the use of land during their lifetimes or during their widowhood. Fifty daughters inherited land from their fathers, and thirteen women other than wives and daughters inherited men's property. The only identifiable case of landownership by a black woman was documented in her father's will. Andrew Elliott of Savannah, a mariner, left all of his real estate to Isabella, the daughter of Sylvia Elliott, a free Negro woman living in Gambia.[49] Thus, although men apparently often ignored dower rights when disposing of property in their wills, women did control and manage considerable amounts of land through inheritance.[50] Women whose husbands died intestate received through their dower rights at least one-third of the husband's property while they lived, although many inherited more.

During Georgia's royal period approximately seventy thousand acres were granted outright to women.[51] So far as civil status could be determined, 80 percent of the women receiving grants were feme soles, either widows (60 percent) or spinsters (20 percent). In a new colony with few extended families, the practicality of single women receiving land to support themselves and their families is obvious. The cultivation of land brought self-sufficiency, which was desirable both for the women and for society as a whole.

The remaining 20 percent of grants to women whose marital status is identifiable went to feme coverts, an unusual practice. Many of these requests involved land of former husbands or of male relatives. A grant established clear title to the land, especially in cases when the deceased had petitioned for a grant, had the land surveyed, but had not received final title. For example, in August 1770 Judith Polson received a grant for two thousand acres that had been surveyed for her father, Mark Carr, and on which he had erected a sawmill before his death.[52] In

February 1762 Ann Green, wife of Thomas Green of Savannah, obtained a grant for a town-garden-farm lot in Savannah as the sister and heiress of Edward Jenkins.[53] But some grants to feme coverts have no apparent explanation. Equally puzzling are several grants made to husbands and wives in both names. George and Jane Delegal received a joint grant in 1769 for a 582-acre tract at Little Ogeechee "for their joint Lives and the life of the longest liver of them and to the Heirs of their Bodies."[54] Ann and Allen Stuart petitioned that they had lived in Georgia for some time, but neither had received any land. Having five Negroes and desiring land for cultivation, they requested and received 450 acres in joint tenancy.[55] Joint tenancy was evidently given to those who requested it, but the reason for such requests is unclear.

In the early years of royal Georgia town-garden-farm lots constituted the majority of grants to women. In the royal period, 64 percent of all town lots were granted from 1755 to 1765. Most women stayed in Savannah and the surrounding towns, but there were women landowners in Augusta and later in Wrightsborough, both in the backcountry. Women who came with various religious groups settled with their people in such communities as Ebenezer, Vernonburgh, and Midway. Women who owned town lots survived economically in a variety of ways—cultivating their garden and farm lots and participating in businesses. They were midwives, storekeepers, tavernkeepers, seamstresses, and millowners.

The number of women requesting farm acreage increased steadily throughout the royal period. Of the 164 who received grants from 1755 to 1775, 122 got farm acreage. After 1770 women even began to ask for farmland in the upcountry—St. Paul's Parish—and by the Revolution women owned 4,650 acres there on the edge of the frontier, most in small farms. Women who requested farm acreage from 1755 to 1760 owned five hundred or more acres. But the trend for female ownership of small and medium-sized farms increased steadily; grants for under five hundred acres represented 62 percent of all grants in the last five years before the Revolution compared with only 41 percent in the first five years of the royal period. Landholding became increasingly prevalent among middle-class women. The owners of these small farms seldom requested subsequent grants but cultivated what they had. The deeds and conveyances of the royal period contain little evidence that these women purchased additional slaves or acres, as did larger landholders.

The lives of these silent women can be only partially reconstructed through scattered records. For example, Ann Moodie and her husband Robert immigrated to the Georgia province in 1764 and rented land for eighteen months. Robert died, leaving Ann with six children to support. She petitioned the governor and council for a grant of two hundred acres of land to cultivate at Beaver Dam in St. Matthew Parish, which was granted. Her will indicates that she lived on her land, cultivated it, and acquired a respectable amount of livestock— fifteen cows, six sows and pigs, a bay mare, and a chestnut sorrel mare.[56]

Between 1755 and 1775 thirty-one Georgia women received fifty-three grants ranging from 500 to 999 acres. These women obtained additional grants after successful management of their initial grants, although not with the frequency of wealthier landowners with over one thousand acres. Sarah Bevill inherited 450 acres from her husband. In her own right she received a grant of 300 acres because she had nine slaves and five children.[57] By 1774 she had twelve slaves so her plantation must have achieved some success. In addition to farming, she had joined with Nathaniel Miller, William Coulsen, and Abraham Lundy in petitioning the governor and council for permission to purchase 1,000 acres of pine land in St. Matthew Parish in 1767. After receiving the grant, they had built a sawmill by January 1768.[58]

Women also owned some of Georgia's larger colonial estates. Sixteen accumulated tracts of one thousand or more acres each. That these women received a total of sixty-one separate grants is indicative of the success of their operations. Several received numerous grants over a ten- to fifteen-year period, proof of an economic success in their farms and usually an increase in the number of slaves they owned.[59]

Mary Musgrove Mathews Bosomworth, one of the most colorful and controversial characters in early Georgia and perhaps the most important woman in the colonial Georgia story, also owned a large amount of land. The child of an Indian mother and a white father, Mary was living with her husband John Musgrove on Yamacraw Bluff when Oglethorpe landed with Georgia's first colonists. She proved to be an invaluable asset to the struggling young colony, for in addition to aiding in the negotiations with the Indians to obtain permission for the English to settle at Savannah, she provided the colonists with food, liquor, and other "necessities." Mary was a constant source of help to the Georgia authorities, serving as an interpreter on innumerable occasions and as an adviser on Indian relations throughout the colonial period. Mary and her last two husbands became involved in a prolonged and bitter controversy with the Georgia government over land claims, but in 1760 as a compromise and a compensation for her past services, Mary received the largest single grant given a woman—St. Catherines Island, 6,200 acres.[60]

Equally impressive were the holdings of Elizabeth Butler. On December 7, 1758, Elizabeth Elliott, daughter of a South Carolina planter, signed a marriage agreement with William Butler protecting her inheritance of twenty slaves and twenty head of cattle.[61] William died in 1763 leaving her more than three thousand acres of land. As a widow with one daughter and 111 slaves she received twelve grants from 1763 to 1772, totaling 5,320 acres, one thousand of which were pine lands that she intended to use for a sawmilling business. She continued to accumulate land and slaves, and the versatility of her operation made her one of the more prosperous and successful of colonial Georgia's planters and an obvious contributor to the economic growth of the colony.[62]

Women in colonial Georgia came to own and manage land in a variety of ways—through inheritance, grant, and purchase. Most acquired land through inheritance, and although widows often had no control over the disposal of their land after their deaths, they managed the property during their lives. Because most of Georgia's men died intestate, their widows controlled at least one-third, often more, of their property through dower rights. Georgia's women also gained land through outright grants, particularly in the royal period, when the headright system allowed grants to any head of household, based only on ability to cultivate the land. Women also increased the size of their holdings through purchase of additional property, but this was usually a secondary alternative used by wealthier women who had already obtained all land they were eligible for under headright. Although most of Georgia's women landholders were feme soles, married woman did exercise some control and ownership of property. Many set their land apart by marriage agreements, some petitioned for joint tenancy of grants with their husbands, and all had dower rights, which gave them some control over alienation of land. Some women built large plantations, but those of more modest means constituted most of Georgia's women of property. Like their male counterparts, they quietly cultivated their holdings and raised livestock to provide for their families, surviving in a new and often hostile environment.[63] Their stories show hardship and stamina, success and sometimes failure. But they formed an integral part of the society of colonial Georgia and as landholders, farmers, and businesswomen they were significant in the ultimate success of the Georgia venture.

NOTES

1. Elizabeth Dexter, *Colonial Women of Affairs* (Boston, 1924), 98–125.
2. Helen Bartlett, "Eighteenth Century Georgia Women" (Ph.D. dissertation, University of Maryland, 1939).
3. Robert Lipscomb, "Landgranting in Colonial Georgia" (M.A. thesis, University of Georgia, 1970).
4. Ibid., 4–9.
5. [Benjamin Martyn], *An Account Showing the Progress of the Colony of Georgia* . . . in Trevor R. Reese, ed., *The Clamorous Malcontents: Criticisms and Defenses of the Colony of Georgia, 1741–1743* (Savannah, 1973), 186.
6. E. Merton Coulter, ed., *The Journal of Peter Gordon, 1732–1735* (Athens, 1963), 26.
7. Samuel Urlsperger, comp., *Detailed Reports of the Salzburger Emigrants Who Settled in America* . . . , ed. George Fenwick Jones et al., 7 vols. to date (Athens, 1968–), 1:54.
8. Coulter, ed., *Journal of Peter Gordon*, 26.
9. *Minutes of the Common Council of Trustees, 1732–1752*, CRG, 2:7.
10. Coulter, ed., *Journal of Peter Gordon*, 26.
11. Lipscomb, "Landgranting in Colonial Georgia," 40.
12. Entry Books of Commissions, Powers, Instructions, Leases, 1732–38, Ms. CRG, 32:139–40.
13. James Oglethorpe to Trustees, September 27, 1733, Egmont Papers, 14200, pt. 1, 117.
14. Pat Bryant, comp., *Entry of Claims for Georgia Landholders, 1733–1755* (Atlanta, 1975).
15. Original Papers, Correspondence, General Oglethorpe, Others, CRG 25:174.
16. *CRG*, 2:185.
17. Ibid., 96.
18. Letter Books of Trustees, 1745–1752, Ms. CRG, 31:35.
19. *CRG*, 2:229.
20. Bryant, comp., *Entry of Claims*, 23–24.
21. Original Papers of Governor John Reynolds, 1754–1756, CRG, 27:77–99. Four additional grants to widows in Vernonburgh have been located in *Proceedings of the President & Assistants*, CRG, 6:56.
22. Original Papers, Correspondence, Trustees, Others, CRG, 21:467.
23. *CRG*, 27:75.

24. Coulter, ed., *Journal of Peter Gordon*, 27.

25. Ibid., 55.

26. *Original Papers, Correspondence, Trustees, Others, CRG*, 22, pt. 1:348.

27. Lipscomb, "Landgranting in Colonial Georgia," 46.

28. J. R. McCain, *Georgia as a Proprietary Province* (Boston, 1917), 229–30.

29. Lipscomb, "Landgranting in Colonial Georgia," 51–52.

30. Patrick Tailfer, *A True and Historical Narrative of the Colony of Georgia*, in Reese, ed., *Clamorous Malcontents*, 86.

31. Reese, ed., *Clamorous Malcontents*, vii–xvi.

32. McCain, *Georgia as a Proprietary Province*, 243.

33. E. Merton Coulter, *Georgia: A Short History* (Chapel Hill, 1933; rev. ed. 1960), 77.

34. Bryant, comp., *Entry of Claims*. Town lot is used to refer to the town-garden-farm lot combination, which totaled fifty acres.

35. Sarah B. Gober Temple and Kenneth Coleman, *Georgia Journeys, 1732–1754* (Athens, 1961), 207–11.

36. Colonial Dames of Georgia, comp., *Abstracts of Colonial Wills of the State of Georgia, 1733–1774* (Hapeville, Ga., 1962), 49; and Mary Warren, ed., *Marriages and Deaths, 1763–1820* (Danielsville, Ga., 1968), 36.

37. E. Merton Coulter and Albert B. Saye, eds., *A List of the Early Settlers of Georgia* (Athens, 1949), 5.

38. Temple and Coleman, *Georgia Journeys*, 178.

39. *CRG*, 28, pt. 1:366, 368; and Bryant, comp., *Entry of Claims*, 13.

40. Mortgages, 1770–1785, book W, pp. 204–5, Georgia Department of Archives and History, Atlanta.

41. Lipscomb, "Landgranting in Colonial Georgia," 4–7.

42. *Proceedings of the Governor and Council, October 12, 1741 to February 13, 1782, CRG*, 7:512, 681; 8:42, 210; 9:232; 10:161, 167, 608; Bonds, 1765–1772, book R, pp. 107–8, Georgia Department of Archives and History, Atlanta.

43. Frederick D. Kempin, Jr., *Historical Introduction to Anglo-American Law* (St. Paul, 1973), 143–44.

44. *Statutes Enacted by the Royal Legislature of Georgia, 1754–1768, CRG*, 18:417–420.

45. Conveyances, 1750–1766, vols. C-1 and C-2, Georgia Department of Archives and History, Atlanta.

46. "Marriage Agreements, 1748–1783," in William H. Dumont, *Colonial Georgia Genealogical Data, 1743–1783* (Washington, 1971), 1–5.

47. Bonds, 1772–1777, books Y-1 and Y-2, pp. 220–21, Georgia Department of Archives and History, Atlanta.

48. Conveyances, book C-1, pp. 40–41, Georgia Department of Archives and History, Atlanta.

49. Colonial Dames, *Wills*, 44.

50. Ibid., passim.

51. Marion R. Hemperley, *English Crown Grants in Georgia, 1755–1775,* 9 vols. (Atlanta, 1974), passim; and *CRG*, vols. 7–12, passim.

52. *CRG*, 11:103, 249.

53. *CRG*, 8:647.

54. *CRG*, 10:818.

55. *CRG*, 11:397.

56. Bonds, 1765–1772, Book R, pp. 350–51, Georgia Department of Archives and History, Atlanta.

57. *CRG*, 9:674.

58. *CRG*, 10:41, 386.

59. Hemperley, *English Crown Grants*, passim.

60. *CRG*, 4:8, 26, 27; E. Merton Coulter, "Mary Musgrove, 'Queen of the Creeks': A Chapter of Early Georgia Troubles," *GHQ* 11 (1927):1–30; and John P. Corry, "Some New Light on the Bosomworth Claims," *GHQ* 25 (1941):196–224.

61. Bonds, book J, p. 409, Georgia Department of Archives and History, Atlanta.

62. *CRG*, 9:23–26; 10:117, 121, 370, 609, 970; 11:418; 12:201; and Conveyances 1771–1774, X-1, 533–34, Georgia Department of Archives and History, Atlanta.

63. In most grant requests women said they were "desirous of cultivating land." Women are also listed among the stockholders of Georgia.

W. CALVIN SMITH

The Habershams: The Merchant Experience in Georgia

 HEN JAMES HABERSHAM first arrived in Georgia in 1738, he came as a missionary, not a merchant. Although in London he had been a merchant-apprentice, he had journeyed to the colony for spiritual, not temporal, reasons as a companion of the budding evangelist George Whitefield. Perhaps such an introduction was fortunate because although the Savannah that greeted him may have been a suitable missionary field, it was assuredly not a commercial dream. To the newcomer from the hectic world of the London merchant, it could only have looked like a disaster area for a hopeful entrepreneur. It had developed but little in the five years since its founding by Oglethorpe and his small band of settlers. There was no wharf, warehouse, or much indication of business activity. Only some rough steps led up the forty-foot bluff, and a cranelike device was used to lift goods from boats tied up at the crude landing to the town.[1] To reach the city, Habersham had had to complete his journey in a ship's boat from Tybee.[2]

But when Habersham first viewed Savannah, it was not with the eye of a merchant, and evidence indicates no disappointment. For here was a true vineyard for the missionary-teacher who had left his London commercial background for "reasons known only to God and his own soul" to accompany Whitefield to Georgia.[3] Together they had persuaded both Habersham's family and the Trustees that Georgia needed a teacher and minister. Once in the colony, they agreed on the necessity of both a school and an orphanage. When, after several months, Whitefield returned to England for ordination into the priesthood, Habersham became director of a school, caretaker of orphans, and sometime spiritual overseer of Christ Church Parish.[4]

Apparently, he was never totally comfortable with the last position because Savannah had too many unregenerates to suit this Whitefield convert, and he was relieved to transport the "orphan-family" in 1740 to Bethesda, the site ten miles from Savannah on which the orphanage would be built.[5] Habersham remained there as superintendent for the next four years, struggling with limited supplies, the Georgia climate, and occasional interference from the Savannah authorities over the spiritual life of Bethesda's inhabitants. Whitefield's absences made Habersham increasingly concerned with the daily physical needs of his "family" while Jonathan Barber, a New England dissenter, took care of spiritual needs.[6] In these circumstances, Habersham's business talents rose to the fore once again.

By 1742–43, Bethesda was in serious financial difficulty, and its temporal superintendent was worried about its survival. The "orphan-family" now contained more than fifty children, and Habersham prayed for help to lighten the financial burdens and pressures on the institution.[7] His relief came by a series of coincidences that brought Habersham gradually, almost incidentally, into the Savannah commercial community. While he fretted about supplying Bethesda, the Trustees' store in Savannah curtailed its operations. One of its former clerks, Francis Harris, began his own storekeeping operation in mid-1742 with his pay in kind from the Trustees' enterprise.[8] At nearly the same time, Habersham received a financial gift for the orphanage, which he used to purchase a schooner and a large stock of provisions in Charleston for Bethesda's use.[9] The continuing need to obtain goods from Charleston for both Bethesda and Savannah brought the talents of Harris, who was a friend of the Bethesda family, into a natural association with Habersham that blossomed into Trustee Georgia's best-known commercial concern.

During the early months of the Habersham-Harris liaison, Habersham made most of the trips to Charleston to fetch supplies for the orphanage and for the Savannah store, while Harris handled the merchandising for the partnership. The profit from this Charleston-Savannah commerce was sufficient to convince Habersham to pursue his "worldly business" more vigorously.[10] By the spring of 1744, the partnership's trade was "considerable" and the envy of such Savannahians as William Stephens, president of the Trustees' Board of Assistants in Georgia. Stephens hinted that Habersham would abandon Bethesda, but the orphanage superintendent remained at his post. Convinced that God had led him into trade so he could help Bethesda survive, Habersham both superintended the orphanage and financially maintained it with his share of Harris and Habersham profits before Whitefield's return to America late in 1744.[11] Only then did Habersham obtain release from full-time supervision of Bethesda so that he could move to Savannah to take greater responsibility for his merchant affairs there. Yet throughout his life he continued to keep a watchful eye on Bethesda and contributed generously to its financial needs.[12]

Habersham's decision to move to Savannah was wise because he and Harris needed to plan continuously to avoid the pitfalls that had plagued other would-be Georgia merchants. Although they had made a steady profit from the resale of dry goods and foodstuffs purchased in Charleston and brought to Savannah, they had had no opportunity to open direct connections with England and attempt to match the thriving Charleston merchants engaged in the normal patterns of eighteenth-century trade.[13] They did aspire to that day of direct trade when they might compete with their Charleston counterparts,[14] but for the moment they had to devise ways of dealing with the idiosyncrasies of commerce in Trustee Georgia, particularly the distinctive money system and the disadvantage of conducting all external trade via Charleston. These two obstacles could be overcome only with perseverance, determination, and cooperation from the Trustees.

Harris and Habersham possessed a good deal of the first two qualities, but cooperation from the Trustees was often as slow in arriving as the quarterly shipments of "sola bills," the unique paper medium that the Trustees had devised for their Georgia experiment. This troublesome currency had originated with the Trustees' desire to keep close watch on their philanthropic venture. Fearful of ill results and adverse publicity if bad debts arose in their colony, the Trustees refused to allow bills of exchange to be drawn on themselves. Instead, they deposited Georgia funds in the Bank of England and used the bank's resources to print their "Sola Bills of Exchange payable in England." They then sent these bills by quarterly shipment to Georgia, where, once endorsed by the province officials, they circulated as a medium of exchange.[15] On paper the fiscal situation looked workable; but a distance of three thousand miles, resulting in a time lag of two to three months, frequently made London plans inapplicable or outmoded in the New World.[16]

Certainly the time and distance from England made the sola bills a headache for James Habersham, who kept the books for the partnership. The bills usually arrived late and sometimes not at all because of losses at sea.[17] In addition, Charleston merchants were often hesitant about accepting the notes when Harris and Habersham used them to settle accounts. The reliability of the Georgia firm gradually broke down Charleston resistance, but the merchants there still would usually take the bills only at a rate substantially lower than their face value.[18]

This constant devaluation increased trade difficulties for Harris and Habersham, who resorted to using whatever currency they could to conduct business with their Charleston creditors. If lucky, they might get a little Spanish bullion. Not infrequently, they had to rely on General Oglethorpe's old military money notes; and occasionally, they had their own notes printed for small amounts.[19] To ensure that the firm's creditors would accept its notes, Habersham began a correspondence with Harman Verelst, the Trustees' accountant in England, requesting him to use his good offices to see that bills and notes from Georgia were honored by English merchants. He pointed out the hardships of conducting business in Savannah with sola bills arriving late and other currency scarce, and he recommended that "indubitable" bills of exchange, well-recognized abroad, be allowed in Georgia if the Trustees wished to see trade expand.[20] The Trustees' willingness to do so may be doubtful, as Milton Ready has indicated,[21] but it is certain that if Harris and Habersham had been forced to wait for the Trustees to stop using sola bills, their enterprise would have folded. Only near the end of the Trustee era, and after Harris and Habersham had used their own initiative to open a direct trade with London merchants, did the sola bill difficulty begin to dissipate.[22]

Opening direct trade between London and Savannah was also the obvious solution to the disadvantage of conducting business via Charleston. Yet until the partners could convince a London factor that Savannah was worthy of risk, they had to contend with transshipment from Charleston. This situation was cumbersome and costly and, as Habersham frequently noted, a great handicap to his and Harris's business efforts.[23] They had to bear the additional expenses of Charleston warehouse storage as well as extra freight charges from Charleston to Savannah. Shipping delays caused them to miss market opportunities when their Savannah products arrived in Charleston after oceangoing vessels were already loaded with Carolina goods. Further, they often could not collect insurance on spoiled or damaged items sent them by way of Charleston because storage in Charleston warehouses ended the original shipper's liability. Unless shipments to their firm were opened and inspected at the South Carolina port, another burdensome expense, it was impossible to prove when and where the damage occurred. As a result of these expenses, Habersham asserted that charges from Charleston to Savannah could amount to more than one-third the charge from Charleston to Philadelphia.[24]

To make their enterprise a success, Harris and Habersham did much more than complain about sola bills and shipping expenses. They checked with Trustees' local clerks and correspondents to learn what payments were due to which prospective Harris and Habersham customers. When satisfied that an individual had a claim on Trustee funds, Harris and Habersham extended that person's credit, ordinarily for less than the amount due from the Trustees. Then, when sola bills arrived, Harris and Habersham would balance accounts with their Savannah debtors.[25] This system worked in spite of objections from some indebted colonists that Harris and Habersham enriched themselves at Trustee expense by supplying Georgia with overpriced goods bought "second-hand in Charleston."[26] On the transatlantic scene, the partners promoted commercial development as early as 1746 by sending Harris to London to engage a business connection there. John Nickleson, a Mansfield Street merchant and factor known to James Habersham from his merchant-apprentice days, agreed to handle their orders and help them cut out the Charleston middlemen. Still, it was not until the winter of 1748–49 that Harris and Habersham felt economically stable enough to direct their London connection to charter a ship for them to load at Savannah the following winter with rice, lumber, deerskins, and whatever else they could obtain.[27]

Subsistence-level production in Georgia had caused much of the delay in their transatlantic commercial development, but Habersham felt the key to breaking this trade barrier was to make Savannah into a true marketplace where industrious laborers could sell their produce. He confided this view to John Martin Boltzius, the Ebenezer Salzburgers' leader, who was in good favor with the Trustees and who used his influence to laud Harris's and Habersham's commercial efforts.[28] Boltzius's praise eventually had a positive effect. Even though the Trustees were near the termination of their charter in the late 1740s, they apparently wanted to end their era with some sign of success and yielded to the commercial requests of Harris and Habersham. In 1749, the Trustees moved to assist the firm both directly and indirectly: they arranged to station troops from South Carolina in Georgia and authorized Harris and Habersham as provisioners; they granted frontage freely on the Savannah River for the partners' proposed wharf; they gave Habersham authority to endorse and issue sola bills;

and finally, they named him to the Board of Assistants, their official governing agency in Georgia.[29]

Habersham was delighted with this change in fortune, which he attributed to his analysis of needs for Savannah's commercial development, and he anticipated greater ease in business dealings with Georgia officials now that he was one himself. He proceeded eagerly with the firm's plans for a wharf and the initiation of its direct transatlantic trade. In so doing, he revealed how well he knew the benefits of having "government support" for his business. When the Savannah River was found to have sandbars obstructing vessels of more than ten to twelve feet draft, Habersham persuaded his fellow assistants to have the river surveyed to determine the best shipping channels and to request the Trustees to bear the expense of deepening those channels.[30]

Even though such subsidy was unlikely because the Trustees were preparing to unburden themselves of Georgia in the early 1750s, Habersham felt confident of his economic future in the colony. He and Harris were by then trading directly with the West Indies in lumber and other goods, and they owned a sloop, the *Georgia Merchant,* which they used along with the "orphanage schooner." Their trade had increased to the point of hiring a clerk to handle their correspondence.[31] Habersham's optimism was admirable considering that the company still had to ship and receive a good deal of its wares by way of Carolina and that it could load seagoing vessels only to twelve feet draft in Savannah. Nevertheless, Habersham had become by this time a genuine promoter of Savannah. He repeatedly asserted in glowing terms the bright future of the town and predicted that once Savannah had been settled as long as Charleston, "we shall not be thought to make a contemptible figure in the mercantile world."[32]

It is obvious that by 1752 James Habersham had used both commercial skills and political connections to survive—and thrive—in Savannah business where others had failed. He had advanced from orphanage manager to prosperous merchant and governing assistant. He had acquired stores, houses, town lots, and country acreage. If material prosperity is the measure of success, it is fair to say that Habersham's was among the foremost in the few success stories of Trustee Georgia. It is also fair to state that he did not "rest on laurels." He kept his finger on the pulse of political and economic activity in Savannah as the colony changed hands. He became virtually the political head of the caretaker regime until the arrival of the first royal governor.[33] In addition, he began to emulate Charleston merchants in yet another way.

Those "grandees" had grown rich as rice planters using slave labor; Habersham intended to do the same.

Rice development had been long awaited in Georgia, and now at the end of Trustee rule with its restrictions on landholding and its prohibition against black slavery, both older Georgians and newer settlers aspired to the rice riches of "Carolina Gold." Habersham, who had acquired lands with his business profits, needed time to develop rice-growing plantations. Accordingly, he and Harris curtailed their store-keeping functions in Savannah and embarked on new careers as planters. Wisely, however, Habersham decided not to give up all business connection but to become with Harris a "silent associate" of a newly arrived Savannah merchant-hopeful, Thomas Rasberry, in the firm of Rasberry and Company.[34] He and Harris ended their business arrangement and name, turning over to Rasberry and Company the management of their stores and British accounts. Their former trade name supplied the necessary credit and connections for establishing Rasberry and Company with business correspondents in England. In turn, both Habersham and Harris obtained an outlet to ship rice and receive finished wares without paying extra commissions to another colonial merchant.[35] By remaining a silent partner, Habersham saved middleman costs while allowing himself freedom from the headaches of daily commerce. The arrangement enabled him to reside at Silk Hope, his plantation outside Savannah, where he could directly oversee the growth of his rice crops.[36]

And grow they did! For the remainder of the 1750s and into the 1760s, the merchant rapidly became an accomplished planter. Habersham devoted himself to rice culture with the same diligence he had shown in commerce. By careful management, knowledge of markets, and working slaves more by encouragement than by driving, Habersham became one of the leading planters in the colony.[37] By the early 1760s he had acquired well over two thousand acres, centered in the rich, black, fertile soil of the Little Ogeechee district, and seventy slaves to work that acreage.[38] As his merchant and planter skills merged, he produced by mid-decade seven hundred barrels of rice annually "without hurry and too much driving." Georgia's prosperous era of the 1760s saw Habersham continually increase in wealth and prominence to the point that he had his clothes tailor-made in England, his portrait painted in Charleston by Jeremiah Theus, and his table set "handsomely" enough for dining with a royal governor.[39]

Nevertheless, Habersham did not long remain away from the rapidly growing merchants' world of Savannah. In 1763 his wife died, and her passing made life at Silk Hope increasingly disagreeable to him. Soon he was again residing in Savannah, spending no more than one night out of fourteen at his country house.[40] At about the same time, his business associate Rasberry died; his nephew, Joseph Clay, arrived from England with a request for help in getting started in business; and his own sons' economic future began to concern him. He felt he could handle these challenges better by becoming a "perfect Citizen of Savannah" again and leaving direct supervision of planting to overseers and drivers.[41] He knew it would be easier to maintain contact with his two older sons in school at Princeton, to find a tutor for his youngest child, to aid his nephew in commerce, and to fulfill his government functions as councillor if he lived in Savannah.[42] For all these reasons, he returned to the town life and business in which he had been "unavoidably immersed" from youth.[43]

Having passed the age of fifty by mid-decade, Habersham watched sharply for ways to launch his sons' business careers. He knew that the counting house was the business finishing school of his day and a step to continued fortune for his offspring, and he intended for them to be well placed with all the necessary opportunities in commerce.[44] In 1764 he brought his oldest son, James, Jr., back to Georgia to join Joseph Clay in a partnership which he promised to aid with all his "Interest, Experience, and Advice." Habersham advanced the young partners cash and the credit of his name and planned to build brick stores for them on his corner lot. He knew the Clay-Habersham association appealed to his nephew, who had lacked the capital to accompany his talent for business, and he hoped that Clay's ability in trade would be a good example for James, who showed promise in business affairs but seemed too much of a "good-natured gentleman" for his own benefit.[45]

But it was not James, Jr., or "Jemme" as he was called, that fretted Habersham most as the decade progressed but his second son, Joseph, whom he had brought back to Georgia in 1767. After several years at the College of New Jersey, Joseph (Joe) had become a "tolerable classical scholar" but was poorly trained, his father complained, in penmanship, accounts, and English. Consequently, the senior Habersham set his son to studying accounts and mercantile practice with Clay and James, Jr. A few months later Habersham decided other arrangements should be made. Clay liked having another cousin in the business well enough, but Habersham had some doubts. Not only was

James, Jr., already a partner, but thirteen-year-old John had been made a clerk-apprentice in the firm. Having all three brothers in the same company might be troublesome. Even though they got along well, their father was fearful that "the subjection necessary to bring lads up to business would be difficult for one brother to exercise over another," so he sought the assistance of Charleston merchant Henry Laurens to get Joe placed with a Charleston company.[46]

Although Laurens opened his home to Joseph and agreed to seek a proper firm for the youth in Charleston, he advised Habersham that most of the companies there were already committed to take in the "sons, nephews, or relatives" of their principal partners and customers.[47] Disappointed in this effort, Habersham reluctantly decided to send Joseph to London for placement with his business contact there, Graham, Clark, and Company. He asked his longtime London friend and associate, William Knox, to take Joe under his care and help him get situated. Knox agreed, and seventeen-year-old Joseph sailed for England in mid-1768, armed with his father's advice to "be industrious and diligent" and avoid "idle men," "sharpers," and "those of a lower class" who lurked on the London street corners.[48] With unfeigned relief, James Habersham, who knew the dangers of sea travel, welcomed word from Knox in midsummer that Joe had reached London, was well, and under Knox's care.[49]

For the next three years, Joseph Habersham learned the merchant's skills under the watchful eyes of his temporary guardian, Knox, his uncle, Ralph Clay, and his father's friend and business associate, John Clark. These gentlemen saw that he behaved with "proper civility" and reported that by 1770 he had developed into "a very good lad [who] has left off to be an American much easier and earlier than any youth . . . that ever . . . came here."[50] Joseph's subsequent career in the Revolution suggests that this estimate was exaggerated. He appeared glad to leave England in 1771 when his father suggested he return to Georgia and enter trade with his brother because the partnership of Clay and James, Jr., had dissolved in 1770.[51]

Although that company had successfully operated for five years, had its own sloop, the *Industry*, and co-owned the 280-ton ship *Georgia Packet*, there is evidence of friction because James, Jr.'s preoccupation with being a "gentleman" stood in contrast to the efforts of the "excellent businessman" Joseph Clay. James may not have liked being junior partner to his cousin because he immediately attempted a co-partnership with Richard Wylly. That effort failed to establish any

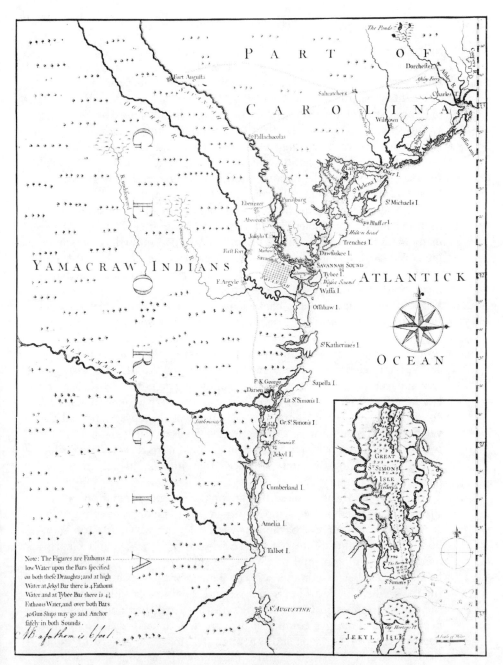

A map of Georgia and part of Carolina drawn by R. W. Seale, ca. 1743.
(Courtesy of Special Collections, University of Georgia Libraries.)

satisfactory arrangement with a London merchant, the prerequisite of successful trade for a colonial firm, and James, Jr., persuaded his father to enter commerce again as his partner under the firm name James Habersham, Jr., and Company.[52]

James, Sr., reluctantly agreed to reenter the business in 1771. He would soon be sixty, his health was not robust, and his colonial political burdens were increasing. Although he could not refuse his son, who had a "growing family" and was at the time "out of all kind of Business," he intended to remain active in trade only until Joseph or John could join "Jemme." Further, to save himself the embarrassment of debt, he determined to limit the business to small importations until its trade built up sufficient capital to warrant more. He believed too many American merchants had been ruined by importing too much on credit without adequate capital.[53] By the time Joseph arrived in Georgia in the fall of 1771, his father and brother had made arrangements with John Nutt of London to serve as the firm's connection in England, and the business, backed by the income from Habersham's rice plantations, was off to a respectable, if modest, start.[54]

Joseph and John were soon working in the business with their brother, as well as assisting their father with plantation supervision and secretarial duties. The arrangement, however, did not last. Joe was apparently not satisfied to be a junior partner to his brother and late in 1772 asked permission to form a five-year partnership with his cousin, Joseph Clay. Habersham, Sr., approved because Clay had developed the "best business connections" of anyone in Georgia, and it would be desirable to have these connections more directly accessible. Accordingly, James Sr. and Jr. agreed that Joe should become Clay's partner as of January 1, 1773.[55]

All in all, the future looked bright for the second-generation Habershams in Savannah's merchant world in 1773. Georgia was enjoying an economic boom, and Savannah was no longer a "Charleston satellite." Customs officials cleared 217 vessels during 1772–73, and Georgia merchants, owning a total of thirty-five ships, were considering establishing a chamber of commerce.[56] To James, Sr., it was a far cry from the days when he and Harris had struggled with sola bills and loaded their one schooner in Charleston. From that small beginning, his connection with Georgia commerce had grown to two well-established companies involving sons and a nephew trading in a variety of goods from all over the British Empire. Pleased with his sons' prospects at last, his thoughts turned more and more to retirement and travel, perhaps to his "native country," England, to improve his declining health.[57]

Events external to business disrupted James Habersham's final plans. The nagging trouble between Great Britain and some of her more northerly colonies began to be felt in Georgia by 1774. Although British commercial policies did not in general conflict with Georgia's economic interests, political policies involving taxation aroused emotions, particularly when urged on by "the fiery Patriots in Charleston."[58] Even Georgians who were doing well financially or growing rich such as the second-generation Habershams became concerned with abstract questions of right and wrong. Joseph Clay affirmed this concern in concluding his order to a London factor early in 1775 with the comment, "We write for these things on presumption public matters may not grow worse. . . . but if otherwise, we should have nothing to do with business . . . [since it is] hardly possible to suppose we should be suffer'd to remain tame spectators while (the) rest of the continent are engaged in opposition."[59]

The elder Habersham, who dreaded to see trade embargoes and associations ruining his offsprings' businesses, was shocked to learn that his son Joseph and his nephew supported and even led opposition to England. He had launched his son and his nephew in business as best he could. If they were determined to ruin themselves by rebellion, he felt too old and ill to prevent them. Heartsick to see his family divided politically, and made infirm by gout and age, he decided to travel north by sea for his health in the summer of 1775, hoping to escape for awhile the heat of both revolutionary passions and Savannah summers. He did not survive the voyage, however; he died off the coast of New Jersey in July.[60] Nor did the businesses he had helped to begin survive the War for Independence. Despite the efforts of some of Savannah's merchants to continue in trade as long as possible, that war, as Joseph Clay succinctly phrased it, "in a manner put an end to all business."[61]

Yet there remains a final notation on the Habersham experience in colonial commerce: the payment of prewar debts. At the war's end, only Joseph Clay sought actively to clear his accounts and reenter business. The Habersham brothers preferred plantation life and federal jobs to the insecurity of commerce in late eighteenth-century Savannah.[62] Neither did they concern themselves much with unsettled accounts. Although the treaty ending the war provided for no impediments to debt collection, few British creditors had much success in recovering losses. In the South, their legal efforts were met with arguments that property had been destroyed, crops wasted, and estates ruined by their own king's troops.[63]

Nevertheless, once federal courts were functioning and the political climate changed by time and Jay's Treaty, some British creditors saw an opportunity to clear old accounts. Although frequently prevented from bringing their cases in civil law because of statute limitations, vanished companies, or scattered partners, creditors could and did bring suits in equity before federal courts. The Habersham brothers were struck in this way in 1798, when John Nutt and Company of London brought suit in chancery against the estate of James Habersham, Sr. The firm to which the senior Habersham had confided his wish not to be embarrassed by debt demanded payment of an alleged balance due from James Habersham, Jr., and Company of £27, 333.9.4. Nutt's bookkeeper claimed that this balance had been guaranteed by the estate of James, Sr., and was equal to $117,143.30 United States currency as of August 31, 1797.[64]

The Habershams protested the suit and fought the case in court for the next six years. They argued that much of their father's property had been destroyed by British forces in the Revolution, they had borne heavy burdens and expenses during that war, and they still had financial encumbrances to counter the demands of John Nutt, who, they said, had "slept upon his right upwards of twenty-five years."[65] The court failed to sustain the Habersham pleas of wartime sacrifices and the passage of time to block collection of this prewar debt, and litigation continued. Finally, in 1805, after claim and counterclaim, demurrer and replication, Joseph Habersham, the last survivor of the second generation, paid Nutt and Company with court approval an agreed-upon modified claim of $24,000.[66] In so doing, he closed the books on the Habersham experience as merchants in colonial Savannah.

The Habershams' commercial success had grown with Savannah. From the almost forced involvement of the senior Habersham in trade in the early 1740s to the post–revolutionary war settlement of debts by his offspring, the Habershams' commercial fortune was linked to that of Savannah. Their story is the story of the rise of commerce in that colonial town. It reveals the business accommodations made by Savannah merchants with British counterparts to overcome trade obstacles in the colony's early history. It shows in compressed fashion how Georgia, once free of Trustee limitations, followed the pattern of merchant-capitalist development that occurred throughout colonial America. As such, the Habersham experience is an excellent example of the transatlantic ties, the merchant-family connections, and the commercial details that made the British mercantilist system work in Georgia until abruptly ended by revolution and war.

NOTES

Research for this article was supported in part by the University of South Carolina Office of Sponsored Programs and Research.

1. E. Merton Coulter, ed., *The Journal of Peter Gordon, 1732–1735* (Athens, 1963), 35.

2. Iain Murray, ed., *George Whitefield's Journals* (London, 1960), 152.

3. James Habersham to the Countess of Huntingdon, December 10, 1770, "The Letters of Hon. James Habersham, 1756–1775," *Coll. GHS,* 6:103; James Habersham to Christopher Bagwith, January 1739, quoted in William Bacon Stevens, "A Sketch of the Life of James Habersham," *GHQ* 3 (1919):153.

4. Stevens, "Life of James Habersham," 153; *CRG,* 5:46–47; George Whitefield to Harman Verelst, May 17, 1737, *CRG,* 21:395; James Habersham to a friend in London, January 14, 1739, quoted in Stevens, "Life of Habersham," 154–55; Murray, ed., *Whitefield's Journals,* 156–59, 164; James Habersham to Countess of Huntingdon, May 15, 1771, *Coll. GHS,* 6:128; Harman Verelst to General Oglethorpe, August 11, 1738, to George Whitefield, August 11, 1738, *Cal. SP,* 44 vols. (London, 1880–1969), 44: 191–92.

5. *CRG,* 4:214–15, 219, 487–90; 4, Supplement:21; Stuart Henry, *George Whitefield: Wayfaring Witness* (New York, 1957), 38–39; James Habersham to John Wesley, June 20, 1739, James Habersham Papers, Georgia Historical Society, Savannah; Murray, ed., *Whitefield's Journals,* 395; James Habersham to George Whitefield, October 21, 30, 1740, quoted in James F. Cann, *Bethesda: A Historical Sketch, with Incidental Recollections of Whitefield and Habersham, Its Founders* (Savannah, 1860), 22–23.

6. *CRG,* 5:359, 673; 4:521, 539–40; James Habersham to George Whitefield, June 11, October 2, 1741, *The Works of the Reverend George Whitefield, M.A.,* 6 vols. (London, 1771–72), 3:441–42, 445; James Habersham, *A Letter from Mr. Habersham, (Superintendent of Temporal Affairs at the Orphan-House in Georgia), To the Reverend Mr. Whitefield* (London, 1744), 3–4, 10–11, 14–15; E. Merton Coulter, ed., *The Journal of William Stephens, 1741–1745,* 2 vols. (Athens, 1958–59) 2:81.

7. Habersham, *Letter,* 3–4, 10. Not all fifty were orphans. Some were offspring of the staff, such as Habersham's own child by the wife he married in 1740.

8. Coulter, ed., *Journal of Stephens*, 1:119, 132; Milton L. Ready, *The Castle Builders: Georgia's Economy under the Trustees, 1732-1754* (New York, 1978), 182-83, 187.

9. Habersham, *Letter*, 11-12.

10. Ibid.; Coulter, ed., *Journal of Stephens*, 1:132, 137, 218-19.

11. Habersham, *Letter*, 12; William Stephens to Harman Verelst, October 17, 1744, *CRG*, 24:334.

12. Coulter, ed., *Journal of Stephens*, 2:190-91, 197, 236; George Whitefield to James Habersham, September 21, 1748, *Works of Whitefield*, 2:179; John W. Christie, "Newly Discovered Letters of George Whitefield, 1745-1746," *Journal of the Presbyterian Historical Society*, 32 (1954):241-42.

13. Coulter, ed., *Journal of Stephens*, 2:81-82; Leila Sellers, *Charleston Business on the Eve of the American Revolution* (Chapel Hill, 1934), 49.

14. James Habersham to Revd. Mr. Bolzius, September 25, 1747, Peter Force Transcripts, Georgia Miscellaneous, 1732-96, Library of Congress, Washington, D.C.

15. William E. Heath, "The Early Colonial Money System of Georgia," *GHQ*, 19 (1935):145-46, 150-51.

16. Daniel J. Boorstin, *The Americans: The Colonial Experience* (New York, 1958), 1, 72-84, 95-96.

17. William Spencer to the Trustees, July 31, 1746, *CRG*, 25:87; Heath, "Colonial Money System," 152-54, 159; Klaus G. Loewald, Beverly Starika, and Paul S. Taylor, trans. and ed., "Johann Martin Bolzius Answers a Questionnaire on Carolina and Georgia, Part II," *WMQ* 3d ser., 15 (1958):243.

18. Heath, "Colonial Money System," 151-52; Loewald, Starika, and Taylor, "Bolzius Questionnaire," 243.

19. Heath, "Colonial Money System," 152-54, 159; Loewald, Starika, and Taylor, "Bolzius Questionnaire," 243.

20. James Habersham to Harman Verelst, September 6, 1746, *CRG*, 25:100-101.

21. Ready, *Castle Builders*, 175-76.

22. Harris and Habersham to Benjamin Martyn, February 13, 1749, James Habersham to Benjamin Martyn, May 24, 1749, Harris and Habersham to Harman Verelst, July 10, 1750, *CRG*, 25:115-16, 389-91; 26:28-31.

23. James Habersham to Revd. Mr. Bolzius, September 25, 1747, Force Transcripts; James Habersham to Benjamin Martyn, May 24, 1749, *CRG*, 25:390-91.

24. James Habersham to Revd. Mr. Bolzius, September 25, 1747, Force Transcripts.

25. Patrick Houstoun to Harman Verelst, February 26, 1745, *CRG*, 24:367-68; *CRG*, 6:156-57.

26. Patrick Houstoun to Harman Verelst, February 26, 1745, William Spencer to Harman Verelst, July 31, September 12, 1746, CRG, 24:367-68; 25:88, 106-7.

27. James Habersham to Harman Verelst, September 30, 1746, Harris and Habersham to Benjamin Martyn, February 13, 1749, James Habersham to Benjamin Martyn, May 24, 1749, *CRG*, 25:129–30, 359–60, 390–91.

28. James Habersham to Revd. Mr. Bolzius, September 25, 1747, Force Transcripts; John Martin Bolzius to Benjamin Martyn, August 29, September 3, 1747, *CRG*, 25:206–7, 214; James Ross McCain, *Georgia as a Proprietary Province* (Boston, 1917), 170.

29. Harman Verelst to James Habersham, July 6, 1749, to president and assistants, September 29, 1749, Ms. CRG, 31:316–17, 348; James Habersham to Benjamin Martyn, May 24, 1749, *CRG*, 25:389–90.

30. James Habersham to Benjamin Martyn, July 7, 1749, Harris and Habersham to Harman Verelst, January 1, 1750, *CRG*, 25:389–90, 449–50. The planned wharf was to be three times the size of the public wharf and to have stores and docking facilities (ibid.); James Habersham to Benjamin Martyn, January 24, March 8, 1751, *CRG*, 26:137–42, 180–81.

31. Harris and Habersham to Harman Verelst, January 1, 1750, James Habersham to Benjamin Martyn, June 13, December 18, 1751, *CRG*, 25: 449–50; 26:241, 320–21.

32. James Habersham to Benjamin Martyn, January 24, 1751, February 3, 1752, *CRG*, 26:137–39, 335–39.

33. *CRG*, 6:461; 26:370–73, 408, 413; E. Merton Coulter, *Georgia: A Short History* (Chapel Hill, 1947), 83.

34. *Ga. Gaz.*, April 28, 1763; James Habersham to Joseph Tuckwell, May 18, 1765, *Coll. GHS*, 6:36–37; Thomas Rasberry to Lt. White Outerbridge, August 12, 1758, in Lilla M. Hawes, ed., "The Letter Book of Thomas Rasberry, 1758–1761," *Coll. GHS*, 13:10–11.

35. Thomas Rasberry to Lt. White Outerbridge, August 12, 1758, to Samuel Lloyd, September 12, 1758, to William Banbury, March 8, 1759, to William Thompson, March 3, 1760, *Coll. GHS*, 13:10–11, 13, 45, 104.

36. James Habersham to Joseph Tuckwell, May 18, 1765, *Coll. GHS*, 6: 36–37; James Habersham Land Grants, Land Grant Record File, Georgia Historical Society; *CRG*, 8:91; "Manuscript Sketch of James Habersham," 18, Robert W. B. Elliott Family Papers, Southern Historical Collection, University of North Carolina, Chapel Hill.

37. James Habersham to Joseph Tuckwell, May 18, 1765, to William Knox, March 9, 1764, November 20, 1770, to James Wright, July 16, 1772, *Coll. GHS*, 6:36–37, 15–17, 95, 190–91; James Habersham to Martin Fenton, October 26, 1768, Etting Collection, Historical Society of Pennsylvania, Philadelphia.

38. *CRG*, 8:380; 9:224, 227, 241; James Habersham Land Grants, Land Grant Record File, Georgia Historical Society.

39. James Habersham to William Knox, July 17, 1765, November 17, 1767, to Jeremiah Theus, July 31, 1772, to Henry Laurens, April 5, 1765, to James Wright, May 30, 1772, *Coll. GHS*, 6:29–30, 38–39, 61–63, 182, 197.

40. James Habersham to William Knox, July 17, 1765, to John Ellis, October 18, 1770, *Coll. GHS*, 6:38–39, 92.

41. "Introduction," *Coll. GHS*, 13:i; 8:7; James Habersham to Ralph Clay, September 26, 1764, to William Knox, July 17, 1765, ibid., 6:26, 39; George Whitefield to James Habersham, November 29, 1762, James Habersham Papers.

42. James Habersham to Mr. Berrien, November 29, 1763, James Habersham Papers; James Habersham to Messrs. Deberdt and Barkit, November 31, 1764, to Ralph Clay, September 26, 1764, to William Knox, May 7, 1768, *Coll. GHS*, 6:20, 26, 67; Erwin Surrency, "The Life and Public Career of James Habersham, Sr." (Master's thesis, University of Georgia, 1949), 66–68, 79–80.

43. James Habersham to John Ellis, October 18, 1770, *Coll. GHS*, 6:92.

44. Robert A. East, "The Business Entrepreneurs in a Changing Colonial Economy, 1763–1795," *JEH* 6, Supplement:19; Reba C. Strickland, "The Mercantile System as Applied to Georgia," *GHQ* 22 (1938):163; James Habersham to John Nutt, July 31, 1772, *Coll. GHS*, 6:195–96.

45. *Coll. GHS*, 8:7; James Habersham to Ralph Clay, September 26, 1764, to William Russell, October 10, 1764, to William Knox, July 17, 1765, to William Symonds, December 4, 1765, *Coll. GHS*, 6:26–27, 38, 51–52.

46. James Habersham to William Knox, May 7, 1768, to Henry Laurens, February 22, 1768, *Coll. GHS*, 6:63–64, 65–69.

47. Henry Laurens to James Habersham, January 25, 1768, George C. Rogers, Jr., and David R. Chesnutt, eds., *The Papers of Henry Laurens*, 9 vols. to date (Columbia: University of South Carolina Press, 1968–), 5:565.

48. James Habersham to William Knox, May 7, 1768, to Joseph Habersham, May 10, 1768, *Coll. GHS*, 6:65–67, 68–70.

49. William Knox to James Habersham, July 8, 1768, James Habersham Papers.

50. William Knox to James Habersham, August 26, 1769, April 5, 1770, Graham, Clark, & Co. to James Habersham, February 13, 1769, March 18, 1769, James Habersham Papers.

51. William Knox to James Habersham, August 6, 1771, James Habersham Papers; James Habersham to Joseph Habersham, October 13, 1770, *Coll. GHS*, 6:90; *Ga. Gaz.*, January 3, 1770.

52. "List of Incoming Ships and Vessels entered at Savannah between April 5–July 5, 1766," *Coll. GHS*, 8:262; "List of Outbound Ships and Vessels at Savannah between April 5–July 5, 1766," *Coll. GHS*, 8:263; East, "Business Entrepreneurs," 20; James Habersham to William Russell, October 10, 1764, to William Knox, May 7, 1768, to Graham, Clark, & Co., February 12, 1771, ibid., 6:27, 67, 120; *Ga. Gaz.*, January 3, 1770.

53. James Habersham to Graham, Clark, & Co., February 12, 15, 1771, to John Clark, June 15, 1771, *Coll. GHS*, 6:120–21, 140–41.

54. James Habersham to John Nutt, July 9, 1771, Habersham Family Papers, Duke University Library; James Habersham to William Knox, November 26, 1771, to John Nutt, July 31, 1772, *Coll. GHS*, 6:151, 195–96.

55. Surrency, "James Habersham, Sr.," 83; James Habersham to John Nutt, January 7, 1773, Habersham Family Papers; Clay and Habersham to Benjamin Stead, January 20, 1773, Joseph Clay Papers, Georgia Historical Society.

56. Barratt Wilkins, "A View of Savannah on the Eve of the Revolution," *GHQ*, 54 (1970):577–80; Milton L. Ready, *The Impact of the Revolution upon Georgia's Economy, 1775–1789* (N.p., 1975), 3; Strickland, "Mercantile System," 160–61.

57. Wilkins, "View of Savannah," 579; Clay and Habersham to Benjamin Stead, January 20, 1773, Joseph Clay Papers; James Habersham to John Nutt, January 7, 1773, Habersham Family Papers; James Habersham to Mary Bagwith, January 7, 1774, *Coll. GHS*, 6:233.

58. Allen D. Candler, ed., *The Revolutionary Records of the State of Georgia*, 3 vols. (Atlanta, 1908), 1:12–13; Ready, *Impact of Revolution*, 11; James Habersham to Messieurs Clark & Milligan, April 7, 1775, *Coll. GHS*, 6:235–36.

59. Strickland, "Mercantile System," 160, 168; Joseph Clay & Co. to Benjamin Stead, May 13, 1775, Joseph Clay Papers.

60. James Habersham to Messieurs Clark & Milligan, April 7, 1775, to Abraham Hayne, April 7, 1775, to John Edwards, April 7, 1775, *Coll. GHS*, 6:235–37; *Ga. Gaz.*, October 25, 1775.

61. William L. Roberts, III, "The Losses of a Loyalist Merchant in Georgia during the Revolution," *GHQ*, 52 (1968):271–72, 275; Joseph Clay & Co. to Bright & Pechin, May 16, July 8, 1775, to Capt. Walker, March 26, 1776, Joseph Clay to Joachim Noel Fanning, October 18, 1785, Joseph Clay Papers.

62. Joseph Clay to Graham & Clark, April 24, 1783, Joseph Clay Papers; Joseph Clay to Nathaniel Hall, April 16, 1783, to Joachim Fanning, April 23, 1783, *Coll. GHS*, 8:184, 186, 190–94; John Habersham to Henry Knox, August 29, 1789, Henry Knox Papers, Massachusetts Historical Society; Wesley Everett Rich, *The History of the United States Post Office to the Year 1829* (Cambridge, Mass., 1924), 173; East, "Business Entrepreneurs," 26.

63. Joseph Habersham, Answer to Bill of Complaint of John Nutt, July 5, 1800, Habersham Family Papers; Charles A. Beard, *Economic Origins of Jeffersonian Democracy* (1915; reprint, New York, 1965), 270–73.

64. James Habersham to John Nutt, July 9, 1771, Affidavit of William Nelson to Mayor of London, September 5, 1797, *John Nutt v. James Habersham Jr. et al.*, April 1798, Habersham Family Papers; Beard, *Economic Origins of Jeffersonian Democracy*, 275–89.

65. Answer of James Habersham, Jr., to Bill of Complaint of John Nutt,

March 12, 1799, Joseph Habersham, Answer to Bill of Complaint of John Nutt, July 15, 1800, Joseph Habersham, Administrator of John Habersham, Answer to Bill of Complaint of John Nutt, May 16, 1804, Habersham Family Papers.

66. *John Nutt* v. *James Habersham Junr. Co. Jos. and John Habersham,* Case File, Records of the United States Circuit Court, District of Georgia, Case A, Box 11, Federal Records Center, East Point, Ga.

GEORGE FENWICK JONES

John Adam Treutlen's Origin and Rise to Prominence

LL THAT IS KNOWN about John Adam Treutlen's birth is its year, 1733, which can be deduced from his age as given on various contemporary records. Two and a half centuries have elapsed since that time, yet we still know neither where Treutlen was born nor where he was buried. In fact, most of what has been published about him is sheer fantasy. The latest article says that he was "a native of Austria, born in Berchtesgaden about 1726," and that his family fled from Salzburg to escape persecution and arrived in Georgia in 1741.[1] As we shall see, he was born neither in 1726 nor in Berchtesgaden, which, incidentally, was not in Austria, nor was he a religious exile, and he did not arrive in Georgia in 1741. The second paragraph of this account tells us that he married Anna Unselt in 1788, which was some six years after his death.

Treutlen's early life is recorded in many documents, most of which, although available, have been largely overlooked or misinterpreted. He appears to have been born somewhere in southern Germany, most probably in the Rhenish Palatinate or a neighboring state; and he left home in 1743 with a large party of Germans who were setting out for Pennsylvania at their own expense. They were hardly off the coast of England before their ship, the *Two Sisters*, Captain John Stedman, was captured by two Spanish privateers and taken to Bilbao. There some of the passengers died, including John Adam's father; and the others lost all their belongings. Finally redeemed by the British, the captives were taken by the cartel ship *Drake* to Gosport, a small town near Portsmouth, where they arrived on March 31, 1744.[2]

Thoroughly discouraged, those who could afford to do so—about half the party—returned to Germany. The rest remained in Gosport until August 1745, supported by the charity of the townspeople and housed in a warehouse belonging to John Carver. Learning of the plight of these stranded people and motivated by charitable as well as practical considerations, the Georgia Trustees accepted a petition from the Germans' spokesmen, Wendall Brakefield (Wendel Brachfeld?) and Matthew Wust (Matthias Wüst), and offered on May 30, 1745, to transport the group to Georgia in exchange for four years of indentured service. Anna Clara, the widow Treutlen, was among the seventy-three who agreed to the very generous articles on August 19, 1745, engaging herself and her sons John Adam and Frederick.[3]

On their ship, the *Judith*, which sailed later in the month under Captain Walter Quarme, were Thomas Causton, the former keeper of the stores in Savannah, Hermann Heinrich Lemke, a replacement for the recently deceased Salzburger assistant pastor Israel Christian Gronau, and Bartholomäus Zouberbühler, a Reformed minister from Appenzell in Switzerland who had returned from South Carolina to England for ordination into the Anglican ministry. Causton, a good friend of the Salzburgers, had been summoned back to England under a cloud of suspicion to have his books audited but had been exonerated. Seeing the valuable human cargo that was to go aboard his ship, Causton had arranged to have Ockstead, his estate near Thunderbolt, declared to be within the district to which the German servants were to be restricted.[4]

The poor immigrants' second voyage was scarcely more propitious than the first: a fever broke out and carried off many of the passengers and crew, including Causton, Captain Quarme, and James Bull of South Carolina, who had been entrusted with the care of the Germans and had been promised the services of one of them.[5] Indeed, with the captain dead and the first mate nearly so, the ship might never have reached its destination had not Zouberbühler, a landlubber from Appenzell, known enough geometry to plot its course with the help of an illiterate seaman. Had the emergency navigator steered even a few degrees off course, he could well have landed his ship on the hostile shore of Florida instead of at Frederica, Oglethorpe's new bastion against the Spaniards, which they reached on January 22, 1746.

A list of the *Judith*'s passengers has long been available,[6] yet no one has recognized the name Treutlen, which was distorted to Frideling. It is possible that the widow Treutlen came from a linguistic area where the diphthong *eu* was pronounced the same as the diphthong *ei* (pronounced "eye")[7] and that the first scribe had heard it as *Tride-*

lin and that a later one miscopied it as Frideling.[8] In any case, during the Revolution, Colonel Archibald Campbell must have heard Treutlen's name pronounced correctly because he referred to his farm as "Troitland's plantation." (Again a final consonant was gratuitously appended!) It is possible that the widow's real name was Treutl or Treutle and that she used the feminine form Treutlin, a form that is attested in Georgia records.[9]

When the indentured servants reached Savannah, some were offered to the British officials, and the remainder were assigned to Pastor Johann Martin Boltzius for distribution among his Salzburgers at Ebenezer and to Michael Burckhalter for distribution among the people of Vernonburg, a town recently established on the White Bluff ten miles south of Savannah for Swiss and German redemptioners who had served out their time.[10] Burckhalter, who had run away secretly from his home in Lützelflüh in Canton Bern in 1735,[11] signed a florid and beautifully penned letter of thanks to the Trustees on March 19, 1746, for the gift of a "Palatine Woman-Servant (and her Three Children)" and for other instances of their goodness "towards us poor German Protestants."[12] Because no Swiss at that time would have called himself a "German" Protestant, it is evident that the letter was written by an English clerk. The words "Three Children" suggest that Anna Clara had taken on an orphan child.

Indentured boys normally served until the age of twenty-one; yet Burckhalter, recognizing John Adam's exceptional intelligence and diligence, sent him to Ebenezer for a good Lutheran schooling, even though he himself was a loyal member of the Reformed or Calvinist faith. At Ebenezer the youngster made a favorable impression on Boltzius, who wrote in his journal on Sunday, June 7, 1747, that, among the children confirmed on that day, was "Johann Adam Treutlen, 14 years old, son of a widow in Vernonburg. He came to this country with the last German people and is serving at our place. He is a pious and dear child, who has learned Christian dogma very thoroughly and to the great joy of his heart. Because of his mother, it was hard to bring him here, but now he is all the happier to be here."[13]

Half a year later Boltzius again mentioned a serving boy, who was surely the same child:

Saturday, the 2nd of January, 1748. Yesterday evening after the public prayer meeting, I was greatly pleased by a little letter from a serving boy at our place who has led a blameless and edifying life since the time of his confirmation before he first participated in Holy Communion and has already experienced the blessing and care of our heavenly Father in a very manifest and pleasing manner. It seems to me that he lacked both time and paper: otherwise he would have revealed even further the present condition of his spirit. Meanwhile, what he has written is already enough and will give me an opportunity to adjust myself in my association with him and in my sermons.[14]

In 1750 the town of Ebenezer was augmented by the "First Swabian Transport," a party of immigrants from Württemberg recruited for Georgia by Samuel Urlsperger, one of the "Reverend Fathers" of the Georgia Salzburgers, together with Chretien von Münch, a banker and benefactor, also of Augsburg. In this party was a young man named Johann Georg Meyer, who served as shopkeeper. It was not long before John Adam was put in the newcomer's service to help him keep shop. On June 16, 1751, Boltzius wrote to Henry Melchior Mühlenberg, the leader of the Pennsylvania Lutherans, who had visited him at Ebenezer on his way to Philadelphia:

> Mr. Meyer has an intelligent and skilful youth whom he employs in his store. We would have liked to help him acquire a good piece of land near his brother in Goshen; but it had been given to someone else. Today he sent me the following letter:
> "I beg you most humbly to pardon me for imposing on you again. My brother sent me word that the land I wished had already been given away. Perhaps it is a dispensation of God for me not to go out there. I am now resigning myself fully to the merciful governance of God: may he do with me as it pleaseth Him. It seems to me that I could not live if I had to leave Ebenezer. Oh, I ask you humbly, for the sake of God and for my immortal soul, which has been entrusted to you, to look out for me. I have no one among mankind to whom I can complain or speak. I shall be obliged to you all my life. I also ask you to let me know if you see anything in me or hear anything about me that is not right."
> This youth is a brother of the young and very talented person named Treutlen, who was very well known to Court Chaplain Ziegenhagen, who wrote not many months ago that he had perished with his master Mr. Carver in the water at Gosport in England.[15]

This letter is the only evidence that Anna Clara had left a son in Gosport as servant to Carver. Mühlenberg later indicated that a daughter may have been left behind in Germany.[16]

Little John Adam served Meyer faithfully, yet he did so well in school that Boltzius retained him as schoolmaster. Boltzius's love waned, however, when his young teacher acquired worldly ambitions. The pastor had agreed to let him augment his meager salary by running a small retail store in his spare time with goods furnished on consignment by merchants in Savannah. Unfortunately, realizing that a man cannot serve two masters, the merchants required John Adam to give up either his classroom or his shop, and the youth chose the more lucrative calling. Boltzius never forgave Treutlen for his decision and henceforth considered him obstinate and unreliable.[17] As a good Pietist, Boltzius considered all worldly concerns to be a snare of the devil, an obstacle he puts in the path of a man on his pilgrimage through this vale of tears in order to distract him from the more important task of preparing for heaven. Unlike Causton, Zouberbühler, the Reformed ministers Henri François Chifelle and Johann Joachim Zubly, and Colonel William Stephens, the president of the council, Boltzius never developed his five-hundred-acre "gentleman's lot" for his own enjoyment. He worked day and night to help his parishioners earn their daily bread but disapproved of such "external" concerns as storing up treasures on earth. Consequently, it was a bitter disappointment when his pious protégé jeopardized his soul in Mammon's service.

In 1751 a second Swabian transport came to Georgia under the guidance of William Gerard De Brahm, who settled the emigrants at Bethany on the Blue Bluff just up the Savannah River from Ebenezer. Little time passed before Treutlen moved to Bethany and opened a store. With the earnings from his store he bought slaves; because he had slaves, he could acquire land for them to cultivate.[18] In a short time he was the wealthiest man in St. Matthew Parish, as the region around Ebenezer was called.

Treutlen's only worthy competitor in Ebenezer was Johann Caspar Wirtsch, later Wertsch, who came to Georgia in 1749 on the *Charming Martha*, Captain Peter Bogg, with a group of Palatine redemptioners that included the Heidts, Michlers, Kugels (Gugels), Mohrs, Schubdreins, and Seckingers.[19] Wertsch was given to Carl Flerl, the schoolmaster on the plantations across Abercorn Creek; and, like Treutlen, he soon advanced from schoolmaster to storekeeper, at which profession he gradually amassed considerable money.[20] Wertsch endeared himself to the English authorities by taking over the silk industry, which they were anxious to establish. James Habersham, who had also worked up from schoolmaster to merchant and was then act-

221

ing royal governor, wrote on October 3, 1771, to Governor James Wright in England that Mr. Wertsch had sent 438 pounds of raw silk to London and promised even more; and he reminded Wright that "you know him to be a worthy, prudent, and Cautious Man."[21] Wertsch also strengthened his ties with the older Salzburgers by marrying Hanna Elisabeth Gronau, the daughter of the late, lamented second pastor, whereas Treutlen had married an outsider, Marguerite Dupuis, who brought no political backing.

Despite his apolitical marriage, Treutlen had certain advantages over Wertsch: he had come three years earlier with an even larger party, one strongly united through their ordeals of captivity in Bilbao, exile in Gosport, and sickness on the *Judith*. Many Bilbao captives settled in Ebenezer, among them the Bohrmanns, Ihles (Illys), Portzes, Stäheles (Staleys), Walthauers, Wiesenbachers, and Wüsts (Wests), all of whom became prominent inhabitants of Ebenezer.[22] During his nearly a year and a half at Gosport, John Adam must have played with the English children and mastered their language, for he later conversed easily with the Englishmen in Georgia and was never accused of having a foreign accent.

Treutlen's and Wertsch's relative standing in their power struggle is indicated in the Jerusalem Church records[23] by the number of children for whom each stood sponsor; for, possibly as a result of pre-Christian tribal customs, German parents became politically bound to the persons they chose as godparents. According to this reasoning, Treutlen became allied with the Kieffers, Wüsts, Schades, Kornbergers, Bechtles, Kleins, Ihles, Leimbergers, Rheinländers, Rabenhorsts, Paul Zittrauers, Heinrich Meyers, and Martin Taeschers (Dasher), as well as with Gertraut Boltzius, the pastor's wife. He also had a claim on the loyalty of his brother Frederick's kinsmen through baptism.

Wertsch, too, formed a faction, which included the Fischers, Greves (Graves), Hangleiters, Webers, Paulitschs, Zettlers, Zimmerebners, Metschers, Greiners, Birks, Resters, Buntzes, Michael Riesers, Balthasar Riesers, Johann Flerls, Johann Caspar Walthauers, and Johann Georg Zittrauers. Thus most of Ebenezer's inhabitants seem to have become clients of one or the other of these two prominent men. These ties were made even firmer whenever one of them stood as sponsor to successive children in a single family. Despite their rivalry, the Treutlen and Wertsch families long remained amicable: in 1760 Treutlen asked Mrs. Wertsch to be godmother to his daughter Elisabeth, and in 1762 he asked Wertsch to be godfather to his daughter Dorothy, and in

1766 he asked Mrs. Wertsch to be godmother to his daughter Hanna. This friendship was, however, to turn into hostility.

The pastors in Ebenezer had lived harmoniously for thirty-five years. Gronau and his successor Lemke had worshiped their autocratic first pastor, Boltzius, and had gladly accepted his domination; and even Christian Rabenhorst, who had arrived as chaplain of the third Swabian transport in 1752, had fallen in line. After Boltzius died in 1765, the Reverend Fathers in Germany saw that Lemke was failing and that Rabenhorst would be unable to minister alone to the growing and widespread congregation, so they decided to send a third pastor. For want of any other candidate, they chose Christian Friedrich Triebner, even though Hermann August Francke, the head of the Francke Foundations in Halle where Triebner taught, had found him greedy and emotional.

Arriving at Ebenezer in 1769, Triebner immediately established himself by marrying Friederica Maria, another daughter of the late Gronau; and thus he became the brother-in-law of Wertsch, the husband of Hannah Elisabeth Gronau. Wertsch stood as godfather to Triebner's firstborn, Christoph August Gottlob, on August 8, 1770; and two weeks later Mrs. Triebner stood as godmother to Wertsch's daughter Hannah. After that the two couples often sponsored each other's offspring or those of other Ebenezer inhabitants.[24]

Triebner learned that Rabenhorst was managing the grist and lumber mills, Ebenezer's two chief industries; and, without closer inquiry, he wrote to Francke accusing his older colleague of trying to gain personal possession of them. Believing the charges, Francke ordered the mills to be turned over to Triebner; but the local mill board, which was better informed about the situation, disregarded the orders of the benevolent but misguided benefactor in Halle. Triebner enjoyed Wertsch's patronage in this dispute, and Rabenhorst enjoyed that of Treutlen, who had chosen him and his wife Anna Barbara as godparents to his son John Adam. Thus the sides were drawn, and hostilities were sure to follow.

The dispute that had begun as an economic matter degenerated into a holy war when the hotheaded young Triebner began denouncing his opponent from the pulpit in most scurrilous terms. To prevent such abuse of clerical power, Treutlen and his party stood guard one Sunday morning with drawn swords and prevented the new minister and his followers from entering the church. Meanwhile, both parties were bombarding the authorities in Germany with so many conflicting accusations and denunciations that the Reverend Fathers had to request the now elderly Muhlenberg to make the long and arduous trip to Ebenezer to restore order.[25]

As soon as the venerable clergyman reached Charleston, a Mr. Philips, who had just arrived from Savannah, told him on October 10, 1774, that Wertsch and Treutlen were at the bottom of the whole affair in Ebenezer. Both were justices of the peace and wealthy merchants who had the common people under their sway, and Philips contended that the great majority of the German inhabitants and all the English had an especial affection and regard for Pastor Rabenhorst.[26] Muhlenberg remained in Savannah long enough to have each of the feuding ministers report to him individually and acknowledge his authority to arbitrate the issue. He then proceeded to Ebenezer and held several meetings with the two ministers and the two sets of feuding vestrymen.

During these long and painful sessions, Muhlenberg acquired a high regard for Treutlen. When Triebner chided Treutlen, the latter

> replied coolly and laconically, for he possesses native intelligence. He has lived in this neighborhood for almost twenty-nine years; he knew the late pastor, is a confessor of our religion, has attended our religious services for many years back; has observed what was good and what was bad; for a number of years he has been a justice of the peace and member of the provincial *assembly*. He was a deacon of the congregation during Pastor Boltzius' lifetime and still is at present, and he is accustomed to demand sufficient reasons concerning any matter. Such a man who is at home in the English ways does not easily permit himself to be shouted down with *declarations*, etc., still less can he be won over by untimely reprimands given in the manner in which gentlemen are accustomed occasionally to convince their bonded servants.[27]

After conferring with Treutlen on November 19, Muhlenberg confided in his journal: "It is a peculiar pleasure for me to confer with a man who possesses an enlightened reason, Adam's natural intelligence and ability to give a name to every animal, knowledge of the laws of the land, and some discernment of practical religion."[28]

As a consequence of these heated sessions, Rabenhorst's management of the mills was judged to have been in order and Triebner was reprimanded for maligning so good a man. The mills were then rented out to a tenant, much to the chagrin of Triebner and Wertsch. In addition to helping Muhlenberg settle this shameful controversy, Treutlen helped him save Jerusalem Church for Lutheranism, for Wertsch and

Triebner, no doubt inadvertently, had allowed the words "Evangelical Lutheran" to be omitted from the new church charter, thereby incurring the risk that the beautiful new church building might escheat to Zouberbühler's Anglican church, which had become the established church when the colony reverted to the crown.

The remainder of Treutlen's career is easily traceable in English documents.[29] He embraced the Whig party and worked toward independence from Great Britain. Triebner remained loyal to the king. Treutlen, who had had legislative experience in the assembly, was acceptable to yeoman farmers and small planters and to Germans and Englishmen. In 1777 he became the first elected governor of the state of Georgia. His tenure of office, which lasted less than a year, was not particularly memorable, except for a large financial grant from the Continental Congress to conduct the war in Georgia and the thwarting of the attempt by William Henry Drayton and other South Carolinians to persuade the Georgians to join their state to their larger neighbor to the north.[30]

During his term as governor Treutlen's first wife, Marguerite Dupuis, mother of his eight children, died. On January 14, 1778, he married Anna Unselt, the widow of David Unselt, who had died in 1771 when thrown from a horse. By a peculiar coincidence, Treutlen lost an intended son-in-law when a similar accident befell Israel Heintzelmann, a preacher's son from Philadelphia who was serving in Treutlen's store and had been chosen to marry Treutlen's daughter Rachel.[31]

When Savannah and Ebenezer fell to the British at the end of 1778, Treutlen withdrew to Orangeburg County in South Carolina, where his son owned a plantation. In the spring of 1782 he was elected to represent his constituency at the assembly at Augusta; but before the assembly met, he was dragged out of his house at night and brutally murdered. Family legend says he was killed by Tories; but Tory activity was minimal at that time and place, and he may have been murdered by personal enemies, possibly by a jilted suitor, for he had married for a third time only a few days earlier. Treutlen's untimely death was a great loss to Ebenezer and the Georgia Germans.

NOTES

1. James F. Cook, *Governors of Georgia* (Huntsville, Ala., 1981), 31. "R," the author of an article on Treutlen in *Der deutsche Pionier* 7 (1875):

303–18, gives a complete and "documented" (and erroneous) account of Peter Treutlen, Johann Adam's father, a druggist who was claimed to have been expelled from Berchtesgaden and traveled with the third Salzburger transport to Ebenezer, where he established an apothecary shop and died in 1754.

2. *CRG*, 1:467–71, 474; Ms. *CRG*, 31:9, 25–28, 30–31, 41, 45–48, 294–310.

3. Ms. *CRG*, 31:47.

4. "In Which District Mr. Thomas Causton's Settlement may be considered," *CRG*, 1:470; Ms. *CRG*, 31:27.

5. *CRG*, 25:8; Ms. *CRG*, 31:30–31.

6. Ms. *CRG*, 31:45–48.

7. Those who sing *O Tannenbaum, O Tannenbaum* at Christmas will know that *ein Baum von dir mich hoch erfreut auch im Winter, wenn es schneit.*

8. In 1757 Frederick Triedling sold a lot at Goshen to Matthias West (Pat Bryant, comp., *Entry of Claims for Georgia Landholders, 1733–1755* [Atlanta, 1975], 189), this sale being recorded elsewhere under the name of Frederick Tradling (*English Crown Grants in St. Matthew Parish in Georgia, 1755–75* [Atlanta, 1975], 181). In 1755 John Caspar Both bought a lot at Goshen from Frederick Trith (F. H. Beckemeyer, ed., *Abstracts of Georgia, Colonial Conveyance Book C-1, 1750–61* [Atlanta, 1975], 168). In 1758 Frederick Tritlen, laborer, and his wife Margaret sold land to James Whitefield (ibid, 251).

9. Treuttlin (Bryant, comp., *Entry Claims*, 47, 49, 50). Triebner referred to Treutlen as Treutle (Hermann Winde, "Die Frühgeschichte der Lutherischen Kirche in Georgia," [Ph.D dissertation, University of Halle, 1960], 60). On the other hand, it was not unusual for Swiss and South Germans to drop the final nasal of their names. For example, Ambrosius and Johann Jacob Zueblin of Ebenezer were the uncles of Johann Joachim Zubly of Savannah, and Gregorius Stierle of Ebenezer had spelled his name Stierlin when he lived in Switzerland (A. B. Faust and G. M. Brumbaugh, eds., *Lists of Swiss Emigrants in the Eighteenth Century . . .* [Baltimore, 1976], 1: 37). If the *in* was a feminine ending, the British authorities, and perhaps John Adam himself, thought it a part of the name. Later Muhlenberg (T. G. Tappert and J. W. Doberstein, trans., *The Journals of Henry Melchior Muhlenberg*, 3 vols. [Philadelphia, 1945], 2:553) referred to Treutlen's second cousin Jacob Treutlen in Philadelphia, who was probably the same Jacob Treuttle who had arrived in Philadelphia in 1765 on the ship *Polly* (Ralph Strassburger and John Hinke, *Pennsylvania German Pioneers*, 3 vols. [Baltimore, 1980], 1:704).

10. *CRG*, 1:471. For the founding of Vernonburg (Dutchtown), see George F. Jones, "The Georgia Palatines," in *Yearbook of German-American Studies*, forthcoming.

11. Faust and Brumbaugh, eds., *Lists of Swiss Emigrants*, 2:38.

12. *CRG*, 25:29–30. The original letter is in PRO, Kew (CO 5/642, p. 5).

13. Samuel Urlsperger, ed., *Ausführliche Nachricht von den Saltzburgischen Emigranten* (Halle, 1735), 13th Continuation, p. 141.

14. Ibid., 268.

15. Samuel Urlsperger, ed., *Americanisches Ackerwerck Gottes* (Augsburg, 1755), 34.

16. On September 26, 1773, Muhlenberg inserted a memorandum into his journal stating that he had received a letter of September 6 from Treutlen asking him to inquire of a Mr. Paris concerning his second cousin, Jacob Treutlen, who had sent him an obscure letter. He continued, *Wegen seiner Schwester in Deutschland soll er ihm Nachricht geben, und wenn sie zu ihm kommen will, so will er die Fracht von London bis Savanna bezahlen.* Tappert's translation (Tappert and Doberstein, *Journals of Muhlenberg*, 2:553) states, and the destination suggests, that the letter concerns Treutlen's sister, but grammatically it could just as well refer to Jacob Treutlen's sister. It seems strange that a man as successful as Treutlen would have to hear about his sister from a remote second cousin. Treutlen's reaction is more that of a dutiful second cousin than of a man who has not seen his sister for more than thirty years. Possibly he offered to pay his second cousin's passage to Georgia so that she could pay it off by working for him. It is significant that the Jacob Treuttle mentioned in note 9, surely her brother, was indentured. The original of Muhlenberg's clearly written letter is in the Lutheran Archives Center in Philadelphia, to which I am indebted for a copy.

17. Winde, "Die Frühgeschichte der Lutherischen Kirche in Georgia," 306.

18. In the decade 1757–67 alone he received eight grants (*CRG*, 28, pt. 1:109, 319; pt. 2:82, 85, 212, 267, 280). Eleven are listed in *English Crown Grants*, 181–83.

19. *CRG*, 26:49–51.

20. When Muhlenberg returned in the winter of 1773–74, Wertsch gave him a greatcoat from his store.

21. "The Letters of the Honorable James Habersham, 1756–1775," *Coll. GHS*, 6:146.

22. All these families appear in my *Salzburger Saga* (Athens, 1984).

23. C. A. Linn, ed., *Ebenezer Record Book*, trans. A. G. Voigt (Savannah, 1929).

24. These data can be found through the index in ibid.

25. Muhlenberg devoted many pages of his journal to this difficult task; see Tappert and Doberstein, *Journals of Muhlenberg*, 2:585–686.

26. Ibid., 584–85.

27. Ibid., 611.

28. Ibid., 624.

29. See *CRG*, esp. vols. 7, 8, 10–12, 14, 18, 19, 28, and Ms. CRG 38, and all three vols. of Allen D. Candler, ed., *The Revolutionary Records of the State of Georgia* (Atlanta, 1908).

30. See Kenneth Coleman, *The American Revolution in Georgia, 1763– 1789* (Athens, 1958), 86–87, 90–91.

31. Linn, ed., *Ebenezer Record Book*, 83, 106. On October 4, 1777, Triebner reported that Treutlen had proposed to Salome, the late Pastor Lemke's youngest daughter, but that she had declined on the grounds that she was too sickly to manage his large household (*GHQ* 49 (1965):434). Perhaps her real reason was that she preferred the poor young schoolmaster David Weidmann, whom she married on the twenty-eighth of the same month! (Linn, ed., *Ebenezer Record Book*, 84).

The Late Colonial Period and the Coming of the Revolution

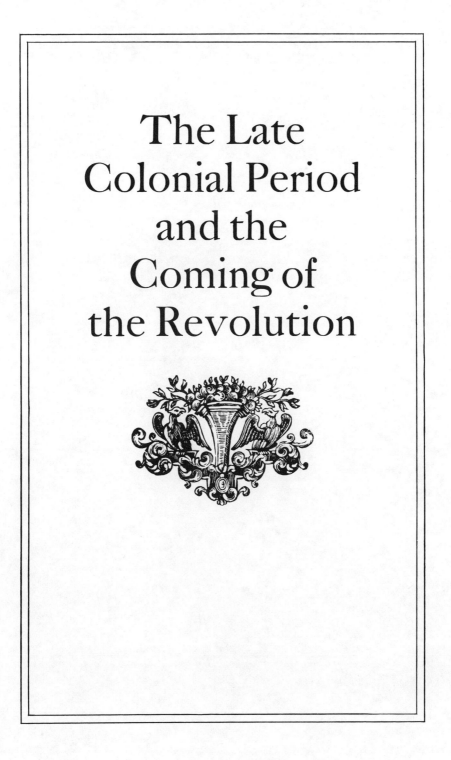

U ntil recently students of colonial Georgia have tended to emphasize events taking place along the coast, especially in and around Savannah, because that was the domain of the powerful merchant-planters and also the seat of government. The back-country—that ill-defined area extending from the tidewater to and beyond the fall line—was usually considered only in relation to the east, which resulted in a somewhat warped perspective of the growth of the colony and of the nature of its people. In his essay Edward J. Cashin examines the evolution of this often neglected region, whose growth after 1763 was so rapid that by the eve of the Revolution its white population may well have equaled that of the coast, and discusses the forces that shaped the upcountry parishes and their citizens. More significant, however, is Cashin's analysis of how and why most people in the west, although apparently dependent on the royal government for protection from the Indians, rose in rebellion against the source of their support. Cashin's thoughtful explanation of these Westerners' decision to aid the American cause, a decision that has perplexed historians for decades, reveals much about the origins and impact of the American Revolution in Georgia.

Just as earlier historians have tended to view Georgia's colonial past from the coast, they have also seen much of it through the eyes of the royal governors, whose letters and reports provide some of the best resources for studying the colony. But as most scholars who have used these papers realize, they present a one-sided and distorted view of the events unfolding—as well as of the Georgians who decided to rebel. Harvey H. Jackson has chosen to approach the problem of Georgia's political development and the accompanying drift toward revolution from a position outside the executive establishment, and to do so he has focused on the development of the Whig movement in the prov-

ince. By examining its origins as the assembly-based Liberty party and then tracing its activities through the War for Independence, the author increases our understanding of the aims and ambitions that compelled Georgians, both on the coast and in the backcountry, not only to rise against the most powerful nation they had ever known but to struggle with equal resolve against those within their own ranks with whom they did not agree. Through this examination of the key men and events in the evolution of Georgia Whiggery Jackson reveals how the movement and the factions within it rose from the colonial political system to shape the course and conduct of the struggle for freedom on the southern periphery.

EDWARD J. CASHIN

Sowing the Wind: Governor Wright and the Georgia Backcountry on the Eve of the Revolution

 OVERNOR JAMES WRIGHT was hailed as a hero when he returned to Georgia with royal permission to proceed with a land cession in 1773. It seemed a perfect triumph. The Cherokees no longer needed land above the Little River, they wanted to pay their debts to the traders, the traders owed money to the Augusta storekeepers, the Augusta suppliers had debts due to the British merchants in London. All of them, Indians, traders, Augustans, and Londoners, had been mobilized to support Governor Wright in presenting his case to the king's ministers. Furthermore, Governor Wright estimated that ten thousand prospective purchasers were itching to buy the land at six pence an acre. The government would simply take their money and pay the Indians' creditors. The population influx would make the frontier secure against any future Indian attack. The entire enterprise would cost the crown nothing. Nor would the royal government be obligated to assume any payments. No wonder praise was heaped upon Governor Wright from Whitehall to Savannah; no wonder he was dubbed Sir James by an appreciative sovereign.[1]

And yet this princely achievement was fated to plunge the backcountry into turmoil that contributed directly to the area's involvement in the Revolution and the loss of Georgia to His Majesty's government. The reason was that two very important segments of the backcountry population were unhappy with Governor Wright's cession of 1773: the Creeks resented the Cherokees giving up land jointly claimed by both nations, and the Crackers were angered at being excluded from the new lands by a price they could not afford.

Most if not all of the histories that deal with the coming of the Revolution concentrate on the British efforts to tax the colonists and the American reaction. The backcountry is treated as the appendage of the more politically sophisticated lowcountry, dragged reluctantly into war. I will argue here that British policy was responsible for a series of miscalculations which precipitated a war in the backcountry. The seeds of future conflict were sown in the year of the first great Indian congress at Augusta.

In 1763 the royal governors of Virginia and North and South Carolina would have chosen the more comfortable Charles Town for a meeting, but the Indians preferred to meet in Augusta, which had always been their town. White settlement outside Augusta had never been agreed to by the Creeks, and they were in no mood to yield land in 1763. According to Governor Wright, they wanted the Savannah River to be the dividing line between their lands and those of the English and all trespassers removed from their side.[2] They were reluctant to come to Augusta because they were afraid they would lose their land. John Stuart assured them, in the king's name, that "your lands will not be taken from you." Nevertheless, by the Treaty of Augusta, the English obtained all the land above Augusta as far as the Little River and west to the Ogeechee. In return, according to the treaty, "it is agreed on the part of his majesty King George that none of his subjects shall settle upon, or disturb the Indians in, the grounds or lands to the westward of the lines herein before described."[3]

The Creeks stressed that the trading path from Augusta was to remain "straight and white to the nation."[4] Although the treaty did not use the language of the Creeks, it bound the Indians not to molest the traders and pledged the English to put to death any white man who killed an Indian. Direct trade in town was forbidden, but it was understood that Augusta would continue to be open to the Indians, who could come and go freely along the great trading paths. This free Indian traffic gave Augusta traders an advantage their Carolina competitors envied. After 1762 Indians were forbidden to enter white settlements in Carolina, but they were entertained, sometimes lavishly, by the principal Augusta traders.[5] Even when the Cherokees were on the warpath in the winter of 1760, Creek Indians were so continuously in Augusta that they took credit for preventing a Cherokee attack on the town.[6] During the same alarm, the Chickasaw Indians at New Savannah just below Augusta had vowed to live and die with the people of Augusta and had been granted a plot of land under the protec-

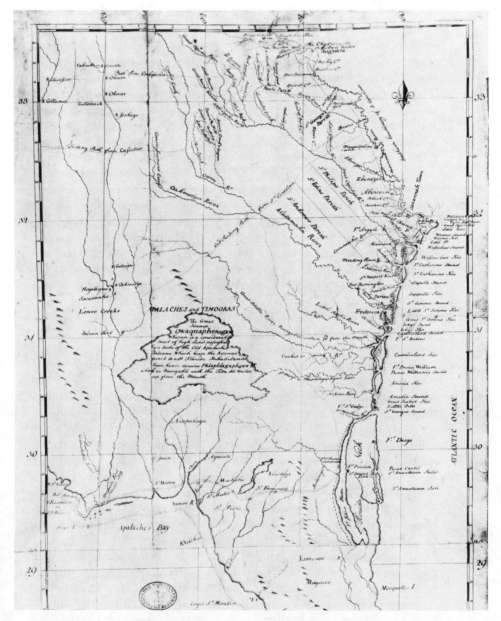

Portion of a map of Georgia and Florida by Thomas Wright, 1763.
(Courtesy of the Georgia Department of Archives and History.)

tion of the fort for their wives and children. Like the Creeks, they considered Augusta their town.[7]

Thus after the peace settlement of 1763, Augusta was something of an anomaly. Governor Wright insisted that Fort Augusta be garrisoned because the town was a frequent resort of Indians. General Thomas Gage was committed to a policy of maintaining forts out in the Indian country, and he saw no purpose in keeping soldiers in a well-settled area. To please Governor Wright, however, he stationed a company of Royal Americans at Augusta.[8] Neither Gage nor Wright seemed to be aware that they were sowing seeds of conflict by permitting Indian traffic in an area of rapidly increasing white settlement. The problem was aggravated by the famous Proclamation of October 7, 1763, which promoted the formation of two antagonistic classes in the Georgia backcountry. Based on a visionary ideal of free trade, the proclamation threw open the Indian trade to any licensed person. The result was a multiplication of small traders and packhorsemen, the "white Indians" who were scorned by the old settlers and feared by the new, and whom Governor Wright called "generally the worst kind of people." During the Revolution many of these men of the forests would be known as Tories by backcountry Georgians. In this usage, the term connoted half-civilized whites who rode with the Indians and fought for the British.[9]

Another provision of the Proclamation of 1763 was fraught with even greater consequence for the Georgia backcountry. By limiting white settlement to the Appalachian divide, the proclamation directed the tide of frontier migration into Georgia. The result was an immediate increase of the yeoman farmer class, which Governor Wright called the "middling sort." These were newcomers who took care to petition for land grants of one hundred acres for each family head and fifty acres for each member.[10] There was also a large mass of squatters who were called by several names, all of them invidious. James Habersham depicted them as follows to Governor Wright: "The present intruders I am informed are persons who have no settled habitation and live by hunting and plundering the industrious Settlers. . . . You will easily distinguish that the people I refer to are really what you and I understand by Crackers."[11] Even the Indians despised these people, whom they called "Virginians." "English men and Scotch Men, I have been long acquainted with, and always found them to be good men," observed a Creek chief. "But these Virginians are very bad people, they pay no regard to your laws."[12]

Sowing the Wind

The Georgia Assembly recognized that Augusta was a dangerous place for peaceable people but was of two minds about what to do. Because it was understood that Indians would continue to visit the town and that Indians were as fond of rum as whites, the best that the assembly could do was to pass legislation for the repair of the old fort at Augusta in 1765 and to oblige white males "to carry firearms to places of public worship." The "Act for Encouraging Settlers to Come into This Province," passed in 1766, was certain to increase friction between Indians and whites because it sought to establish compact townships upon the borders of the Indian line.[13] This plan followed the New England pattern of settlement. Slaves were to be taxed, but white settlers were exempt for ten years. Townships never worked well in the South, and Georgia's were soon dissipated because the settlers sought more land. Of the two townships established under the law, Wrightsborough was the more successful. It was established when fifty Quaker families from North Carolina applied for a reserve of land in 1767. By 1775 Wrightsborough's total population exceeded six hundred. Although the well-behaved Wrightsborough people managed to get along with the Indians, their pacifist views exposed them to hostile treatment by their more violently inclined white neighbors. They were a unique patch in the emerging social quilt of the back-country.[14]

The second township on the Indian line was Queensborough, the brainchild of two successful Augusta traders, John Rae and George Galphin. Protestants from the north of Ireland were recruited in the hope that they would produce Irish linen. The first contingent arrived in 1768, and by 1774 there were approximately nine hundred Scotch-Irish immigrants, although they were already beginning to scatter by then.[15] The Irish settlers were not restrained by pacifist scruples, and friction with their Indian neighbors was inevitable. More obnoxious, as far as the Indians were concerned, were the many squatters who ignored the boundary and settled on the Indians' reserve.

Governor Wright at first refused to believe the Indians' complaints of trespassers upon their lands. In 1767 he sent a party of rangers to look for any such intruders. The rangers reported that they found no white settlers across the line of the Ogeechee, but there was an Indian town near the river which invited attack. Governor Wright tried to persuade the Creeks to pull their Indians back, "for the white people sometimes get drunk as well as the Indians and it is not good that they should live too nigh each other."[16] Before the Indians could abandon their village, if they had a mind to, a group of settlers took matters into their own hands and burned the place down. Governor Wright called upon the Augusta magistrates to discover and punish the ringleaders and asked his superiors for more soldiers for Augusta. In outlining the situation to Lord Shelburne, Wright revealed the result of the contradictory policies his government had been following without betraying any awareness that the policies were at fault. "Augusta, my Lord, appears to me to be a place of some consequence and I consider it as a kind of frontier town or settlement, it is a receptacle for goods of considerable value for the Indian trade and the general resort of the Indians themselves and in the neighborhood of a set of almost lawless white people who are a sort of borderers and often as bad if not worse than the Indians."[17] The governor and the minister might blame the lawless Crackers, but it was their own policy that sought to maintain an Indian rendezvous, open to Indian traffic, while attracting people who hated and feared Indians into the same area.

Governor Wright's request for troops in 1767 prompted an exchange with General Gage, which had the quality of high comedy. Gage replied that he would not increase the size of the garrison until Georgia provided "barrack necessaries" for the men already in Augusta.[18] The officer in command reported that the men had to sleep on the floor and fetch their own firewood. Furthermore, he said the men were continually being "seduced" to desert by the townspeople. The report concluded that the soldiers were not needed in a town where most of the men were better armed than they were and where some of the gentlemen had better forts than the king's.[19] Governor Wright promised to make amends, and he did persuade a reluctant Georgia Assembly to provide money for better accommodations for the military. After meeting all of Gage's objections, Wright was astonished to learn that the troops would be removed from Georgia regardless. Wright argued that the new policy of centralizing the troops in the north was "extremely mistaken," and perhaps it was. Without troops, how was he to prevent a clash between the Crackers and the Creeks?[20]

Governor Wright was never at a loss for ideas, and his next was more sensible than it might seem. He proposed to mark the 1763 boundary line clearly. The line along the Little and Ogeechee rivers was clear enough, but there was a difference of opinion as to the location of the line connecting these rivers. Trees were blazed by a team of surveyors, and on November 12, 1768, a congress was held in Augusta to secure the Indians' ratification of the demarcation.[21] The visible line, however, was no more effective than an invisible one in restraining people who paid no attention to laws.

More curious in this story of contradictions was Governor Wright's own violation of his boundary agreement. By 1771 he had granted lands as far as forty miles beyond the line. A Creek chief complained that white people had encroached "two days march" beyond the land that was given to them. He charitably supposed that they had not seen the line, "which Mr. Stuart said should be like a mountain, not to be passed, or they certainly would not have done so." The chief, Emistisiguo, reminded the royal authorities of their promise that the trading path to Augusta "should be always free for their friends the Indians to pass and repass upon."[22]

The settlers could be justified for complaining of the policy that limited whites, except for traders, to the Ogeechee while permitting Indians to wander into Augusta and for the policy that permitted traders to place guns and ammunition in the hands of Indians who were likely to turn the weapons upon the settlers. In the spring of 1770 a party of irate frontiersmen marched into Augusta and forcibly unloaded packhorses bound for the Indian country. During that same year another Creek village on the Oconee was burned. Isolated acts of violence kept the frontier in a state of tension during the next two years.[23]

The new settlers who moved into the Georgia backcountry after 1763 differed from the older inhabitants in several important respects. They did not want to do business with the Indians, whom they feared and hated, and they wanted the land the Indians occupied. After 1770, the British authorities seemed more sympathetic to the Indians than to the settlers. Referring to Creek attacks on trespassers, General Thomas Gage remarked to the Earl of Hillsborough, "If all the Indians confine themselves to this method without proceeding further, it might save us trouble by preventing our vagabonds from strolling in the manner they do."[24] Most of the trespassing occurred on the Indian land above the Little River. James Habersham, acting governor in 1772, issued a proclamation requiring the intruders to remove themselves as "idle and disorderly vagrants."[25] Of course, they paid no attention.

Thus the seeds of war had been sown by an official policy that sought to protect the Indian trade while promoting rapid settlement by people hostile to the trade. In this context Governor Wright's dramatic achievement, the land cession of 1773, occurred. This apparently brilliant piece of work led directly to the revolt of the backcountry because the Creeks and the Crackers were left out of it.

The initiative for the cession came from the Cherokees. In 1770 they indicated that they would give up some of their land east of the mountains to a trader to whom they owed a large debt. Private cessions were forbidden by the Proclamation of 1763, but the Cherokee offer set off Wright's imagination. As he put it, "The matter was set on foot."[26] The Cherokees were told to make a formal offer to the king through Governor Wright and John Stuart for cancellation of all their debts in return for a larger cession north of the Little River and entirely within Georgia. In a moment of candor Wright confessed to Lord Hillsborough, "I did not choose to tell the Creek Indians that I had anything to do with the affair of the Land, but that it had proceeded entirely from the Cherokees."[27] Wright tried to improve upon the opportunity by obtaining the stretch of land between the Ogeechee and Oconee, hunting grounds dear to the Creeks but not highly valued by the Cherokees. He attempted to bring the Creeks around by the time-tested device of using the Augusta traders to convince them. But the Creeks were still opposed to any cession in 1771, when Wright left for England with the intention of securing approval for the transaction. Wright returned to Georgia with permission to negotiate for lands already privately ceded to the traders. The Creeks, of course, had made no private cession. Before the conference, the Georgia Assembly reminded the governor of his opportunity to try for the land to the Oconee.[28]

The Indians began to gather in Augusta around the middle of May. The peripatetic naturalist William Bartram was there and rhapsodized about the beauties of nature in springtime. His journal reveals the fatal flaw in the negotiations: "The merchants of Georgia demanding at least two millions of acres of land from the Indians as a discharge of their debts, due and of long standing, the Creeks, on the other hand, being a powerful and proud spirited people, their young warriors were unwilling to submit to so large a demand, and their conduct evidently betrayed a disposition to dispute the ground by force of arms."[29] Although the Creeks were finally brought around by liberal presents, they refused to yield any property beyond the Ogeechee, except for a rectangular slice of land in the lowcountry. Governor Wright had to settle for just over two million acres instead of the five million he had hoped for. Worse, the Creeks left Augusta in a surly mood. William Bartram was warned by John Stuart that he should not travel just then into Creek County.[30] Before the year was out small bands of disgruntled Creeks would bring terror to the frontier.

The Crackers were the uninvited guests at the banquet table. No one wanted them on the new purchase. John Stuart suggested that they be barred in favor of industrious people from Britain, Ireland, or Germany. The fact was that several thousand of these "banditti," as Governor Wright called them, ignored Acting Governor Habersham's proclamation banning settlement and were already occupying the new cession. Governor Wright then adopted stronger measures: he ordered a troop of rangers to be raised to police the new cession and proposed to tour the country himself, hoping "it will deter the bad and encourage the good."[31]

Wright made his tour and in the process laid out a new town named Dartmouth in honor of the new secretary of state for the colonies. His visit to the new purchase stimulated the interest of potential settlers, and Wright reported that he had received applications for three hundred thousand acres on the first day his land office was open. He guessed that as many as ten thousand appropriate settlers were ready to purchase land.[32] Essential to Wright's plan was settlement by the better sort, who could pay for the land and thereby raise money to reimburse the traders. With prospects so propitious, the Creek attack on an outlying settlement on Christmas Eve was a major blow to Wright's hopes. In January the Creeks struck again. In a pitched battle at Sherrill's Fort near Wrightsborough seven settlers were killed and five wounded. Several days later the Creeks routed a force of Georgia rangers and militia of 101 men, killing 3 and wounding 1. The men were "struck with such a Panick," in Governor Wright's words, "that neither fair means nor threats could prevail on them to stay." Wright was convinced that the outbreak was caused by "runagate" Indians who were determined to prevent settlement of the ceded lands.[33]

If Wright had to deal only with the Creeks, he might have worked out the conflict successfully. But an additional problem was presented by the Crackers, who were reluctant to enter the fight themselves but anxious to keep the war going in the hope of getting more land from the Creeks. When a Creek chief walked into Augusta in March on a peace mission, he was treacherously slain by one Thomas Fee. Governor Wright offered a reward for Fee's arrest. Fee was apprehended and jailed at Ninety-Six, South Carolina, only to be liberated by a mob who considered him a hero.[34]

Since Wright was unable to obtain troops, he resorted to the next best expedient. He obtained the grudging consent of the military and the cooperation of the other southern governors in putting a stop to the Indian trade. This move could not have failed to delight the hearts of settlers, Crackers and all. When some of the Augusta traders defied Wright's proclamation and continued a clandestine trade, the Crackers found themselves on the same side as the governor, with the traders in the unaccustomed role of the lawless ones.[35] Wright had to employ a company of rangers to enforce his ban. Thus when in August the Savannah merchants protested the Intolerable Acts, the backcountry settlers were quick to sign counterpetitions, arguing that the Savannah merchants did not have to worry about Indians and they did. They depended upon "such powerful aid and assistance as none but Great Britain can give."[36] The canvass for signatures, which had Governor Wright's approval if not his actual instigation, might be regarded as the first thoroughgoing effort to organize the backcountry politically. Ironically, the same petitioners would put together a revolutionary organization a year later.

The Creek crisis in 1774 hastened the political maturity of the backcountry in another way. Not all of the Crackers fled from the ceded lands at the first war whoop. Evan Haines was a lad of eighteen and one of the settlers on Fishing Creek, near the present city of Washington in Wilkes County. When the alarm was raised, the settlers built a fort for their protection. In Haines's words, "So soon as the Fort was completed the people living convenient to it moved into it and there organized themselves and chose their officers."[37] Thus were launched the careers of John Dooly and Stephen Heard, who were elected colonel and lieutenant colonel and who were fated to play major roles in revolutionary Georgia. This scene was duplicated all over the backcountry as a network of forts was erected.

Governor Wright was delighted with the success of his embargo when the Creeks put to death their guilty people and sued for peace. The backcountry Georgians were delighted, too; they confidently expected a new land cession as a condition of peace. They were bitterly disappointed when the treaty drawn up in Savannah on October 20, 1774, simply reopened the trade in return for the Creeks' pledge not to molest the settlers or their cattle. In what must have seemed a backward step, the government agreed to prevent the settlers from hunting in the Oconee-Ogeechee strip.[38]

The Savannah treaty marked the end of the brief alliance between the settlers and the governor. The backcountry's case was presented in a petition subscribed by "the Inhabitants of the Parish of St. George, and St. Paul, including the ceded lands in the Province of Georgia." In their opinion Sir James Wright had yielded to the "self-interested" entreaties of the Indian traders and merchants and had failed to take advantage of the opportunity to secure the Oconee lands, which "nature formed for the benefit and advantage" of the settlers. The resumption of the Indian traffic was "of utmost prejudice" to the petitioners and benefited only those engaged in the trade. As the Indians came and went along the Augusta road, they were likely to commit all manner of mischief, including murders and robberies.[39] By the year's end a Savannah Whig could report that most of those who had expressed loyalty to the crown in August had changed their opinion and that "two of our back Parishes which made the most noise are now come over to us." He meant that the backcountry was ready to join in the Continental Association against trade with England.[40]

The backcountry's disenchantment with Governor Wright was reciprocal. When the settlers resumed their interrupted wanderings, Wright became exasperated with them. He asked the assembly in January 1775 to pass legislation "to prevent encroachments and trespasses and other irregularities" by "disorderly people."[41] Such language and such measures further strained the relations between the settlers and the government. Backcountry people were disposed to believe that their rulers preferred the Indians and the Indian trade to the interests of the settlers.

Thus policies adopted by Governor Sir James Wright had by 1775 created a tinderbox which was about to explode. The last volatile element was Wright's determination to locate the "better sort" of persons on the ceded lands. English gentlemen and Crackers were not good neighbors. For an example of what happened when the two groups came together one might look at the settlement along Kiokee Creek above Augusta. Twenty-five families had been granted land along Kiokee and its tributary Greenbriar Creek by early 1775. Others had not bothered to register their claims or their claims have been lost. The most important of these was Daniel Marshall, who led a group of separate Baptists into Georgia in 1772 and erected the first Baptist church in Georgia between the Greenbriar and Kiokee forks. Marshall was arrested for preaching without a license but was released by a magistrate who admired his piety. Marshall, his son Abraham, and many of his Baptist followers would take the Whig side in the ensuing struggle.[42] So would other neighbors such as Daniel Coleman, Sherwood Bugg, and Zachariah Lamar. Into this nest of independent settlers were introduced some of the "better sort" who were attracted to Georgia by Governor Wright's energetic advertising of the ceded lands. At least two important newcomers set up their plantations along the Kiokee. These two were William Manson and Thomas Brown; both of them and especially the latter would play major roles in the dramatic events to follow. Manson was a sea captain who heard about the new cession while his ship was at Savannah. With the financial backing of partners in England, Manson was responsible for bringing nearly one hundred indentured servants to Georgia in 1775.[43]

Just beyond Manson's land on the Greenbriar lay Brownsborough, the plantation of Thomas Brown. A descendant of Sir Anthony Browne, master of horse to King Henry VIII, Brown comported himself with the assurance of one to the manor born. With the financial backing of his father, Jonas Brown, a wealthy alum manufacturer and shipowner of Whitby in Yorkshire, Brown recruited seventy-four persons in Yorkshire and the Orkney Islands and brought them to Georgia in September 1774 while the Indian scare was still potent. All were indentured to Brown, as was another contingent of seventy-five scheduled to arrive the following year. Brown set his servants to work immediately building a plantation house, thirty-six farm houses, a barn, stables for his fine English horses, kitchen, outhouses, and the other structures found upon a typical Yorkshire estate.[44] Brownsborough was in fact a transplanted manor, and Thomas Brown fit the image of the gentleman planter Governor Wright had hoped for. His suspicious neighbors, however, whispered that he was the illegitimate son of Lord North.[45]

If the unlettered Crackers wondered about Thomas Brown, Brown's servants were in positive awe of them. One servant wrote home: "This is a good poor man's Country when a man once gets into a way of Living, but our country people knows nothing when they come hear, the Americans are Smart, Industrious, hardy people and fear nothing. Our people is only like the New Negroes that comes out of the Ships at first when they come amongst them."[46] This was a country where men could hit a dollar from three hundred yards with a rifle and where even little boys carried guns and shouted "Liberty or Death."

Thus by 1775 the frontier had been shaped by a well-intentioned but contradictory British policy. The social matrix included gentlemen planters, indentured servants, slaves, traders, packhorsemen, Quakers, Anglicans, Protestants of the Great Awakening, a class of drifters, and, of course, the Indians, who came and went along the trading path that was forever to be kept white and clean.

The spark that ignited this explosive mixture was the rumor that the king's agents were about to launch an Indian war upon the frontier people. As Governor Wright phrased it, "The Liberty people have now got another pretense for raising men, they assert that Mr. Stuart the Superintendent has been endeavouring to raise the Cherokee Indians to come down against them."[47] That this incredible report was taken seriously reveals that the settlers were already convinced that the government had abandoned their interests in favor of the Indian trade. The rumor, false though it was, was the most effective weapon the liberty faction could have used to win over the people of the frontier. Fear of Indians had kept the frontier loyal in 1774; fear of Indians would sever that loyalty in 1775.

Under the leadership of the revolutionary Council of Safety in Savannah, committees were elected in each town and district to enforce the Continental Association. Liberty Boys used physical force to persuade people to take the oath. The leader in rallying the backcountry against the association was Thomas Brown. According to a member of William Manson's party, Brown, "being a warm stickler for Government, got several thousands in the Back Country brought over to that interest."[48] James Grierson, militia colonel in Augusta, wrote to Governor Wright that Brown's effective recruiting "Irritated the People about this place."[49]

The number of Liberty Boys who marched out to confront Thomas Brown is a measure of their irritation and of their respect for him. Around 140 armed men demanded that Brown sign the association. He defied them all. Thereupon they fell upon him and tortured him unmercifully, scalping, stabbing, and burning. According to James Grierson, he was also tarred and feathered and hauled about the streets of Augusta in a cart. It is a wonder Brown lived, and it is no wonder that he set out as soon as he could to gain vengeance.[50] The "better sort," the large planters and Augusta merchants, tended to sympathize with Brown but did not take up arms. "Your friends impatiently await for the arrival of the regulars," an Augustan informed Brown after fighting began. The "lower sort" of settlers opposed the king. It was customary for Governor Wright and his friends to heap scorn upon the rebels, citing their bad manners and low birth. Brown's correspondent informed him that the new rebel battalion was "chiefly composed of shirtless Crackers unaccustomed to restraint." Brown's servants went over to the rebels, by choice or constraint. Even his fine English horses were impressed to draw wagons in Augusta.[51]

When Thomas Brown sought allies to stand up for the king, he found them among the traders and packhorsemen and among the Creeks and Cherokees. Brown believed that there were thousands of backcountry people living in dread of the rebels who would declare their loyalty when the king's troops arrived. This notion, which became a cardinal point of British policy, proved a will-o'-the-wisp as far as the Georgia backcountry was concerned.[52] The people of the frontier would not ally themselves with the Indians. Indeed, the supposition that they would, a supposition held by Brown, Governor Wright, and the British ministry, was the latest in the series of miscalculations by which the British lost the backcountry. They had sown the wind; now they must reap the whirlwind.

NOTES

1. Lord Dartmouth informed Wright that the king, relying upon Wright's zeal and integrity, had given him charge of the treaty negotiations (Dartmouth to Wright, December 12, 1772, Ms. CRG, 38, pt. 1A:31–35).

2. Wright to Earl of Egremont, June 10, 1763, to Francis Fauquier, June 22, 1763, Ms. CRG, 37, pt. 1:50–53, 57–60.

3. *Journal of the Congress of the Four Southern Governors and the Superintendent of that District with the Five Nations of Indians at Augusta 1763* (Charles Town, 1764), 14, 40; James Wright, Arthur Dobbs, Thomas Boone, Francis Fauquier, John Stuart to My Lord, November 10, 1763, Ms. CRG, 37, pt. 1:62–65.

4. Talk of Emistisiguo, May 1771, in Philemon Kemp to governor of Georgia, June 6, 1771, K. G. Davies, ed., *Documents of the American Revolution*, 21 vols. (Shannon, Ireland, 1972–81), 3:118–21. The same expression was used by the Mortar in a talk delivered by Handsome Fellow at Fort Augusta, in Wright to Thomas Gage, August 28, 1764, Gage Papers, William L. Clements Library, Ann Arbor, Michigan.

5. Memorial from Carolina Traders in John Stuart to Thomas Gage, July 21, 1767, Gage Papers.

6. White Outerbridge to William H. Lyttelton, February 16, 1760, in Lyttelton Papers, William L. Clements Library, Ann Arbor, Michigan.

7. White Outerbridge to William H. Lyttelton, September 11, 1756, December 19, 1759, Henry Ellis to William H. Lyttelton, November 25, 1759, Lyttelton Papers. There were ninety Chickasaws at New Savannah in 1765 (Samuel Frink to Society for the Propagation of the Gospel in Foreign Parts, June 1, 1765, Journal of the Society for the Propagation of the Gospel, 17:424–26, microfilm, University of Texas Library, Austin, Texas).

8. Thomas Gage to Lord Shelburne, April 3, 1767, Gage Papers.

9. Wright to Shelburne, November 29, 1766, Ms. CRG, 37, pt. 1:146–49. The Georgia Assembly described the Indian allies as "hellish and diabolical fiends" (Allen D. Candler, ed., *The Revolutionary Records of the State of Georgia*, 3 vols. [Atlanta, 1908], 2:384–86).

10. Wright to Halifax, December 23, 1763, to Shelburne, May 15, 1767, Ms. CRG, 37, pt. 1:69–71, 206–12.

11. Habersham to Wright, August 20, 1772, *Coll., GHS*, 6:203–7.

12. Louis De Vorsey, Jr., *Indian Boundary in the Southern Colonies* (Chapel Hill, 1966), 160–61.

13. *CRG*, 18:639–40, 743–44; 14:191–92.

14. Kenneth Coleman, *Colonial Georgia: A History* (New York, 1976), 227–28.

15. Ibid., 226–27.

16. Wright's reply to talks of Talechia, Chehaw King, White King of the Cowetas, Sempoyaffee, the Young Lieutenant, Hitchetaw King, and the White King of the Cussitas, January 3, 1767, Ms. CRG, 37, pt. 1:170–73.

17. Wright to Shelburne, August 15, 1767, ibid., 240–42.

18. Gage to Wright, April 30, 1767, Gage Papers.

19. Wright to Gage, August 6, 1767, citing Capt. L. Valentine Fuser to Wright, July 24, 1767, Ms. CRG, 37, pt. 1:250–52.

20. Wright to Gage, December 1, 1767, June 12, August 25, 1768, Wright to Fuser, April 16, 1768, Gage Papers.

21. Wright to Hillsborough, September 17, 1768, Ms. CRG, 37, pt. 2:371–72; De Vorsey, *Indian Boundary*, 156–57.

22. Philemon Kemp to Governor of Georgia, June 6, 1771, Davies, ed., *Documents*, 3:118; *CRG*, 28, pt. 2:365–69.

23. John Richard Alden, *John Stuart and the Southern Colonial Frontier* (New York, 1966), 297; Wright to Hillsborough, August 22, 1770, October 8, 1770, Ms. CRG, 37, pt. 2:474, 483–85.

24. Gage to Hillsborough, June 4, 1771, Davies, ed., *Documents*, 3:104.

25. Habersham to Hillsborough, August 12, 1772, and "A Proclamation by His Honor James Habersham Esquire, President and Commander of his Majesty's said province of Georgia. Chancellor, Vice Admiral and Ordinary of the same," August 4, 1772, Ms. CRG, 38, pt. 1A:4–10.

26. "List of Papers Relative to My Memorial about Indian Affairs and with Some Notes and Remarks Thereon," in Wright to Hillsborough, re-

ceived December 12, 1771, Ms. CRG, 28, pt. 2B:669–73; also in *CRG*, 28, pt. 2:358–60.

27. Ms. CRG, 28, pt. 2B:789.

28. *CRG*, 15:425–26.

29. Francis Harper, ed., *The Travels of William Bartram* (New Haven, 1958), 22.

30. De Vorsey, *Indian Boundary*, 170.

31. Wright to Dartmouth, August 10, 1773, Ms. CRG, 38, pt. 1A:80–82; Coleman, *Colonial Georgia*, 227.

32. Wright to Dartmouth, December 27, 1773, Ms. CRG, 38, pt. 1A: 158–60.

33. Wright to Dartmouth, January 31, 1774, ibid., 163–71.

34. Wright to Dartmouth, April 18, May 24, 1774, ibid., 239–43, 286–87.

35. Proceedings of Council, September 8, 1774, Ms. CRG, 38, pt. 1B:316–22; *CRG*, 12:406–10; Alden, *Stuart and the Colonial Frontier*, 309–10; John Stuart to Dartmouth, September 12, 1774, Davies, ed., *Documents*, 7:608, 680.

36. A Protest of Declaration of Dissent of the Inhabitants of St. Paul's Parish, *Ga. Gaz.*, October 12, 1774.

37. Petition of Evan Haines, Revolutionary War Pension Claims, Record Group 15, National Archives, Washington, D.C.

38. Wright to Dartmouth, September 23, 1774, Ms. CRG, 38, pt. 1B: 326–27; Wright and Stuart to Dartmouth, October 21, 1774, ibid., 335.

39. The Petition of the Inhabitants of the Parish of St. George and St. Paul, including the ceded lands in the Province of Georgia, July 31, 1776, in *Collections of the New York Historical Society for the Year 1872* (New York, 1873), 181.

40. Extract of a letter from Savannah to a gentleman in Philadelphia, December 9, 1774, Peter Force, ed., *American Archives*, 4th ser. (1837–46) 1:1038–39.

41. Wright to Dartmouth, December 12, 1774, Address to Assembly, January 18, 1775, Ms. CRG, 38, pt. 1B:359–60, 375–79.

42. Waldo P. Harris III, "Daniel Marshall: Lone Georgia Baptist Revolutionary Pastor," *Viewpoints: Georgia Baptist History* 5 (1976):51ff.

43. William Manson to Dear Mother, April 8, 1776; Deposition before Thomas Winstanley, Charleston, June 27, 1781, William Manson Papers, Orkney Island Archives, Kirkwall, Orkney, transcripts in possession of Heard Robertson, Augusta, Ga.; grantees to land on the Kiokee may be found in Marion R. Hemperley, *English Crown Grants in St. Paul Parish in Georgia, 1755–1775* (Atlanta, 1974). William Manson's American adventures did not interfere with a generally successful career. He returned to his native town, Kirkwall in the Orkneys, and became comptroller of the

customs. His wife Elizabeth was a member of the distinguished Balfour family, and their daughter Mary married the scion of the Balfours, her cousin William. Manson's handsome house is the Customs House on Albert Street today. This information was gleaned from several local histories in the Kirkwall Library.

44. Brown's lands are described and his servants listed by name in the Supplemental Memorial of Lieutenant Colonel Thomas Brown (n.d.), PRO, AO 13/34. Brown's father, Jonas Brown of Whitby, was a Georgia promoter. An advertisement noted the sailing of the *Marlborough* for Georgia and added, "Any persons, desirous of a particular information of the situation, quality and mode of purchasing these lands, will have the fullest intelligence by applying to Mr. Jonas Brown at Whitby" (*York Chronicle*, June 10, 1774, North Yorkshire County Library, York, England). Interestingly, one of the captains employed by Jonas Brown since 1765 was the same William Manson who attempted to settle near Thomas Brown on the Ceded Lands (A. A. Berends, "The Stone Horse Had Like to Been Down," Whitby Literary and Philosophical Society *Annual Report* [1982], 16–19). It was no accident that Brown's servants were recruited from Brown's Yorkshire and Manson's Orkney Islands and Caithness region. That Brown founded Brownsborough is mentioned in an unsigned review of Brown's career, probably by one of his children, among the family papers, Thomas Alexander Browne Collection, in possession of Mrs. Anthony Lancaster, formerly of Nassau, Bahamas, now of London, England. Brown refers to Brownsborough in a letter to his father, November 10, 1775, in the same collection. Brownsborough's location is fixed in postrevolutionary plats, Deed Book R, pp. 23, 24, 26, Columbia County Courthouse, Appling, Ga. The Yorkshiremen among the newcomers must have had some inkling of the nature of the country they were going to because a local paper carried an account of a skirmish between whites and Indians on the Oconee (*York Chronicle and Weekly Advertiser*, April 9, 1773, North Yorkshire County Library, York, England).

45. Thomas Brown to Lord Cornwallis, July 16, 1780, Cornwallis Papers, PRO, CO 5/82, microfilm, South Carolina Department of Archives and History.

46. Baikia Harvey to Thomas Baikia, Esq., December 30, 1775, William Manson Papers.

47. Wright to Dartmouth, June 20, 1775, *Coll. GHS*, 3:189.

48. Extract of a letter from Savannah, December 26, 1775, to Mr. Morrison of Birtley White House, near Newcastle, Margaret Wheeler Willard, ed., *Letters on the American Revolution, 1774–1776* (Boston, 1925), 345–46.

49. Grierson to Wright, August 6, 1775, Ms. CRG, 38, pt. 1A:583–85.

50. Ibid.; Wright to Dartmouth, August 17, 1775, *Coll. GHS*, 3:206–9;

Ga. Gaz., August 30, 1775; Heard Robertson, "A Revised or Loyalist Perspective of Augusta during the American Revolution," *Richmond County History*, Summer 1969, 5–24.

51. Extract of a letter from a friend in Georgia, Thomas Brown to Patrick Tonyn, November 8, 1776, East Florida Papers, PRO, CO 5/557.

52. Heard Robertson, "The Second British Occupation of Augusta, 1780–1781," *GHQ* 58 (1974): 422–46.

HARVEY H. JACKSON

Georgia Whiggery: The Origins and Effects of a Many-Faceted Movement

N February 1776 Joseph Habersham, scion of one of Georgia's oldest, most influential families and an outspoken critic of British colonial policies, wrote his South Carolina counterpart, William Henry Drayton, of the sad state of affairs south of the Savannah. To Habersham the Whig movement seemed in chaos, and he was not optimistic about the future. "I am sorry to inform you," the Georgian cynically reported, "that we are at present a little unhappy in our C[ongre]ss, owing to the ambitious views of some of our leading people. I think this province is remarkable for a number of parties and I am afraid we shall find it too true that a house divided against itself can never stand."[1]

Joseph Habersham's fears soon seemed confirmed, for within the year these "parties" and their "ambitious" leaders were locked in the struggle that has made revolutionary Georgia a laboratory for the study of Whig factionalism and its effects. Recent scholars, first attracted by its intensity, then intrigued by its accomplishments, set out to use this inter-Whig conflict over "who would rule at home" to assess the nature of the War for Independence in Georgia. As a result of their efforts factionalism is now generally accepted as a critical factor in determining the course and conduct of the Revolution on the southern periphery and in shaping the system of government the Revolution created. Although historians have not asserted that this internal contest alone explains Georgians' particular responses to the pressures of independence and self-government, their work has confirmed these Whig divisions as essential to the understanding of the transition of Georgia from colony to state.[2]

Yet most studies of this phenomenon have focused on factionalism during and after the conflict, which helped explain the wartime evolution of Georgia Whiggery but left unexplored the nature and impact of its colonial antecedents. This focus was unfortunate, for though Whig factionalism was obviously shaped by the dynamics of the Revolution, the divisions Habersham decried were equally products of the past. The ambitions, attitudes, and uncertainties that moved their individual members to rise in rebellion had dictated and would continue to dictate how the groups collectively responded to British policies and to each other. The nature of these parties, and to no small degree their ultimate composition, was greatly determined during the short, significant period of social, economic, political, and ideological conditioning that preceded the conflict. Such divisions existed because the forces that caused the American Revolution in Georgia existed, and for that reason the origins and development of these Whig factions deserve more than casual consideration.[3]

Although his letter seemed to imply otherwise, Joseph Habersham was a member of one of the factions that plagued Georgia politics, and even though he was only in his mid-twenties, many colonists counted him among the "ambitious" who aspired to lead the Whig movement. He belonged to a coalition of individuals and interests associated with the older areas of the colony and led by Liberty Boys from Savannah and surrounding Christ Church Parish. Included in their ranks were men such as Noble Wimberly Jones, Jonathan Bryan, John Houstoun, and Joseph Clay, men whose circumstances and connections placed them among the provincial aristocracy and whose support for the cause gave Whiggery a credibility not provided by lesser lights. But Habersham and his colleagues did not consider their coalition to be a "party." To them it was the movement, and they expected others to follow their lead.[4]

Not all Georgia Whigs shared this point of view, and from this body of dissenters emerged the alliance which modern historians have designated the "radicals." Initially a small group led by men from St. John Parish, this element appeared as a separate entity during the summer of 1774, when Georgians gathered in the capital to protest the Intolerable Acts. At first their opposition was little more than a nuisance to Savannah Whigs, who sponsored the meetings and who, with

their allies, dominated proceedings at the outset, but as tensions between colony and crown increased that situation quickly changed.
Inspired by future signers of the Declaration of Independence Lyman
Hall and Button Gwinnett, who advocated more substantive alterations in the political system than establishment Whigs were willing to
accept, this faction set out to convince other Whigs "that the views
and interests of the town of Savannah were different from those of
the State" and that to gain the freedom they sought Georgians had to
oppose arbitrary rule both by Great Britain and by the Christ Church
coalition. By early 1776, as Joseph Habersham's fears confirm, their
efforts had begun to bear fruit.[5]

Further muddying Georgia's political waters was the collection of
elements which contemporaries identified, with revealing imprecision,
as the "western members." These frontier factions embraced such a
diverse group of interests and classes as to prove the contention that
the colony was "remarkable for a number of parties." At the time
Habersham wrote Drayton, some of these western members, especially
those belonging to the region's Cracker–small farmer majority, had
joined the radicals, convinced by their leader, George Wells, that that
faction would be more attentive to their demands for land than coastal
conservatives and would pursue an aggressive policy toward the Indians who threatened western expansion. Others from that region,
chiefly members of the rising trader-planter class, who had earlier
seen no conflict in electing such men as Savannah merchant Edward
Telfair to represent them in the assembly, continued to function as
part of the Christ Church coalition. And naturally some rejected both
sides and charted their own course. The situation was so fluid that
anything seemed possible, and Joseph Habersham's concern was well
founded.[6]

Yet many Whigs saw Habersham and others of his class as the movement's natural leaders. They were heirs to a tradition dating back to
the last years of Trustee administration, when Georgia's absentee executors relaxed their grip and prominent men from the Savannah area—
particularly longtime residents James Habersham, Sr. (Joseph's father),
Francis Harris, and Noble Jones—became more active in colonial affairs. During this interim, "although some little squables happened
between the Governing & Governed, . . . such animosities were stifled
in their very Cradle" and the province enjoyed a period of political calm.
Newly arrived planters such as Jonathan Bryan from South Carolina and
Clement Martin from St. Christopher's Island added substance and sta-

bility so that when it was announced that royal authority would be extended south of the Savannah, the nucleus of a provincial aristocracy was ready to play the political role they perceived being played by counterparts in other colonies.[7]

It was hardly surprising, therefore, that when Georgia's first royal chief executive, John Reynolds, arrived in 1754 local leaders "received [him] with the greatest Satisfaction." Believing their credentials as men of influence and authority would dispose the governor to turn to them for aid and advice, they assumed his administration would reflect their interests and ideals. They were disappointed. Although Habersham, Harris, Jones, Bryan, and Martin were named to the royal council and others of similar status were elected to the Commons House of Assembly, Reynolds soon concluded that they were out to "depreciate" his authority and resolved to oppose them. To counter what he considered "exorbitant Claims" to undeserved privileges, Governor Reynolds encouraged his private secretary, William Little, to organize backcountry legislators and other dissidents into a faction that would, with the governor's help, challenge the Savannah establishment and its allies.[8]

This open effort to create a "governor's party," combined with a general antipathy toward Savannah on the part of the administration (Reynolds even suggested the capital be moved to Hardwick, a new town on the Ogeechee River), soon made enemies of the very men who should have and probably would have been the executive's friends. As it became increasingly obvious that Little's tactics might well succeed, those being attacked initiated efforts to convince London that the governor should be restrained or removed. Their cries of protest did not go unheeded, and late in the summer of 1756, after having considered a memorial presented on behalf of "most of the Councillors, Representatives, Public Officials, & Planters of Substance & Character" in the colony, which detailed the abuses charged to the administration, the Board of Trade ordered John Reynolds to return to England "to answer for his Conduct in his Government." His legacy to Georgia was the foundation of the first Christ Church coalition—an alliance of the colony's principal people, who were determined to see that in the future Georgia's government would reflect the views and desires of like-minded men.[9]

The new governor, Henry Ellis, avoided his predecessor's mistakes and set the colony on a course as noted for cooperation as Reynolds's was marred by conflict. A talented politician and a shrewd judge of the people with whom he had to work, Governor Ellis demonstrated an ability to lead without commanding that served him well, particularly in his relations with the men Reynolds had alienated and whose cries of protest led to the first governor's downfall. Realizing that members of the council were the executive's natural allies, Ellis restored Noble Jones (an opponent Reynolds had earlier dismissed) to the board, removed some of the former governor's allies, and dealt with all who remained in a manner so evenhanded that few had reason to complain. Thus Ellis surrounded himself with members of Georgia's embryonic aristocracy, and to maintain their loyalty he pursued policies accepted by most as good for them and for the colony. They responded by rallying to their new executive and throughout his term in office proved to be his staunchest supporters.[10]

Winning over the Commons House of Assembly, however, presented more of a challenge. In the last days of his tenure Reynolds had allowed the legislature to assume certain executive functions—the auditing and paying of accounts and the nominating of justices of the peace—which his supporters who remained in the House were loath to surrender. Determined to undo this extension of power, Ellis moved to reaffirm his authority while the assembly was not in session so his enemies could not stop him. In this action he displayed the sense of timing and tact for which he became noted, but his success did not rest entirely on his skill and subtlety. Within the House was a Savannah-oriented clique not unlike that which now dominated the council. Its members, including Noble Wimberly Jones (son of Noble Jones), had also tried to cooperate with the first governor, were rebuffed, and now considered themselves victims of his policies. Seeking Ellis's support against the remnant of the Reynolds faction, they willingly abandoned earlier encroachments into executive affairs. With their help, or at least acquiescence, the governor's powers and prerogatives were restored, and in return Ellis quietly but effectively sponsored their domination of the legislature.[11]

In addition, with the governor's approval, Georgia's body politic underwent a major transformation. Parishes replaced the cumbersome district system that had existed since the Trustee era, and new lines were drawn and representatives allocated to give the colony's principal port and that city's allies control of the House, while making it difficult for competing parties to undo these measures.[12] It was an impressive victory for what could now be accurately called the Christ Church coalition. Talk of moving the capital all but ceased, and Savannah stood unchallenged as the center of the colony's social, economic, and political life. The turmoil that previously plagued the province virtually disappeared, and when Ellis resigned in 1760, pleading ill health, he left his successor a colony still poor but improving. He also left behind a Savannah-led colonial elite convinced that further improvement could be accomplished only with their help. To keep the political peace, the new governor had only to involve these men in the political process and make them beneficiaries of it.[13]

Georgia's third and last royal governor, James Wright, at first appeared to the colony's emerging aristocracy to be an ideal administrator. Determined to "make sure his government served the best interests of those who were in a position to make Georgia productive and prosperous," he saw the wisdom of Ellis's policies and initially continued them, to the great satisfaction of the Christ Church coalition. Supported by his council and a generally agreeable assembly, Wright enjoyed a five-year "honeymoon" during which he was able to reduce tensions in relations with the Indians in the backcountry, divert a significant portion of tribal trade from Charleston to Savannah (which strengthened the natural tie between the capital and Augusta), and put into effect policies that enhanced the economy of the colony as a whole and of the seat of government in particular. To Georgia's planters and merchants James Wright seemed to be a champion who would take the steps necessary to guarantee them the progress and prosperity they deserved. Equally important, Governor Wright seemed willing to accept colonial leaders as partners in this process. Prominent Georgians felt more in control of their own destinies than ever before.[14]

Then, in the fall of 1765, Wright's alliance with the Christ Church coalition was put to the test, and although it seemed to survive, cracks formed in its façade which in time would bring the entire edifice crumbling down. The point of contention has been described elsewhere. As late as September James Wright was "universaly respected by all the inhabitants," yet by January 1766 an armed mob had gathered outside the capital and "Faction & Sedition" were in the wind. The issue was the Stamp Act, a measure most Georgians objected to yet one Wright felt duty bound to enforce. The governor thus proved that though he would act to see that his colony received the same advantages as her sister provinces, he would not allow colonists to violate policies and procedures determined upon by the king and Parliament. So long as Georgians accepted the relationship between crown and colony, governor and governed, which Wright thought was the foundation of an orderly, progressive society, they had his energetic aid and support; but if their desires came in conflict with those ideals, they could expect little help from the governor.[15]

Wright's intransigence put the Christ Church coalition in an uncomfortable position. Many of its members had reservations about the Stamp Act but were unwilling to risk what they had gained by taking part in protests conducted outside accepted channels and over which they might have little control. As a result, Noble Jones, James Habersham, Sr., John Graham, Lewis Johnson, and others cast their lot with the system they had helped create, leaving open opposition largely in the hands of rural Liberty Boys and the "incendiaries. . . . Sent here from Charles Town," whom Wright claimed inspired them. The governor, with support from these and other "well disposed Gentn.," carried the day, but his victory proved a hollow one.[16] To his dismay the Stamp Act was soon repealed, which caused many Georgians, including some who had reluctantly accepted British taxation, to doubt the governor's ability to anticipate and interpret royal policy. It also left the impression that protest, if pressed, could accomplish its goals. Nevertheless, the impact of these events would not have been so great had not other forces been at work within the Christ Church coalition.[17]

Although royal Georgia was scarcely a decade old when the Stamp Act was passed, time and events had already begun to alter the Savannah-led faction. Whereas once the coalition was coextensive with the colony's provincial aristocracy, population growth, economic expansion, and social mobility had broadened the party's base and brought into its ranks rising planters and merchants whose attitudes toward the allocation and application of local authority were not always one with those of the colony's established leaders. By the mid-1760s many of the coalition's older "guiding lights" were secure in council positions or held other offices at the governor's pleasure, so their support for Wright could make them appear as little more than extensions of the executive. The response of these "well disposed Gentn." to the Stamp Act could not have helped but raise concerns among many Georgians that Wright had succeeded where Reynolds, well within the memory of most, had failed—he had created a "governor's party" strong enough to thwart the will of the people and their representatives. The old guard's capacity to represent and defend provincial interests was thereupon called into question, which made their position as spokesmen for the Christ Church coalition and the colony all the more vulnerable. The door was thus opened for a challenge not only to the governor but also to the authority of provincial leaders who supported him, and it is in that challenge that the origins of the Whig party in Georgia may be found.[18]

As founding members of the coalition were drawn closer to the governor and his policies, another group, younger in most cases and often recently arrived, began to make its presence known. Still led by men economically and socially associated with the capital, on the surface this group of dissidents, whose ranks eventually included future revolutionaries Noble Wimberly Jones, Archibald Bulloch, Edward Telfair, Samuel Elbert, and Button Gwinnett, along with former Councillor Jonathan Bryan, whose public opposition to the Townshend duties got him removed from the council and subsequently elected to the assembly from Savannah, seemed cut from the same cloth as the original Savannah-led alliance. But soon it was obvious that they were moved by motives far different from those of their predecessors. Their ideas and opinions were formed during the Stamp Act controversy and shaped by subsequent crises, and they increasingly acted as though interest and ideology had combined to produce a plan for the future— a future they were convinced could be theirs. Discovering an outlet for their ambitions in the Commons House of Assembly, they soon gained control of that body and, fearing that Wright's unyielding stand on the Stamp Act only foreshadowed future trouble, they began to seek ways to limit his authority and increase their own. They did not have to look far for an example of how to proceed. In other colonies—especially South Carolina whose precedent loomed large for Georgia—men in similar circumstances had slowly and systematically been curtailing the power of the executive and his supporters and expanding that of the assembly. These rising members of the Christ Church coalition set out to emulate that success.[19]

These legislative leaders created a second Christ Church coalition, and this group, later identified as the Liberty party, soon established itself as Georgia's champion of local control and legislative supremacy. During the following decade these assemblymen attempted time and again to expand their authority at the expense of the executive and his "party," but with little success. Governor Wright, more independent and perhaps more determined than his counterparts in other colonies, was able, with the consistent support of his council, to beat back their efforts.[20] As a result, by 1774 Christ Church–led legislators, who had hoped to bring the assembly to a position comparable to that enjoyed in other colonies, found themselves politically little better off than when they began. Efforts to accomplish their aims within the system had come to naught, and some among them, frustrated by their impatience, were beginning to conclude that if success was to be theirs, more extreme measures might have to be taken.[21]

The inability of the assembly's Christ Church–led coalition to advance its cause was not entirely the result of the strength and resolve of the governor and his council. Within the Liberty party there were many who were unwilling to carry the fight to the point of alienating the executive or bringing down the wrath of officials in London. This attitude was prevalent among lawmakers who represented the upriver parishes of St. George and St. Paul and the town of Augusta—the area loosely defined as the backcountry. Often these parishes selected Savannah residents to represent them in the assembly, a testament to the common concerns of the regions, but as time passed one issue came to influence the west far more than it did the coast. As the population of the inland parishes grew, confrontations between frontiersmen and Indians made defense the critical issue in the upcountry. Most westerners believed their security depended on the governor—the commander in chief of the colony and symbol of the presence of Great Britain. Therefore, though they might agree with the goals of their coalition counterparts, they could hardly be as active in pursuit of those goals.[22] Before they could support any policy that might cause the governor to reconsider his commitment to them, they would need assurance that the new arrangement would not put their persons and property in jeopardy.

Yet on the whole, tidewater members of the second Christ Church coalition seemed to take their upcountry allies' conditional support for granted because during the movement's formative period, and in some cases up to the eve of the Revolution, coastal Liberty people were only slightly more aggressive than the western members. In fact, when compared with their counterparts in South Carolina, whom they continued to emulate, Georgia's neophyte Whigs appear so classically conservative that their lack of success may have been caused more by their own timidity than anything else.[23] But they had reason for caution. Although they wanted to redistribute power in their favor, they had no desire to emasculate the executive or overturn the system it represented. They were part of that system, and it protected the status they enjoyed—a status which, in a colony so poor and exposed, was

far from secure. Therefore, western and coastal leaders worked together, and their cooperation obscured the divisions that would come
to the surface in more trying times. It is hardly surprising, then, especially when seen in the light of events in other colonies, that Whig
activities in Georgia often seemed halfhearted and that by 1774 they
had produced more symbolism than substance.

These reluctant revolutionaries became aggressive advocates of a
new order less because of their philosophical commitment to a system
they concluded could occur only with independence (though that
commitment was real enough) than because of the realization that, as
Robert Livingston recognized in New York at about the same time,
"they should yield to the torrent if they hoped to direct its course."[24]
Their decision came as a result of events set in motion that critical
summer of 1774, when meetings called by some of the coalition's
members were held in Savannah to denounce the Intolerable Acts and
thereby strike a blow at Wright and his royal establishment. From
these gatherings, which were boycotted by other coalition Whigs who
felt they set a dangerous precedent, there emerged the party whose
position, when compared with that of Christ Church and her allies,
has earned it the epithet "radical."[25] This faction more than any other
force put Georgia on the road to revolution, for its attitudes and activities set standards which Whigs who wished to deserve the name
could not ignore. It unleased the "torrent" that forced more conservative Liberty people to meet the issues of the era head-on.

This new party, like the coalition it challenged, had roots deep in
Georgia's colonial experience. Its leaders were from St. John, a parish
located some forty miles south of the capital, which was settled in the
1750s by Dissenters whose search for a place "suitable for the convenient and compact settlement and support of a congregation" led them
from Massachusetts to South Carolina and from there to Georgia.[26]
Seeking to insulate themselves from the pressures of modernization—
diversity and pluralism—which threatened their way of life, they
founded the town of Midway and began to build a plantation system similar to but apart from that operating in older areas. Supplied
through their own port, Sunbury, which they built as much to avoid
Savannah as to complement her, St. John's Puritans seemed determined
to create and preserve the self-contained, congregation-based community that had eluded their earlier attempts. In the process they also preserved the "tincture of Republican or Oliverian principles" which for
some became a hallmark.[27]

In the light of these goals it is hardly surprising that the first delegates St. John sent to the assembly neither joined nor opposed the Christ Church coalition. They seemed willing to let others dominate legislative affairs so long as their interests were respected and they were otherwise left alone. Yet in a province where religious dogma was declining in significance and where clannish societies were reorganizing in the face of increased social interaction, the modernizing forces these refugees feared could not be avoided for long. St. John's population grew rapidly, and by the mid-1760s lists of parish office-holders began to contain the names of men who either were not part of the Midway congregation or, if they were, did not share the attitudes of its founders. Joined by other settlers to whom change was not an entirely negative process, this new group, more concerned with progress than preservation, sought an expanded role in the governing of the colony. They found, however, that the obvious avenue for their ambitions—the assembly—was coming increasingly under the control of the Christ Church–led Liberty party.[28]

Yet at the outset Savannah's domination of the Liberty movement and that movement's extraordinary influence in the assembly posed no particular problem for the reconstituted St. John's delegation. Benjamin Andrew, legislator and member of the Midway congregation, appears to have comfortably cooperated with the capital faction, as did Joseph Gibbons, a Savannah resident who served capably as a St. John representative. Even Button Gwinnett, who later led his parish's opposition to the Christ Church coalition, seemed to have no trouble working with leading members of the assembly. Son of an Anglican minister, Gwinnett settled on St. Catherines Island in the mid-1760s, became active in local politics, and in 1769 was chosen to represent St. John in the assembly. Although he served only one term before financial troubles caused him to withdraw from politics, during that brief tenure he energetically supported Liberty party efforts to have representation extended to parishes unrepresented in yet taxed by the assembly—an issue that served to rally many of the colony's future revolutionaries. After 1770, however, Gwinnett and Gibbons faded from the scene, leaving Andrew as the parish's only representative of any influence. In contrast, the power of the Christ Church–led Liberty party continued to grow so that by 1774 it was clearly the dominant force in the assembly and had come to be considered by concerned Georgians as the defender of American rights in the colony.[29]

The ascendance of Christ Church presented a dilemma for St. John

Whigs who were not part of the coalition. If they supported the Liberty party in its efforts to limit executive authority and enhance that of the assembly, they might do nothing more than replace one form of arbitrary government with what some considered to be another and thus be no better off politically than they were before. But to support the governor or to do nothing would only perpetuate a system that most had concluded was becoming increasingly at odds with local needs and desires. The problem, however, was soon resolved for them. When Savannah-led Whigs called for meetings to denounce British abuses in Massachusetts, the rules which to that point had governed the internal political struggle in Georgia were suspended. Organized protests now moved outside the confines and the security of the assembly, fissures formed in the Liberty party, and dissidents from St. John stepped forth to earn the name "radicals."[30]

The events of the following eighteen months provided the grist for Joseph Habersham's early 1776 assessment of Georgia's "remarkable" political factionalism. After the initial protest meetings, some prominent Liberty people began to urge caution and even signed petitions denouncing their counterparts' actions. Meanwhile, increasingly vocal dissidents from St. John attacked Christ Church Whigs for blocking efforts to send a Georgia delegation to the Continental Congress, which, they charged, revealed their opponents' lack of commitment to the cause of American liberty. The Whigs who were under attack responded by attempting to carry the protests to the assembly, where their majority coalition could deal with them in its own way and in its own good time. But Governor Wright prevented that ploy by proroguing the legislature, and the Christ Church coalition was left with the alternatives of accepting another defeat at the hands of the chief executive or of seeking redress outside the system.[31]

While all this was taking place, Georgia's "western members" were engaged in a struggle of their own. Some from that region quickly joined counterparts on the coast who cast their lot with king and constitution, thus becoming part of the large Loyalist element that was to plague the Revolution in Georgia. Another group, composed largely of Augusta-based merchants and nearby planters who had been important, although sometimes unenthusiastic, supporters of the Christ Church coalition's Liberty Boys, concluded that their interests lay with the Whig movement's more conservative faction and gave it their support. But these two groups hardly represented the point of view that prevailed in the backcountry. In recent years the western population had grown far faster than that of the rest of the colony, and this influx of immigrants had not only changed the composition of up-country society but had altered longstanding political relations as well. Many of these new arrivals, especially those belonging to the small farmer and Cracker classes, doubted if those "elites" who joined the Loyalists or those who led the Christ Church coalition could be counted on to consider the concerns of "middling" and "meaner" western members. Believing the rumor that the British were "endeavouring to raise the Cherokee Indians to come down against them" and fearing that the Christ Church coalition would cater to the demands of Indian traders (as they felt the British had done) they rejected traditional leaders, Whig and Tory, and responded instead to the call for out-groups like themselves to unite with coastal radicals. Led by their champion, farmer and Indian fighter George Wells, these western Whigs set out to shape the movement in their own image. Their entry into the arena further complicated the already complex situation.[32]

These, then, were the parties that confounded Joseph Habersham early in 1776. They reflected the interests and ambitions of the men who filled their ranks, as well as the desire for legislative supremacy and local control which motivated Whigs everywhere. But these par-ties, their origins, and their subsequent response to the pressures of revolution revealed another fundamental characteristic of Georgia and Georgia Whiggery. Despite the evidence recently mustered to show that Georgia's institutions were maturing as the Revolution approached, beneath that institutional maturation was a society in a near constant state of flux. With a population so small that almost any immigration threatened to upset what sociopolitical balance might exist, the colony attracted new settlers at such a rate that between 1753 and 1776 her citizens increased nearly tenfold (from 2,381 whites to more than 20,000). Most of these people arrived with high expectations, received liberal land grants, and in many cases experienced the material prog-ress enjoyed by older colonists. Their sense of achievement, however, was all too often negated by a political system that allowed them little more than token participation. They found that as Georgia society be-came more varied and complex, Georgia government, especially at the upper levels, became increasingly closed and homogeneous.[33]

The paradox and the problem are obvious. Although provincial lead-ers invited and encouraged the diversity described in this collection of essays, the institutions through which they governed offered this di-versity few outlets. Henry Ellis, the most politically astute of Georgia's royal governors, early seemed to recognize the danger in this trend and, apparently without consulting London, enlarged the legislature and expanded the offices available to ambitious colonists.[34] His example, however, was not followed. James Wright had little of his predecessor's spirit of innovation and accommodation. In 1770, for example, when the Liberty party–led assembly sought to extend representation to parishes south of the Altamaha River, Wright, although apparently feeling the need for such expansion, refused to act without prior approval from his superiors. A confrontation ensued which gave Whigs in the assembly yet another example to add to their growing list of actions by an arbitrary executive—an example made all the more vivid when the crown subsequently instructed the governor to allow what he earlier refused. As he had during the Stamp Act crisis, James Wright appeared unresponsive to those he governed and out of touch with those who governed him. More important, such action led many to conclude that the system as constituted could not cope with conditions it helped create.[35]

By 1774 Georgia's government seemed frozen at almost every level. The executive establishment offered assembly leaders little hope for advancing beyond where they were already, while the Christ Church–led coalition which dominated the legislature was equally inflexible when dealing with counterparts from St. John or with western members who refused to follow directions from the coast. And of course for many these and any other offices appeared beyond reach. Thus as Georgia's population grew, opportunities at every level seemed to shrink and frustrations with the system that confined them mounted.

British policies of the period accentuated this discontent not only because they threatened concepts of local government and legislative supremacy on which so many hopes depended but also because Georgia Whigs, and those who would be Whigs, knew that James Wright and his supporters would enforce such policies to the letter. That knowledge made changes in the internal balance of power increasingly important. Finally, the Intolerable Acts made it obvious that Parliament considered its authority and the authority of the king and his appointees to be superior to that exercised by colonists who claimed their mandate to govern came from those they governed. Aware at last that the issue was drawn, the more committed of the Christ Church faction responded with a vigor unseen in their earlier efforts, and Whiggery south of the Savannah became a revolutionary force.

Yet as J. Franklin Jameson noted half a century ago, "The stream of revolution, once started, could not be confined within narrow banks, but spread abroad upon the land."[36] That is what occurred in Georgia. Even as they organized for what proved to be the final assault on the system that confined them, Georgia Whigs, true to their principles (and also aware that they could never succeed alone), invited others who had been politically excluded to join them. In December 1774 Christ Church Liberty people, among them some of the movement's more conservative members, called for the election of a Provincial Congress and declared that "every Free White Man, liable to pay towards the General Tax, within said Town and District, be admitted a Vote." This extension of the franchise, however, would hardly have made the impact it did if these Whigs had not realized that many now wished to play a more active role in what was taking place and that if they were not accommodated, they might be alienated. To give them the opportunity to participate, Whigs adjusted the size of the Congress, so that when it met in January, although only five of the colony's twelve parishes were represented, forty-five delegates attended— over half again as many as sat in the assembly. When a second Congress gathered in the summer of 1775 ten parishes elected more than one hundred representatives. The doors to wider political opportunity had been flung open, and Georgians were crowding to get in.[37]

As significant as the increased number of offices were the characteristics of the people who filled them. James Wright spoke for most Loyalists and for some conservative Whigs when he complained that there were "few Men of real Abilities, Gentlemen or men of Property" among those chosen to govern. But for the more radical Whigs that was precisely the point. The provincial aristocrats who "founded" the Liberty party and who helped organize the initial Whig Congresses were not the only ones seeking a greater opportunity to govern their own lives. Men of moderate means, unproven but able, also wanted a chance to advance; when they got it, they seized it, and the results were staggering. These first two Provincial Congresses ushered in a new political generation. Of the forty-five delegates attending the initial gathering only sixteen had previous legislative experience, and of the more than one hundred elected to the second Congress all but thirty-five were new to government at the provincial level. Their very presence in such an assembly was revolutionary.[38]

And as these men advanced, other Georgians, even less experienced and in most cases less "acceptable," stepped forth to take their place. In Savannah a parochial committee was organized to enforce Whig directives, and although a few of its members were, according to the governor, the "better Sort of Men and Some Merchants and Planters," most were "a Parcel of the Lowest People Chiefly Carpenters, Shoemakers, Blacksmiths &c." "It is really Terrible my Lord," Wright wrote the Earl of Dartmouth, "that such People Should be Suffered to Overturn the Civil Government and most arbitrarily determine upon and Sport with Other Mens Lives Libertys and Propertys."[39] The "stream of revolution" was lapping at its banks.

Early in 1776 James Wright fled the colony, leaving government in the hands of the Whig Congress and a Christ Church–controlled coalition, which then dominated it as a similar coalition once led the assembly. But in the fall this conservative faction was defeated by an alliance of lowcountry and backcountry radicals whose leaders, Button Gwinnett and George Wells, claimed that Savannah Whigs were seeking to monopolize the government by restricting political opportunity, just as the British had previously done. Promising, among other things, to reform the system so it would better respond to the needs of all the people, the radicals swept the election and secured their victory with a new constitution reapportioning the state along more democratic lines and offering an even wider range of political opportunities for its citizens. Conservatives were outraged. "We are but a few people," wrote Lachlan McIntosh, a prominent member of that faction, "and a plain Simple Form of Government with few Offices or Temptations will . . . suit us best." McIntosh believed the radicals were appealing to man's selfish nature—his "Lust after the old flesh pott"—in an attempt to buy support, but this argument appealed only to those already convinced it was true. The constitution went into effect in 1777, and though the immediate result was not "Stark Naked Democracy" as many feared, what followed seemed to some little better.[40]

Although conservatives continued to struggle against the rising tide of popular participation, the weapons at their disposal were hardly sufficient for the task. Charges that "Gentlemen of ability, whose characters [were] well established" were excluded from office indirectly insulted rising Georgians who now held those positions and who considered themselves as able and established as those claiming to be their betters. Further accusations that these men served only because of "the Extravagent Promises of promotion, & Number of Offices, with the Enormous Sallerys annexed to them" alienated all the more those very people upon whom any successful political movement now depended and reinforced radical counterclaims that their opponents were closer in sympathy to Loyalists than to true Whigs. Finding themselves on the wrong side of what had become for many the critical issue, conservatives were isolated from the political mainstream and by the end of the war had as a group, virtually ceased to be an effective force.[41]

The government, however, which both signified and symbolized the failure of conservatives to control the movement they began, bore and would continue to bear their imprint. The struggle for local control and legislative supremacy which they and their predecessors, the colonial Christ Church coalition and the Liberty party, had carried on long before revolutionary factions divided the state for its spoils, came to fruition with the radical Constitution of 1777. Without the precedents they set, Georgia could never have been changed as it was. This new government, with its weak executive and powerful assembly, owed a far greater debt to the men who opposed its creation than has yet been acknowledged, and the extent of that debt helps explain how and why most later accommodated themselves to the new structure, although they still opposed the men who framed it.

Yet in the prerevolutionary aims and ambitions of those Whigs who became the conservative faction one also finds the seeds of that faction's downfall. Their desire for a government that would allow them to control their own destinies, a desire that was at the heart of Georgia Whiggery, was felt by others who, though not Whigs at the start, could not reasonably nor practically be excluded from the movement. Therefore, when it became apparent their goals could not be achieved within the system, Whig leaders invited—in some cases urged—those even farther outside the colonial political process than themselves to join them, believing (or at least hoping) latecomers would accept the authority of "Gentlemen of ability" under this new arrangement as they had under the old. The extent of their miscalculation reveals how far Georgia had come and how high Whig ideology had raised hopes south of the Savannah. These recent converts quickly concluded that conservatives did not appreciate their needs and, fearing they would fare no better under them than they had under the British, cast their lot with the likes of Gwinnett and Wells—men who had not been members of the prerevolutionary provincial elite and who had no desire to preserve the relationships that gave that elite its authority. Rallying to these rising politicians, "middling and meaner" Whigs created a popular movement where one scarcely existed before. In the process they revolutionized Georgia.

Still, the reduction of conservative Whiggery to a peripheral power did not prevent some of those associated with the defeated group from remaining prominent in state politics. The era's antielitist attitudes notwithstanding, Georgians continued to look to "Gentlemen of ability" for leadership—a testament to the persistence of colonial sociopolitical attitudes. Yet in postrevolutionary Georgia being a "gentleman" or possessing abilities above the average did not assure access to office as they once had. South of the Savannah democracy, albeit free white male democracy, was now a political fact, and those wishing to gain and hold power had, first and foremost, to convince the electorate that once in office they would govern by the will of the people. That some of their former allies could make such a transition caused consternation among those few who remained true to the politics of privilege, but it should not have. Almost from its inception Georgia Whiggery had been democratic, though most of its initial advocates were not. And as radicals proved during the Revolution, democracy could be an effective means of advancing fundamental Whig goals. Therefore, men such as the early conservative spokesman George Walton, finding popular politics not incompatible with their own evolving attitudes and ambitions, abandoned elitist baggage and became leading advocates of popular government.[42]

Thus it was that Georgia Whiggery gave birth not only to a new political order but to a new politician as well. As much a creature of the system as its creator, at his worst he proved a demagogue capable of exciting and exploiting popular prejudices for his own ends. At his best he was a statesman seeking to unite the forces that threatened to divide Georgia and use them for the common good. A complex, often contradictory figure, he was the prototype for the southern planter-politician of the nineteenth century—a slaveholding aristocrat who spoke for the yeoman farmer, an advocate of state rights and the status quo in an age when nationalism was the norm and change was its agent. But despite conflicts that rendered him unintelligible to many, this new arrival on the political scene would, with few exceptions, remain true to the principles for which Georgia Whigs fought their revolution—local government, legislative supremacy, and the opportunity for men to determine their own destinies through participation in the political process. In the new politicians' efforts to govern the state and influence the nation, one may well find the most lasting legacy of Georgia Whiggery.

Georgia Whiggery

NOTES

1. Joseph Habersham to William Henry Drayton in Robert Wilson Gibbes, ed., *Documentary History of the Revolution, 1764-1776* (New York, 1856), 259.

2. See Edward J. Cashin, " 'The Famous Colonel Wells': Factionalism in Revolutionary Georgia," *GHQ* 58 (1974):137-56; Cashin, "Augusta's Revolution of 1779," *Richmond County History* 8 (1975):5-13; Cashin, "George Walton and the Forged Letter," *GHQ* 62 (1978):133-45; Harvey H. Jackson, "Consensus and Conflict: Factional Politics in Revolutionary Georgia, 1774-1776," *GHQ* 59 (1975):388-401; Jackson, "Button Gwinnett and the Rise of the 'Western Members': A Reappraisal of Georgia's 'Whig to Excess,' " *AHJ* 24 (1980):17-30; Jackson, *Lachlan McIntosh and the Politics of Revolutionary Georgia* (Athens, 1979); Jackson, "The Rise of the 'Western Members': Revolutionary Politics and the Georgia Backcountry," paper presented at the 1982 meeting of the U.S. Capitol Historical Society, Washington, D.C., and Ronald Hoffman and Thad Tate, eds., *An Uncivil War: The Southern Backcountry during the American Revolution* (1985); George Lamplugh, " 'To Check and Discourage the Wicked and Designing': John Wereat and the Revolution in Georgia," *GHQ* 61 (1977):295-307; and Robert S. Davis, *Thomas Ansley and the American Revolution* (Ansley, S.C., 1981).

3. Several studies that address other aspects of Georgia politics have also touched on factional development. W. W. Abbot, *The Royal Governors of Georgia, 1754-1775* (Chapel Hill, 1959), approached the subject from the perspective of the chief executive. Jack P. Greene, *The Quest for Power: The Lower House of Assembly in the Southern Royal Colonies, 1689-1776* (Chapel Hill, 1963), looked at general legislative developments, which in Georgia naturally involved factional activity. James M. Grant, "Legislative Factions in Georgia, 1754-1798: A Socio-Economic Study" (Ph.D. dissertation, University of Georgia, 1975), sought to identify the factions and their members and provided much useful data.

4. A brief discussion of this coalition may be found in Jackson, *Lachlan McIntosh*, 21-22. See also Jackson, "Consensus and Conflict," 388-90. For the activities of these and other Liberty Boys see Kenneth Coleman, *The American Revolution in Georgia* (Athens, 1958), and Abbot, *Royal Governors of Georgia*.

5. Jackson, *Lachlan McIntosh*, 22-24; and Jackson, "Consensus and Conflict," 389-91, describe the early activities of this faction. See also Jackson, "Button Gwinnett," and James Harvey Young, "Lyman Hall," in *Georgia's Signers and the Declaration of Independence* (Atlanta, 1981); and "Remarks on a Pamphlet, Entitled 'Strictures on a Pamphlet, entitled The Case of George McIntosh' . . ." (Savannah, 1777), 15.

6. Western radicalism is described by Edward Cashin in " 'The Famous Colonel Wells,' " "Augusta's Revolution of 1779," and "George Walton and the Forged Letter." The Christ Church coalition's western allies and activities are discussed in Lamplugh, " 'To Check and Discourage the Wicked and Designing,' " and Jackson, *Lachlan McIntosh*, 111–35. The interplay of these and other backcountry factions is assessed in Jackson, "The Rise of the 'Western Members.' " Other prominent backcountry delegates who were closely connected to and sometimes lived in Savannah were John Graham and John Shurder. See Greene, *Quest for Power*, 493–95.

7. Abbot, *Royal Governors of Georgia*, 3–33; and Kenneth Coleman, *Colonial Georgia* (Athens, 1958), 89–110; Joseph Ottolenghe to Benjamin Martyn, November 25, 1754, *CRG*, 27:41; and Grant, "Legislative Factions," 206.

8. Abbot, *Royal Governors of Georgia*, 34–56; Jonathan Bryan to the Earl of Halifax, April 6, 1756, *CRG*, 27:114; John Reynolds to Board of Trade, September 22, 1755, March 29, 1756, *CRG*, 27:74, 113.

9. Abbot, *Royal Governors of Georgia*, 49–56; Reynolds to Board of Trade, May 31, 1755, Bryan to Halifax, April 6, 1756, Memorial of Alexander Kellet, July 7, 1756, H. Fox to Board of Trade, August 3, 1756, all in *CRG*, 27:63–64, 114–15, 117, 121.

10. Abbot, *Royal Governors of Georgia*, 57–83; Henry Ellis to Board of Trade, February 10, 1759, *CRG*, 28, pt. 1:181; Orders in Council, May 31, 1759, ibid., 210.

11. Abbot, *Royal Governors of Georgia*, 61–83. In the appendix (pp. 493–95) to *Quest for Power* Jack Greene has compiled a list of the principal assemblymen from Georgia. Under Reynolds's governorship four of the twelve leading legislators were from Christ Church; under Ellis that number increased to six, five of whom were identified as belonging to what Greene classified as the "first rank" of legislators. They dominated the key committees and were influential far beyond their numbers. With allies representing other parishes they were the strongest force in the House.

12. *CRG*, 18:259–60. Albert Saye, *A Constitutional History of Georgia* (1948; rev. ed., Athens, 1970), 58–59. For an example of how Ellis catered to the Christ Church coalition see *CRG*, 13:128–31, 409; James Wright to Earl of Hillsborough, December 26, 1768, Ms. CRG, 28, pt. 2:681–83; and Greene, *Quest for Power*, 184–85.

13. Abbot, *Royal Governors of Georgia*, 82–83. Ellis briefly supported moving the capital but quickly dropped the idea (Ellis to Board of Trade, March 11, 1757, *CRG*, 28, pt. 1:11–14).

14. Abbot, *Royal Governors of Georgia*, 84–102, covers this phase of Wright's administration, during which the influence of the Christ Church coalition grew increasingly. Of the nineteen leading legislators who served during the period, ten were delegates from Christ Church. In addition,

three who represented other constituencies were either from Christ Church or had close ties to it, a trend that would grow. When these assemblymen were joined by others whose parishes were linked to the capital the Christ Church coalition was complete and powerful (Greene, *Quest for Power*, 493–95).

15. John Bartram, *Diary of a Journey through the Carolinas, Georgia, and Florida: From July 1, 1765, to April 10, 1766* (Philadelphia, 1942), 29; Wright to Henry Seymour Conway, January 31, 1766, Ms. CRG, 37:103–9. Wright's role in the Stamp Act controversy is well described in Abbot, *Royal Governors of Georgia*, 103–25. For other aspects of the crisis see Coleman, *Revolution in Georgia*, 18–25; Randall M. Miller, "Stamp Act in Colonial Georgia," *GHQ* 56 (1972): 318–31; S. F. Roach, "*The Georgia Gazette* and the Stamp Act: A Reconsideration," *GHQ* 55 (1971):471–91; and C. Ashley Ellefson, "The Stamp Act in Georgia," *GHQ* 46 (1962): 1–19.

16. Wright to Board of Trade, February 1, 1766, *CRG*, 28, pt. 2:135–36, James Habersham to William Knox, January 29, 1766, *Coll. GHS*, 6:56.

17. Abbot, *Royal Governors of Georgia*, 121–25.

18. Ibid., 126–44; Jack P. Greene, "The Georgia Commons House of Assembly and the Power of Appointment to Executive Offices, 1765–1775," *GHQ* 46 (1962):151–61.

19. Greene, *Quest for Power*, describes the activities of these individuals and compares events in Georgia with those in other southern colonies. Abbot, *Royal Governors*, 126–61, looks at matters through the eyes of Governor Wright. Coleman, *Revolution in Georgia*, 16–38, gives a general overview of the period. See also Wright to Hillsborough, September 20, 1769, March 1, 1770, Ms. CRG, 37:417–18, 436–37; and *CRG*, 15:228.

20. Abbot, *Royal Governors*, 126–61, and Coleman, *Revolution in Georgia*, 16–38. See also Harold Davis, "The Scissors Thesis, or Frustrated Expectations as a Cause for the Revolution in Georgia," *GHQ* 61 (1977):246–57; and Greene, "Georgia Commons House and the Power of Appointment," 151–61.

21. Jackson, "Consensus and Conflict," 388–90.

22. Jackson, "The Rise of the 'Western Members.'"

23. Jackson, "Consensus and Conflict," 390–91; Jackson, *Lachlan McIntosh*, 21–22.

24. Quoted in Norman K. Risjord, *Forging the American Republic, 1760–1815* (Reading, Mass., 1973), 126.

25. Jackson, *Lachlan McIntosh*, 22–24: Jackson, "Consensus and Conflict," 389–91.

26. James Stacy, *History of Midway Congregational Church, Liberty County, Georgia*, 2 vols. (Newnan, Ga., 1903), 1:1–19.

27. Wright to Dartmouth, April 24, 1775, in George White, *Historical*

Collections of Georgia (New York, 1855), 523; Charles C. Jones, Jr., *The Dead Towns of Georgia* (Savannah, 1878), 141–223; and Jackson, "Button Gwinnett," 19–20. See also Richard D. Brown, *Modernization: The Transformation of American Life, 1600–1865* (New York, 1976), 3–22.

28. Only just settled during the Reynolds administration, St. John understandably had no representatives who might be classified among the legislature's leaders. Under Ellis, John Elliott, a prominent member of the Midway congregation and a "trustee" of Sunbury, served on key committees but was never in Greene's "first rank." During the initial years of Wright's administration St. John delegates again disappeared from leadership positions as the Christ Church coalition took control of the assembly, but after the Stamp Act protest parish representatives appeared to be gaining new recognition. Although still not as influential as men from Christ Church, between 1766 and 1770 four St. John delegates were classified among Greene's principal assemblymen—Benjamin Andrew, Joseph Gibbons, Button Gwinnett, and John Smith. Of these only Andrew can be identified as a member of the Congregational church. See Greene, *Quest for Power*, 493–95; Jones, *Dead Towns of Georgia*, 144–46; and George White, *Historical Collections of Georgia* (New York, 1855), 513–23.

29. Jackson, "Button Gwinnett," in *Georgia's Signers*, 38–41; Jackson, "Consensus and Conflict," 389–92; and Greene, *Quest for Power*, 493–95.

30. Jackson, *Lachlan McIntosh*, 21–23.

31. Ibid., Jackson, "Consensus and Conflict," 389–92.

32. Jackson, "Rise of the 'Western Members' "; Wright to Secretary Lord Dartmouth, June 20, 1775, *Coll. GHS*, 3:189.

33. The best description of the general growth of the colony is in Abbot, *Royal Governors of Georgia*, 3–33. For one look at the impact of immigration on Georgia, see W. W. Abbot, "A Cursory View of Eighteenth Century Georgia," *South Atlantic Quarterly* 61 (1962):339–44; and for an example of objections to the lack of political opportunities, see Darien Petition of January 12, 1775, in Lilla M. Hawes, ed., *Lachlan McIntosh Papers in the University of Georgia Libraries* (Athens, 1968), 10–14.

34. See Greene, *Quest for Power*, 184–85; Wright to Hillsborough, December 26, 1768, Ms. CRG, 28, pt. 2:681–83.

35. Greene, *Quest for Power*, 383–84; Abbot, *Royal Governors of Georgia*, 153–54; and Coleman, *Revolution in Georgia*, 32–34.

36. J. Franklin Jameson, *The American Revolution Considered as a Social Movement* (1924; Princeton, 1967), 9.

37. *Ga. Gaz.*, December 7, 1774; White, *Historical Collections*, 60–61, 65.

38. Wright to Dartmouth, December 19, 1775, *Coll. GHS*, 3:228; White, *Historical Collections*, 60–61, 65; Grant, "Legislative Factions," 187–216.

39. Wright to Dartmouth, December 19, 1775, *Coll. GHS*, 3:228.

40. Lachlan McIntosh to George Walton, December 15, 1776, Hawes, ed.,

McIntosh Papers, 24; Henry Laurens to John Wereat, August 30, 1777, Henry Laurens Papers, South Carolina Historical Society, Charleston; and Joseph Clay to Messers. Bright and Pechin, July 2, 1777, in *Letters of Joseph Clay, Coll. GHS,* 8:35. See also Jackson, *Lachlan McIntosh,* 50–70.

41. Col. John Coleman to McIntosh, July 31, 1777, in Force Transcripts, Library of Congress; note by McIntosh, March 1780, *Coll. GHS,* 12:89; Jackson, *Lachlan McIntosh,* 60–70, 111–23.

42. Edwin C. Bridges, "George Walton: A Political Biography" (Ph.D. dissertation, University of Chicago, 1981), is the best treatment of his career. For a thorough analysis of postwar Georgia, see George R. Lamplugh, "Politics on the Periphery: Factions and Parties in Georgia, 1776–1806" (Ph.D. dissertation, Emory University, 1973). A more detailed analysis of what happened both to radical and conservative Whigs, as well as an assessment of the moderating forces that emerged after the Revolution, may be found in Jackson, "Rise of the 'Western Members.'"

Epilogue

In this concluding essay Jack Greene pulls together and assesses many of the elements dealt with in the previous essays, a task for which his abilities to conceptualize and synthesize make him particularly well suited. Greene focuses on the process of identity formation taking place within the colony and on how that process helped shape society south of the Savannah. Looking first at what the colony was to be, then at what the colonists concluded they should be, and finally at what they had (and had not) become by the end of the royal period, Greene gives a unity to the diversity that characterized Georgia. By so doing he renders comprehensible not only what happened to Georgia and her people but how what happened dictated what the colony was and who the colonists were.

Of special interest are Greene's observations on Georgians' efforts to obtain Negro slaves and the impact their success had on this process of collective identity formation. He also reveals that, although Georgians sought to bring their province into the mainstream of British-American colonial development and in many cases made remarkable progress in that direction, they were not entirely successful. To the end of her colonial era Georgia remained different, if not unique.

JACK P. GREENE

Travails of an Infant Colony: The Search for Viability, Coherence, and Identity in Colonial Georgia

 HO WE ARE, what kind of a society we live in, and what sort of a place we inhabit are important, if usually only implicit, questions for the members of all human societies. For new societies such as the early modern British-American colonies, societies initially without clear shape or a well-defined sense of social purpose, these questions take on a heightened importance. The inhabitants of most of the colonies only gradually found satisfactory answers to these questions as their society slowly developed a definition of itself both as a corporate unit—as a place and as a society—and as a collection of inhabitants who shared both common membership in a social order and a set of commonly held values and orientations that provided a basis for approved social behavior and the interpretation of contemporary events and developments. Only as these necessarily stereotypical definitions of the collective self were gradually first articulated and refined by both the inhabitants and outside observers and then internalized by the inhabitants did the settlers begin to understand what they and their societies were about. Eventually, through that understanding, they constructed a coherent sense of themselves and their enterprises—that is, a collective identity.

As the clearest expression of what a people was *"wanting or trying to be, or wanting to do with what it"*[1] was, a colony's corporate sense of self thus provides a key to the contemporary meaning of its inhabitants' collective experiences in founding and developing their new societies. At the same time, the analysis of the changing content of those collective identities reveals, perhaps as well as can the study of any other single phenomenon, the character of their responses to the suc-

278

cessive social and political transformations they experienced. This essay, based on my reflections upon some of the voluminous published contemporary descriptions, analyses, and histories, seeks to describe and explain the changing reputation and identity of colonial Georgia and Georgians from the early 1730s to the mid-1770s.

Two general methodological or procedural points must be stated at the outset. First, as I discovered in trying to construct a much more ambitious analysis of the process of identity formation in three other early modern plantation societies—Virginia, Jamaica, and South Carolina—the collective identities of the new societies of colonial British America can be plotted around the answers to four general questions.[2] The initial question, before the settlers left England, was what they hoped to do in this new place or why they should go there. Second is the question that immediately confronted the settlers upon arrival: what was the place like and what could be done there? The third question arose during the first generations of settlement out of the dialectic between the first two questions: what, given their original intentions and the possibilities offered by the environment, *should* they do there? The final question impressed itself ever more powerfully upon each succeeding generation of inhabitants: who were they, that is, on the basis of their shared experiences in this new place what had they become? From the answers to these four questions—questions about objectives, circumstances, standards, and history—a sense of corporate self in each colony gradually took shape.

My second procedural point is that this process of collective identity formation in new societies seems to go through three sequential but not sharply distinguishable stages. In the first stage, characteristics of place usually assumed primacy. That is, the inhabitants identified themselves and their societies largely on the basis of the nature and potentiality of the places in which they had settled. During a second stage, they tended to define themselves more according to the way they were organizing their social landscapes and the extent to which those landscapes did—or did not—conform to inherited notions and standards. Finally, during a third stage, the inhabitants defined themselves on the basis of their predominant characteristics as a people.

In contrast to many other early modern British-American colonies, the settlers of Georgia from its very beginning had an unusually clear sense of what they hoped to do. Indeed, it is probable that no other early modern British colony began with a more fully articulated set of

Seal of the colony of Georgia, 1732–33.

goals. These goals were revealed in an extensive promotional literature that in volume probably exceeded that for any of the earlier colonies, except possibly Virginia and Pennsylvania. Georgia was the first entirely new British colony founded in America since Pennsylvania almost fifty years before and the last until the establishment of East and West Florida and several new island colonies in the Caribbean at the close of the Seven Years' War. Not since the founding of England's first colony in Virginia at the beginning of the seventeenth century had the establishment of any colony attracted so much public attention in Britain or such wide public support, the extent of which was indicated not only by large private contributions but by an unprecedented outlay of government funds.

In some ways, the initial projections for Georgia do not appear very different from those for most other colonies. Like most earlier colonies, Georgia was intended to enhance the power and wealth of the British nation and to provide an outlet and a field of opportunity for the unfortunate, the persecuted, and the adventurous of the Old World. Its specific strategic role as a barrier to render the increasingly valuable but black colony of South Carolina "safe from Indians and other enemies," particularly the Spanish in Florida, was not unlike that foreseen for Jamaica in the 1650s and New York and the Carolinas in the 1660s. Ever since the establishment of Virginia, moreover, colonies had been seen as "Asylum[s] to receive the Distressed," and, especially since the founding of the Carolinas, New Jersey, and Pennsylvania during the last half of the seventeenth century, they had been promoted as places of religious refuge, where besieged and "distressed Protestants" from the continent of Europe could find "Liberty of Conscience and a free Exercise of Religion."³

Similarly, Georgia's depiction in the promotional literature as a land of promise, a new Eden, was not significantly different from the early portraits of other colonies in regions south of New England. With a warm, temperate climate and rich soil, which required "slight" husbandry and little work to yield a rich abundance, Georgia was presented as a place where the settlers could easily achieve both prosperity and contentment. Not only would its "fertile lands" and generous climate yield up all of the crops and other commodities produced in South Carolina, including corn, grains, rice, livestock, naval stores, and deer skins, it also promised to be suitable for the production of flax, hemp, and potash, which Britain then imported in substantial quantities from Russia. Most important, because it occupied "about the same latitude with part of China, Persia, Palestine, and the Made[i]ras," it was "highly probable," Georgia's promoters predicted, that as soon as the new colony was "well peopled and rightly cultivated," it would supply Britain with many of the exotic products—"raw silk, wine, [olive] oil, dies, drugs and many other materials"—which it then had to purchase at vast expense from other "Southern Countries." Because it already had "white mulberry-trees [growing] wild, and in great abundance," silk, the production of which was "so Easy a work that Every Person from Childhood to old Age can be Serviceable therein," would, it was thought, be to Georgia what sugar was to Barbados and Jamaica, tobacco to Virginia and Maryland, and rice to South Carolina. Georgians would at the same time grow prosperous through such easy and potentially profitable productions and contribute to the prosperity and power of the entire Anglophone world.⁴

Nor until they had succeeded in such enterprises would Georgians have to worry much about either sustenance or defense, "difficulties" that had frequently "attended the planting" of earlier colonies. Just across the Savannah River, South Carolina abounded with cattle, grain, and other provisions that would be easily and cheaply available to feed the settlers of the new colony until they could support themselves. And although they would have to be on guard against the treacherous Spaniards, they had little to fear from Indians. Unlike both Virginians and Carolinians in their early days, Georgians would be "in no danger" from the Indians, whose numbers had so "greatly decreased" over recent decades that they "live[d] in perfect amity with the English." Such a safe and "fine Land . . . in a Temperate Climate" that would yield "a vast variety of Productions fit for the Benefit of Trade and Comfort of Life" was obviously "capable of great improvements." The colony's promoters assured potential supporters and settlers that the newcomers "must in a few Years be a flourishing and happy People." Like Pennsylvania, which a mere fifty years earlier had been "as much a forest as Georgia is now, and in those few years, by . . . wise economy . . . now gives food to 80,000 Inhabitants, and can boast of as fine a City as most in Europe," Georgia could not fail to grow into "a mighty Province."[5]

But the Trustees had no intention of permitting this extraordinary promise to be frittered away in the egocentric pursuit of wealth. They knew that many earlier colonies had been undertaken with the best of intentions and the most elaborate plans and that in every one, with the possible exceptions of the orthodox Puritan colonies of New England, the plans of the organizers had quickly given way before the uncontrollable pursuit of self-interest. Placing their own welfare over all social concerns, the colonists had settled in a pell-mell and dispersed fashion, monopolized as much land as they could, and did everything possible to enhance their own private wealth. With their small white populations, legions of dangerous and discontented slaves, and large concentrations of land in the hands of a few proprietors, South Carolina and Jamaica were exactly what Georgia's organizers were determined it would never become. Having learned from the mistakes of earlier promoters, the Trustees were determined that Georgia would be "founded upon Maxims different from those on which other Colonies have been begun."[6]

The Georgia plan as devised by the Trustees was less a throwback to seventeenth-century ventures than a preview of the later doctrines of "systematic colonization" advocated by Edward Gibbon Wakefield and others for the settlement of Australia and New Zealand in the 1830s and 1840s. In contrast to such places as Jamaica and South Carolina, Georgia was to be "a regular Colony," by which its promoters meant "methodical; orderly"; "agreeable to rule"; "instituted . . . according to established forms of discipline"; "consistent with the mode prescribed"; "governed by strict regulations."[7]

Georgians would have "Civil liberty . . . in its full extent" in the manner of the free people in all British colonies. But this civil liberty would not include the freedom to pursue individual interests at the expense of the Trustees' overall design. Thus the colonists were to be settled "in an orderly manner so as to form . . . well regulated town[s]" and close settlements and not in the dispersed manner that was common in other colonies and for which Virginia was particularly infamous. Experience had "shown the inconvenience of private persons possessing too large quantities of land in our colonies, by which means, the greatest part of it must lie uncultivated" to the prejudice of the "well-settling" of those colonies. The Trustees were therefore determined that Georgia should have "a more equal distribution of lands." To that end they stipulated that land "be divided in small Portions" of fifty acres, none of which could subsequently be united through "Marriage or Purchase." By this "strict *Agrarian* Law," the Trustees hoped to prevent "the Rich [from] . . . monopolizing the Country." Because they had only small tracts, the settlers would not need the slaves that had helped undermine both the social happiness and the individual moral fiber of South Carolina and colonies in the Caribbean. Rather, they would be able and would be expected "to labor themselves for their support." "Like the old Romans," they would not be sucked by slavery into indolence and passivity but would be rendered "more active and useful for the defence of their government." Finally, the Trustees vowed to give "all Encouragement . . . to Virtue and Religion & all Discouragement to Immorality and Profaneness" and to maintain "good discipline" through the introduction of "such regulations . . . as . . . would best conduce to the . . . encouragement of industry and virtue among" the settlers.[8]

As one looks more deeply into the Georgia plan, it becomes obvious that it was designed to avoid not only the mistakes of earlier colonies but the contemporary social evils of Britain as well. As is well known, Georgia was conceived as a charitable trust that would employ a combination of the lightly occupied land between the Savannah and the Altamaha rivers, the private contributions of the benevolent in Britain, and public funds to relieve the nation's growing population of the impoverished and the imprisoned. Hence the founding of the colony was widely heralded in Britain as an act of beneficence by which "many families who would otherwise starve" would "be provided for & made masters of houses and lands," and many other unfortunates then languishing in prison would be once again rendered useful to the nation. That this charitable assistance would also free the British public from some of the economic burdens of poor relief was also a consideration. The cynical could dismiss this aspect of the Georgia enterprise as a clever device to get the poor and the imprisoned out of the country and off the public charge: to rephrase the old aphorism, out of sight, out of mind—and not out of pocket.[9]

But the impulse behind the founding of Georgia obviously went far deeper than such expedient calculations. Established during what one contemporary social critic called "the very age of retention, [an age] in which every man's benevolence is centered in himself, and publick spirit is absorbed by private interest," Georgia was to be not just a model colony but a model society for Britain, a mirror or counter-image that would stand as both a reaffirmation of old values and a repudiation of the baser tendencies then rampant in British life. For throughout the first half of the eighteenth century, one social commentator after another sounded the theme that Britain's rising wealth and growing involvement in an expanding and volatile money economy were the primary sources of the blatant social miseries that Georgia was in part designed to relieve. These developments, critics asserted, had not only produced a decline in virtue and other traditional English values but social evils unknown to earlier generations. As the rich grew ever richer and wallowed in more and more luxury, it seemed, the gap between rich and poor grew ever wider, poverty increased, the number of poor in workhouses, poorhouses, and prisons rose dramatically, and private virtue and public spirit fell victim to a deluge of possessive individualism and a riot of self-indulgence.[10]

The ubiquity of such concerns in Britain strongly suggests the possibility that the Georgia project elicited such deep public resonances and exerted such a powerful and widespread appeal among the comfortable and the wealthy because it proposed to relieve not just some of the nation's growing social problems but also the social guilt created by those problems. By giving money to the Georgia Trustees instead of spending it on "luxury and superfluous expenses," the people considered responsible for the country's social ills could at the same time allay their guilt over their own good fortune in the lottery of life, absolve themselves of any personal responsibility for existing social ills, prove—to themselves and to others—their generosity, and show that, doomsayers to the contrary notwithstanding, all "public spirit" was not "lost" in Britain.[11]

Georgia may thus have become a great national undertaking not only because of the growing appreciation of the worth of colonies and a desire further to enhance the wealth and power of the nation but also because it spoke directly—and positively—to some of the British elite's deepest social anxieties. If Georgia could prove that the habits and character of such "miserable objects" as the poor and the indebted could, under proper regulations, be reformed and such people given a new sense of purpose and self-worth, there was still hope for Britain itself. The "example of a whole Colony" behaving "in a just, moral and religious manner" would, it was hoped, strike a blow against profligacy throughout the entire Anglophone world. Georgia could become a model, indeed, the inspiration, for Britain's own social salvation. As the patrons and promoters of such a glorious enterprise, the Trustees became national social heroes, and James Oglethorpe was lionized for his selfless patriotism and public spirit. "That a Gentleman of his Fortune possessed of a Large and Valuable Acquaintance[,] a Seat in Parliament, with the Genius to make a Figure in any Senate in the World, Should renounce all these Pleasures to cross a perilous Ocean for the Sake of establishing a few distressed families undone by Idleness, Intemperance, Sickness, with other ill habits and all Oppressed with Poverty, to Found a Colony in a Wilderness wholly uncultivated," was, declared one observer, "one of the greatest pieces of Self Denial this Age has afforded."[12]

For more than a decade, people hoped that this ambitious enterprise would succeed in its original design. Indeed, for the first few years, reports from the colony were largely encouraging. "A very pleasant country" with a "good . . . climate" that, one visitor noted, would produce "with God's blessing, everything which grows in the West Indies" and afforded "the opportunity of cultivating olives, grapes, and silk," Georgia seemed to be a "great success." Despite some sickness and predictable intemperance and disobedience on the part of a few of the settlers, Oglethorpe reported to the Trustees eleven months after the arrival of the first settlers that the colony had "increased and flourished." Savannah had been laid out and contained fifty houses; several necessary public works had been begun; the population was approaching five hundred. During the next year, the number of houses in Savannah almost doubled, and many additional settlers swelled population figures. By June 1735, one new arrival claimed that people were flooding in so rapidly "from all parts of America as well as from England" and the Continent that "the builders and brick-makers cannot make and build [houses] fast enough for [all] the [new] inhabitants." "Trade and planting" were developing "very fast"; cattle exceeded two thousand head; naval stores, corn, and peas were being produced in abundance; oranges were coming "on finely"; and silk culture appeared so promising that, it was said, "the name of it fills the colony so full [of hope] that if it goes on so for seven years" Savannah would "be the largest city or town in all the Continent of America."[13]

Although a few lazy and improvident people among the new settlers neglected "to improve their Lands," got into debt, and were "generally discontented with the Country," the "Industrious ones," another visitor told his London readers, "have throve beyond Expectation" and had "made a very great Profit" out of provisions and cattle. Obviously, remarked the young Baron Philipp Georg Friedrich von Reck, who conducted the first transport of Salzburger immigrants to Georgia, God had "so far . . . blessed" the enterprise as to permit industry, justice, and good order to triumph over "[self-]indulgence and idleness," "Discord and disorder." The pious Salzburgers at Ebenezer seemed to do particularly well. When one of them had to travel into South Carolina, he recoiled in horror at the sinful lives of both masters and servants on the rice plantations and vowed to "remain in Ebenezer with water and bread rather than to live in a place [like South Carolina] where people walk[ed] the straight path to hell." By contrast, von Reck concluded, the "arrangements made for Georgia by the Trustees" indeed seemed to be "very praiseworthy and Christian."[14]

Although Georgia continued into the late 1730s to receive glowing reports in the British press,[15] the initial euphoria gave way to doubt as the settlers slowly began to come to terms with the questions of what kind of a place Georgia was and what could or ought to be done there. Reports began to filter back across the Atlantic that all was not well in the new Eden. Within two years, there were complaints about a variety of problems, including incompetent magistrates, ethnic antagonisms, political contention, social dissipation, and the engrossment of trade by a handful of Scottish merchants. Most important were the complaints that, despite all the money being poured into the colony, it was making but "small progress." Contrary to the "extravagant representations . . . in favour of this settlement" circulated in the London press, John Brownfield wrote the Trustees from Georgia in May 1737, a little over four years after the initial settlement, Georgians could not yet feed themselves, few settlers could "subsist independent of" public support, and there was almost no foreign trade and no credit. Instead of becoming the prosperous, well-regulated, regenerated, and contented people initially projected by the Trustees, some significant part of them were slowly falling into an "indolent and dejected" state, and many of the "best workmen" were "beginning to leave the place in order to get employment in Carolina and by that means prevent their families from starving." Far from being "so flourishing as our public papers would persuade us," Georgia was, Brownfield noted, "never yet so low as at this time," and all the inflated reports of its "great improvements" were nothing more than "great chimerical idea[s]" designed to deceive the Trustees and the British public.[16]

Nor, according to a significant and articulate section of the population, did this downward trajectory change over the next few years. The Trustees continued to sponsor publication of favorable reports, which as late as the early 1740s insisted that most settlers had found "Means to live comfortably" and that those of industry and frugality, such as the Salzburgers at Ebenezer and the Highland Scots at Darien, were thriving. Moreover, these reports asserted, continued progress in the culture of silk and wine, the intended "Staple[s] of the Country of *Georgia*," enhanced the hope that with perseverance these two products could yet be brought "to Perfection."[17]

In opposition to such rosy projections, a rising chorus from people the Trustees tried to dismiss as "clamorous malcontents" argued that the colony was an abysmal failure. The first history of Georgia—entitled *A True and Historical Narrative of the Colony of Georgia*, published in Charleston and London in 1741 and composed by three of the Trustees' most vehement critics, Patrick Tailfer, Hugh Anderson, and David Douglas—provided a detailed account of that failure. The promotional literature, these critics complained, had depicted Georgia "as an *Earthly Paradise*, the soil far surpassing that of England; the air healthy, always serene, pleasant and temperate, never subject to excessive heat or cold, nor to sudden changes." Such reports had led the early immigrants to expect a "Land of Promise, overflowing with the abundance of all good things necessary and desirable for the comfortable support of life, and those to be obtained with half the labour, industry and application," required in the Old World "for the lowest subsistance." Instead, the settlers found an excessively hot and, by European standards, inhospitable climate in which sickness and disease were rife and people could feed themselves only with the most debilitating labor without hope of ever achieving more than simple subsistence. Despite the large sums poured into the colony, its critics contended, Georgia during its first decade remained a poor, "miserable colony," a place, indeed, that did not even deserve "the *Name* of a Colony."[18]

The reasons for this failure, according to the malcontents, did not lie in the place. Just across the Savannah River, in South Carolina, people were prospering in the same climate and with the same soil. Nor was the problem the settlers themselves, most of whom had worked hard, and many of whom, having given up on Georgia, had succeeded elsewhere. Rather, Georgia's desolate state was entirely traceable to its initial design and to the implementation of that design by the Trustees and their subordinates in Georgia. Specifically, the restrictions on land acquisition and inheritance had "extinguish[ed] every Incitement to Industry and Improvement" and had been "a *great Means of depeopling the Colony, as fast as you can people it.*" In their passion for system and regularity, the Trustees had assigned lands without regard to fertility or worth and had thus left many people both with inferior plots and at a serious disadvantage. Most important, by excluding black slavery, the Trustees had deprived the colonists of the means to develop their lands in such a hot climate. "It has hitherto been a received maxim in all owr southerne setlements, not only in the West Indies, but also in Carolina," one discontented Georgian noted, "that negroes are much more profitable to the planter (as being naturalisled to the extreame heats) thane any European servants," which were both less reliable and more expensive. Indeed, "without the help and assistance of negroes," the malcontents concluded, it would be "morrally impossible that the people of Georgia can ever gett forward in their setlements or even be a degree above common slaves" because "the people of Carolina, who are remarkable for their industry and who inhabite a country equally as fine and productive as Georgia, will at all times, by the help of their negroes be able to undersell the people of Georgia in any commodities they can possibly raise, at any market."[19]

Finally, as if these difficulties were not enough, the malcontents charged that the interior government of the colony had been conducted in an arbitrary manner that was wholly inconsistent with the customary rights of Britons and was utterly "unexampled under any *British* Government." "While the nation at home was amused with the fame of the happiness and flourishing of the colony, and of its being *free from lawyers of any kind,*" the malcontents reported, "the poor miserable settlers and inhabitants were exposed to as *arbitrary* a government as Turkey or Muscovy ever felt. Very looks were criminal, and the grand sin of *withstanding,* or any way *opposing* authority, (as it was called, when any person insisted upon his just rights and privileges) was punished without mercy." The result was that "for some time there were more imprisonments, whippings, &c. of white people, in that *colony of liberty*, than in all British America besides." Instead of the silkworm, the "Georgia stocks, whipping-post, and logg-house" came to symbolize the colony "in Carolina and every where else in America, where the name of the Province was heard of, and the very thoughts of coming to the colony became a terror to the people's minds." "By all appearance[s]," Georgia thus seemed "to have been calculated and prepared" not as a settlement of British subjects but as "a colony of vassals, whose *properties* and *liberties* were, *at all times*, to have been disposed of at the discretion or option of their superiors." "Not even the flourishing of wine and silk," the malcontents declared, could "make a colony of British subjects happy if they" were "deprived of the liberties and properties of their birthright."[20]

Although first set forth in a conciliatory, even deferential, tone, the criticisms of the malcontents represented a demand for precisely what the Trustees were determined to avoid: placing Georgia on the same "foot of the other American Colonies." In demanding liberty for individuals to acquire as much land as they wished, to dispose of their possessions without restraint, to settle where they liked, to have as many slaves as they saw fit, and, ultimately, to enjoy a government that provided the benefits of British law and assured that they would neither be deprived of liberty and property without due process of law nor governed by laws passed without their consent, they were asking that Georgia be permitted to follow the time-tested pattern of British colonization—the "ancient Custom of sending forth Colonies, for the Improvement of any distant Territory, or new Acquisition," as it had been "continued down to ourselves." "By enjoying the freedom we crave," they declared, "New York and the rest of His Majesty's colonies," including the "famous province of Pennsylvania," were "all doing well," permitting their inhabitants to accumulate "large and plentiful fortunes . . . while this poor province and the people in it, for want of such liberty, are a load and burden to the mother country." South Carolina, which they praised—and not ironically—as "a land of liberty, property and plenty," was a dramatically successful model of the traditional mode of British colonization using slaves to work in the "scorching rays" of the summer sun.[21]

Indeed, the success of all the other British colonies seemed to the malcontents to underline the absurdity and visionary character of the Georgia scheme. Whereas the founders of those colonies "fondly imagin'd it necessary to communicate to such young Settlements the fullest Rights and Properties, all the Immunities of their Mother Countries, and Privileges rather more extensive" so that their colonies would flourish "with early Trade and Affluence," the Trustees, considering "Riches . . . as the *Irritamenta Malorum* . . . that . . . inflate[d] weak Minds with Pride . . . pamper[ed] the Body with Luxury, and introduce[d] a long variety of Evils," had, the malcontents acidly wrote, thus

> *Protected us from ourselves* . . . by keeping all Earthly Comforts from us: You have afforded us the Opportunity of arriving at the Integrity of the *Primitive Times*, by intailing a more than *Primitive Poverty* on us: The Toil, that is necessary to our bare Subsistence, must effectually defend us from the Anxieties of any further Ambition: As we have no Properties, to feed Vain-Glory and beget Contention; so we are not puzzled with any System of Laws, to ascertain and establish them: The valuable Virtue of Humility is secured to us, by your Care to prevent our procuring, or such much as seeing any *Negroes* (the only human Creatures proper to improve our Soil) lest our Simplicity might mistake the poor *Africans* for greater Slaves than ourselves: And that we might fully receive the Spiritual Benefit of those wholesome Austeries; you have wisely denied us the Use of such Spiritous Liquors, as might in the least divert our Minds from the Contemplation of our Happy Circumstances.[22]

After "seven years . . . of fruitless and misspent time and labour," the malcontents declared in 1740, "the present establishment can never answer." Not only the example of other colonies but "trial, practice and experience" in Georgia had shown beyond doubt that the original plan could be dismissed as merely some "noted refiner['s]" "theoretical" and "*utterly impracticable*" scheme. The failure of the Trustees' grand plan had proved conclusively that "all Projects to devise a better Constitution of Government than the *British*, for *British* Subjects," were "sad Quack Politicks," remarkable for at once "destroying or torturing the Patients, and disgracing the Prescriber." Now that a "sufficient Term" had "been allowed for the Experiment," it was time to turn to modes of settlement that had worked elsewhere. Why, they asked, should Georgia, alone among all the British colonies, be "singled out for a state of misery and servitude"? The Trustees' clerical minion John Wesley might desire "*never . . . to see* Georgia *a rich, but a Godly Colony*." The malcontents wanted precisely the opposite.[23]

This frontal assault upon virtually every element that had given the Georgia plan its distinctive character stimulated an increasingly strident and uncompromising verbal battle that lasted for the five years from 1738 to 1743 and produced a continuous round of petitions, counterpetitions and pamphlets. At first, the Trustees and their supporters held fast to all aspects of their initial plan, and, although they eventually agreed to modify the restrictions on inheritance and land distribution, they refused to abandon the prohibition on slavery on the grounds that it was thoroughly "inconsistent" with "the first Design of the Establishment." Not only, they argued, were slaves unnecessary for the production of "Silk, Cotton, Cochineal, [wine,] and the other designed Produces of the Colony," all of which were "Works rather of Nicety than Labour," but they were "absolutely dangerous." Recent "Insurrections of Negroes in *Jamaica* and *Antigua*" had revealed that slaves were "all secret Enemies" who were "apt . . . to rise against their Masters, upon every Opportunity." For that reason, they were wholly inappropriate for a frontier colony such as Georgia. Much more important, however, slavery was a primary source of most of the evils that were present in the other colonies and that the Trustees were determined to avoid in Georgia. Slaves, they argued, citing South Carolina and the West Indies as examples, discouraged white immigration, led to the concentration of wealth and the engrossment of lands in the hands of those who could afford them, destroyed the industry of poor whites, who invariably "disdain[ed] to work like Negroes," and ultimately drove even the slaveholders "to absent themselves, and live in other Places, leaving the Care of their Plantations and their Negroes to Overseers."[24]

Pointing out that "none of our most beneficial Colonies have yielded an early Profit," the Trustees admitted in their counterattacks that Georgia's progress had been slow. But they attributed that slowness not to the prohibition of slaves or to any of the other regulations called into question by the malcontents but to the quality of the early immigrants, many of whom were "low and necessitous People" who had been difficult "to form . . . into Society, and reduce . . . to a proper Obedience to the Laws." The colony's recent problems, the Trustees professed, resulted from the activities and example of the malcontents, those profligate lovers of Negroes, who had fomented a spirit of idleness, dissipation, and contention that discouraged the entire colony. Citing the success of the industrious Salzburgers in Ebenezer and Highland Scots in Darien, the Trustees' protagonists argued that the initial design was viable for any people who were willing to expend the necessary labor and be content with moderate and moral lives. They insisted that Georgia could still be made to work according to its original plan and predicted that silk and possibly even wine would eventually make both the colony and its inhabitants prosperous—without the use of black slaves.[25]

Participants on both sides of this long and bitter public debate agreed on two points: first, that Georgia had not made as much progress in its first decade as had been originally hoped, and second, that it was still a place of extraordinary promise. Their disagreement was over the means by which that promise could best be achieved. When the Trustees continued "their inflexible Adherence to" their "pernicious and impracticable Schemes and Maxims of Government," the malcontents appealed twice to Parliament for redress, in 1742 and 1743. During the second appeal, one member of Parliament indicated in debate that he had "always thought the affair of Georgia a jobb" and averred that the Trustees, though honest men, must have been "misled and misinformed of the [true] state of the colony, or they would [have] change[d] their measures of proceeding." On both occasions, however, Parliament sided with the Trustees on the major issues. Thereafter, the controversy gradually became less intense. Some Georgians continued to press for slavery, but the Trustees resisted their demands until later in the decade.[26]

In the meantime, Georgia continued to grow slowly. By the mid-1740s, Savannah may have had three hundred houses, its famous public garden was still "in a very thriving Way," and in its immediate vicinity were "several very pretty Plantations," including Wormsloe, the seat of the Trustees' treasurer Noble Jones and a place with many "extraordinary" improvements. Nearby was the Reverend George Whitefield's famous orphan house, a large "Superstructure . . . laid out in a neat and elegant Manner" with rooms that were "very commodious, and prettily furnished." Except for Savannah, Ebenezer, and a few other small, scattered settlements, however, the Salzburger spiritual leader Johann Martin Boltzius reported in the early 1750s, that Georgia was mostly "still forests" with "small plantations . . . established only here and there." Between 1740 and 1750, population had increased at a rate of less than two hundred per year, and many settlers, who preferred to "run around rather than work," were primarily hunters with no permanent abode. If, as Boltzius contended, Georgia had "nearly all things" that were "necessary for the wants and refreshments of human life," it was still crude and relatively undeveloped. Almost all of its houses were built of wood; many of its public works, buildings, and fortifications were in disrepair; there was a shortage of craftsmen; and there were few mills or roads. So far, the colony had only two "rich merchants," no ships came directly to Georgia for freight, and there was "very little Business stirring." Although silk production had "for several years . . . rather gathered momentum" and there was "no lack of people who" knew "well how to handle it," the annual volume produced was modest, and Georgia contained no vineyards.[27]

Notwithstanding the colony's slow development, Georgia and the Trustees did not suffer from a wholly unfavorable reputation as a result of the campaign of the malcontents. In the section on Georgia in the second edition of *The British Empire in America,* published in 1741, John Oldmixon praised the Trustees' original design and the colony's subsequent progress. Edward Kimber, whose journal of his visit to Georgia was published in the *London Magazine* in 1745, attributed the fact that Georgia was "so much less flourishing than it was at the Beginning of the Settlement" not to flaws in the Trustees' design but to the "cursed Spirit of Dissension" fomented by the malcontents. The antiquarian John Harris, a friend of Oglethorpe, who included a long section on Georgia in his two-volume library of voyages and travels, published in 1748, was even more lavish in his praise of the Trustees and their "worthy, disinterested, and public-spirited . . . Design." Formed "upon the truest Principles of Virtue, Industry, and Freedom," Harris declared, this design was "the best" of "all the Methods that have been hitherto tried, in fixing Colonies in distant Parts of the World." All it needed "to render it, in every respect, a fertile and a pleasant Settlement" was "a sufficient Number of Inhabitants," and, Harris predicted, it could not "fail of striking firm and deep Root" and "would very soon be full of People, and useful People," not masters and slaves.[28]

But the truth was that the old design no longer had any vigor. Through their intensive public campaign, the malcontents had undermined its appeal, if not its credibility, and that battle had taken much of the enthusiasm for the project out of the Trustees. As a result, Georgia during the 1740s was left without any clear sense of direction. Between an old design that was no longer fully in operation and the alternative model of the ordinary British colony that had not yet been tried, Georgia had no agreed-upon set of goals and priorities, no coherent sense of place, no acceptable collective sense of self. Oldmixon, Kimber, and Harris to the contrary notwithstanding, by the mid-1740s it was clear that Georgia would never become the well-regulated, egalitarian yeoman utopia initially envisioned by the Trustees. Whether it could by another route achieve an equality with other British colonies remained to be seen.

At their first general meeting in July 1732 the Georgia Trustees had ordered a common seal for their new colony. Like all the colonial seals, that of Georgia was a representation of aspirations, an emblem of what its founders hoped Georgia would become. On one side "was a representation of silk worms, some beginning and others having finished their web" with a motto signifying "that neither the first trustees nor their successors could have any view of [private] interest" and that the colony was "entirely designed for the benefit and happiness of" the settlers. The reverse side expressed more directly, one suspects, the expectations of the settlers themselves. It had "two figures resting upon urns, representing the rivers Alatamaha and Savanna, the boundaries of the province." Between them was seated another figure representing "the genius of the colony . . . with a cap of liberty on his head, a spear in one hand and a cornucopia in the other." Liberty, strength, and abundance—these were the qualities, the seal projected, that would form the "genius" of Georgia.[29]

All of these qualities had effectively escaped the colony during its first twenty years. "Great had been the expence which the mother country had already incurred, besides private benefactions, for supporting this colony," one contemporary commentator noted, "and small had been the returns yet made by it. The vestiges of cultivation were scarcely perceptible in the forest, and in England all commerce with it was neglected and despised." When the German engineer William Gerard De Brahm planted a settlement of 160 Germans at Bethany in 1751, he found the colony "so lowly reduced that, had it not been for the few English in the Government[']s Employ, and the Salzburgers," the province would have been "intirely deserted of Inhabitants." De Brahm later recalled that a "few days before he arrived, a Lot with a tolerable House on it in the City of Savannah had been sold for [a] few shillings." He said that he "might have bought at that time with twenty Pounds Sterling nearly half the City." If Georgia had become neither rich nor strong, its inhabitants had also failed to acquire the cap of liberty. Without a representative assembly such as was enjoyed by the other colonies, Georgia, as the New England historian William Douglass remarked disparagingly in the late 1740s, could only be considered as "not [yet] colonized."[30]

Once the Trustees had surrendered their charter, and Georgia, now "new modelled," was finally put upon "the same footing with Carolina," the colony was at last to have a new—the malcontents would have said, a proper—beginning. Following the removal of the restrictions on slavery, De Brahm remembered, "many rich Carolina Planters . . . came with all their Families and Negroes to settle in Georgia in 1752," and "the Spirit of Emigration out of South Carolina into Georgia became so universal that year, that this and the following year near one thousand Negroes were brought in Georgia, where in 1751 were scarce above three dozen." Formal establishment of royal government under the first crown governor, John Reynolds, in late 1754 seemed at last, as one older resident declared, to bring the colony "the greatest prospect to being . . . happy." "People were then crowding in every day, fill'd with expectations of being Settled in a Country which" had "all the Advantages of Air & Soil and was [finally] founded upon liberty"—a country that at last, in Douglass's terms, had been "colonized." But Reynolds turned out to be a disaster, "a lawless tyrant" whose "iron rod" created so much "Discord" and faction that migration once again flowed out rather than in and Georgia, one disappointed inhabitant lamented, seemed likely to "be reduced to as low an ebb as it was under the Late unhappy Constitution under the Trustees." Several more years would have to elapse before the colony would achieve an identity as a free and flourishing place.[31]

If Georgia "drooped and languished" under Reynolds, his term was mercifully short, and under his politically more adroit successor, Henry Ellis, the colony began "to emerge, though slowly, out of the difficulties that [had] attended [it from] its first establishment," and Georgians at last seemed to be acquiring an unambiguous answer to the question of what they ought to be doing. The colony suffered from a very low base of both people and wealth. The population, Ellis reported shortly after his arrival, was small and mostly "so very poor that they but barely subsist themselves." But the Seven Years' War turned out to be a boon for Georgia, which became a refuge for many people fleeing from the warfare along the Virginia and Pennsylvania frontiers. In the two previous years, Ellis reported in January 1759, white population had jumped almost 40 percent to around seven thousand people, and "other things" were "increasing in proportion," the "produce of the Country" having "more than doubled." With growing numbers and production and a new sense of "happiness & tranquillity" in public life, Georgia was finally beginning to manifest "a visible spirit of industry & improvement."[32]

For the last fifteen years of the colonial period Georgia rapidly ac-

quired a reputation for having an abundance of rich land and a growing population, animated by a building "spirit of industry" that was
putting the colony into a "happy" and "most flourishing Condition."
Because the "Climate & Soil is at least equal, the Spirit of Industry
very Great, and the People beginning to have Property & Foundation
Sufficient to Enable them to make Considerable Progress," Governor
James Wright, who, as Ellis's successor, presided over Georgia during
these boom years, observed in early 1763 that "the only thing now
wanting to make this in a few years a Province of as much Consequence to Great Britain as some others in our Neighbourhood" was "a
great Number of Inhabitants."[33]

The close of the Seven Years' War brought peace to the colony and,
by placing Florida under British control, removed all apprehension of
danger from the Spaniards. Wright negotiated a series of treaties with
Indians that brought at least seven million more acres under British
jurisdiction. Spurred by these inducements, inhabitants poured into
Georgia. The number of whites tripled between 1761 and 1773, rising
from just over six thousand in 1761 to ten thousand in 1766 and eighteen thousand in 1773. At the same time, the number of blacks, virtually all of whom were slaves, more than quadrupled, increasing from
thirty-six hundred in 1761 to seventy-eight hundred in 1766 and fifteen thousand in 1773.[34] With these growing numbers, the face of the
landscape changed. The Savannah River and other areas near the coast
now were described as having an "abundance of very fine Settlements
and Plantations." But the most dramatic change occurred in the backcountry, where by 1772 the number of whites substantially exceeded
that of the lowcountry. By 1773, the colony was "well laid out with
Roads," and "the many Plantations and Settlements" along them made
"travelling very convenient and easy." "Increasing . . . extreamly
fast" since 1760, Savannah had many new houses which were spread-
ing west to the new suburbs of "Yamacraw" and the "Trustees Garden," while Savannah Bay was already "nearly fronted with contiguous
Wharfs," all built to handle Georgia's expanding volume of trade.[35]

Indeed, Georgia increased not only in population and settledness
during these years but also in production, credit, shipping, and wealth.
Its rising production can best be measured by the growing value of its
exports, which jumped from around £40,000 in 1761 to almost £85,000
in 1766 to over £100,000 in 1773. The expansion of credit was revealed
by the adverse balance of trade. The annual value of imports often
exceeded that of exports by nearly £50,000, and much of that differ-

ence went for the purchase of slaves, which, in a remark that showed how far Georgia had departed from the Trustees' initial plan, Wright described as the "wealth & strength of the Southern American Colonies" and the "chief means of their becoming Opulent & considerable." Over the period from 1761 to 1773 the number of vessels annually loading out of Georgia rose from 42 to 185. With "Produce & Trade" increasing so "amazingly," personal wealth also grew. Most Georgia planters, the anonymous author of *American Husbandry* reported in 1775, were "very much on the thriving hand." Most were not "yet . . . rich," but a few were doing extremely well. The Savannah merchant James Habersham had an income of £2,000 per year, and Wright had "in a few years" acquired "a plentiful fortune." His "example and success," one commentator noted, "gave vigour to industry, and promoted a spirit of emulation among the planters for improvement."[36]

Silk was of little importance in this expansion. Georgians continued to produce silk until the early 1770s, and, for a time in the early 1760s, it appeared to be "in a Flourishing State." Within the decade, however, Wright had concluded that it was a "Precarious & uncertain" crop and "that nothing but the Bounty of Parliament" kept "Silk Culture alive" in the province. After the bounty was lowered in the late 1760s, production declined precipitously, and Habersham concluded that silk would never become "a considerable Branch of Commerce" in Georgia until, like the Italian silk-producing region of Piedmont, it had "a number of white people of middling circumstances" who would invest the care necessary for its success. Olive trees and vineyards, two of the other exotic staples Georgia had originally been intended to produce, had "not . . . yet [even] become an Object of . . . Attention."[37]

Georgia's new prosperity was based almost entirely upon the same commodities that had been so successful in South Carolina: rice, indigo, naval stores, provisions, lumber, and wood products. "Without Exception," one author proclaimed, all of these commodities could be produced "to the same Perfection, and in every respect equal to South Carolina," and they "arrived at the markets in Europe [and the West Indies] in equal excellence and perfection, and, in proportion to its strength, in equal quantities with those of its more powerful and opulent neighbours in Carolina." Alexander Hewat claimed that because it contained "more good River Swamp," Georgia was actually "a better rice Colony than South Carolina." As proof, several "planters of Carolina, who had been accustomed to treat their poor neighbours with the utmost contempt," had "sold their estates in that colony, and moved with their families and effects to Georgia." Cotton, which in a few decades would be Georgia's premiere staple and was reported to agree "well with the soil and climate of Georgia," was only beginning to be produced in small quantities.[38]

The Georgia seal of 1732 had represented the genius of Georgia as embodying three qualities—abundance, strength, and liberty. The colony's steady growth finally brought abundance and a considerable degree of strength; liberty, that is, the sense of its inhabitants being as much in control of their own destiny and as free as the people of other colonies, was more elusive. With the implementation of royal government in 1754 and the immediate establishment of a representative assembly and a regular judicial system, Georgians appeared finally to have obtained those "English freedom[s]" enjoyed by "all English Colonies"—except Georgia under the Trustees. Once Reynolds was removed as governor, it would be accurate to say, as did a contemporary, that Georgia contained "no trace of a despotic government." But the conversion to a royal colony occurred just when colonial authorities in Britain were strongly advocating limiting the autonomy of all of the older colonies and bringing them under much tighter metropolitan control. The officials who designed and oversaw the establishment of royal authority in Georgia had no intention of permitting Georgians to exercise the same autonomy then enjoyed by the other colonies. Once again, Georgia, along with contemporary Nova Scotia, was to be a model colony, this time a model *royal* colony, a place where "Royal Government" would be "settled in it's [*sic*] greatest purity" and the errors of other governments would be corrected. Georgians were indeed to be "intitled to British Liberty," but their "Mode of Government," as Henry Ellis later declared, was to be "the freest from a Republican Mixture, and the most conformable to the British Constitution of any that obtains amongst our Colonies in North America." In practical terms, this meant that metropolitan officials in the colony—the royal governor and the council—were to have more authority and the representative assembly less than was the case in the other colonies. Even as a royal colony, Georgia would be swimming against the mainstream of British colonial development.[39]

Again, as with the Trustees' plans, however, South Carolina acted as the serpent in Eden. "Influenced by the example of South Carolina," the Georgia Assembly, Henry Ellis complained soon after his arrival in the colony, "was industriously attempting to usurp the same power" enjoyed by the South Carolina Assembly "& had indeed made a considerable progress therein during the Administration of my Predecessor." Indeed, what Ellis called "Carolina notions" seemed in "many instances" to "have prevailed with our people over every other consideration," as Georgians continued "incessantly urging & aiming at the privileges enjoyed there." "It would be happy for us if South Carolina was at a greater distance," Ellis lamented: "So long as our present intercourse with & dependence upon that Province subsists," he despaired that Georgians would ever "alter their ideas" or that he would be able to make the Georgia government conform to the model designed by his superiors in London.[40]

With judicious administration and much help from London, however, Ellis and Wright managed to a remarkable extent to do just that during the late 1750s and early 1760s, albeit the Assembly continued sometimes to grasp "at powers that did not belong to them." When the Treaty of Paris brought many new territories under British control in 1763, the governments of Georgia and Nova Scotia were indeed held up as models for those to be established in the new territories, and a visitor to Georgia just before the Stamp Act crisis found the colony's public life full of "love and unanimity." Its behavior during that crisis seemed to indicate that in Georgia, the only older British continental colony except for Nova Scotia in which the designs of the act were not totally frustrated, the crown's new experiment was working. Georgians did not like the Stamp Act, but, as Habersham said, they did not let their "dislike to this Law" lead them into the "unjustifiable excess[es]" of "the Northern people"—even though "No pains" had "been Spared in the Northern Colonies to Spirit up and inflame the People here." Wright confidently predicted that "A Small Check from Home or disapprobation of their Proceedings" and his own diligent attention would "Set all Right here."[41]

Wright was wrong. Despite several small checks from home, Georgia proved to be "a very fertile Soil" for northern ideas. As the quarrel with Britain intensified during the late 1760s and early 1770s, Georgia came increasingly into the orbit of the discontented colonies to the north until, Wright lamented, "the Spirit of Assuming Power, and Raising the Importance of the Assembly" rapidly became "the Ruling Passion." Inspired by the "Example of . . . Carolina," Georgians seemed to be growing just as licentious as other colonists. In the final crisis in 1774–76, when, partly because of Wright's efforts and influence, Georgians hesitated to throw their unreserved support into the opposition to the Coercive Acts, they were in effect shamed or goaded into doing so by the revolutionary leaders in South Carolina. To prove that they were just as free and just as committed to liberty as people in other colonies, to make it clear to themselves as well as to others that they deserved to wear the cap of liberty displayed by the genius of the colony in their great seal, they had no choice. Georgians could at last become equal to the other colonists in this respect only by being just as firm in the cause of liberty as the others were.[42]

As Georgians, through their economic, social, and political behavior, were establishing during the 1760s and early 1770s the credibility of their claims to the positive attributes of abundance, strength, and liberty forecast by their seal, they also came to a new understanding of their history, of their collective experiences as a people. "Few countries," one commentator remarked during the American Revolution, had "undergone so many changes as Georgia has, in the course of fifty years." But the most dramatic of these changes was the colony's sudden rise to prosperity: "Under the long administration of Sir James Wright . . . it made such a rapid progress in population, agriculture, and commerce, as no other country ever equalled in so short a time." From the perspectives supplied by that change, on the basis of the observable fact that Georgia did not begin "to flourish" until after "the original Constitution framed by the Trustees" had been altered, Georgians and other observers could only conclude that the colony's difficulties under the Trustees were not attributable to the character of the settlers, who with some exceptions had worked hard enough to ensure that Georgia, as De Brahm declared, had been "a Place of Industry ever since its very Beginning." Rather, Georgia's "Backwardness seemed only to be owing, first to the Prohibition of introducing African Servants, [and] . . . secondly for not being governed in a manner as other Provinces [with] . . . Representatives, with the Liberty to make their own Laws." As soon as the colony had been "freed from those Prohibitions, and invested with Privileges and Liberties, as other Provinces," as soon as its "planters," as another writer put it, "got the strength of Africa to assist them" (and it might be said that the planters enjoyed the abundance and liberty forecast by the seal while the Africans supplied the strength), they immediately began to labor "with success, and the[ir] lands every year yielded greater and greater increase." In the face of this success, no conclusions could be drawn other than those put forth by Wright in 1767 to explain the colony's sudden success: the Trustees' plan was obviously "not properly adapted for settling an American Colony," and Georgia's dramatically improved condition was "owing to the great alteration" in that plan.[43]

The writers who supplied the earliest histories of the colony written after the Trustee period—Edmund Burke, John Huddleston Wynne, the Abbé Raynal, Alexander Hewat—all agreed with Wright. They treated the Trustees and Oglethorpe as "humane and disinterested" men whose designs for their new colony could scarcely have been more "Laudable . . . in every respect." "The benevolent founders of the colony of Georgia," wrote Hewat, "perhaps may challenge the annals of any nation to produce a design more generous and praiseworthy than that they had undertaken." Generous and laudable—but not, in Burke's understated phrase, "altogether answerable." Answerable plans for settlement, Georgia's experience under the Trustees powerfully seemed to indicate, had to arise "from the nature of the climate, country, and soil, and the circumstances of the settlers, and [to have] been the result of experience and not of speculation." Certainly, as Wynne remarked, "a levelling scheme, in a new colony," seemed to be "extremely unadviseable," especially, added Burke, when its inhabitants could "see their neighbours . . . in a much more easy condition." The new hero of Georgia, its founding father, became not Oglethorpe but James Wright.[44]

But if the malcontents gained a victory in these early histories, all of which accepted the contention that work in such a hot climate "was too heavy for . . . white men," most of the historians and indeed Governors Ellis and Wright recognized that the Trustees had not been wholly wrong in their intentions. The Trustees' plan had been designed to prevent the irregular settlement, the dispersion, the unequal concentration of property, and the absenteeism and fear associated with a large population of slaves. By 1775 Georgia was displaying strong tendencies in all of these directions; during the period leading up to the Revolution, Georgia's large black population was seen as both a strength and a weakness of the colony.[45]

Notwithstanding the anxieties that slavery brought to the colony, Georgia during the royal period finally achieved a positive sense of itself as a place and as a people. Some areas were unhealthy; indeed, disease seemed to increase with prosperity, population, and trade.[46] As a "young new settled Country," Georgia society was still crude and culturally undeveloped. "We have no Plays, Operas, or public Exhibitions, either in point of Literature or Amusements, to animadvert upon," wrote Habersham in 1772. Or, to put the matter more positively, although Georgia had "some brilliant . . . [public] Assemblys" and at least five "fine [private] Libraries" and there was talk of turning George Whitefield's orphanage into the first college south of Williamsburg, Georgia, in De Brahm's words, had "not as yet [been] debauched by European Luxuries, such as Balls, Masquerades, Operas, Plays, etc.," and Georgians who sought cultural enrichment had little choice but to apply "themselves to reading good Authors."[47]

In spite of these deficiencies in health and culture, Georgia was obviously becoming a place of which its inhabitants could be proud. With large amounts of unoccupied land that, especially in the interior, was said to be "the finest in all America," Georgia was rapidly becoming known and was usually depicted as a "rich and plentiful country" with great opportunity not just for rich slaveowners but even for "people of small fortunes" who did "not dislike retirement" in a place of rural delights. As it became increasingly clear that Georgia was "Making a very Rapid Progress towards being an Opulent & Considerable Province" and that that progress finally afforded Georgians "a Prospect of . . . soon becoming a rich, commercial People," as even outsiders began to suspect that Georgia would "become one of the richest, and most considerable Provinces in British America, and that in a very few years," Georgians gradually acquired a positive sense of themselves as a demonstrably prosperous and liberty-loving people.[48]

At the same time, their home and their society—their country—was gaining an increasingly flattering reputation as a place of opportunity, freedom, and ease. Like all of the other new plantation societies at a comparable point in their development, Georgians had not been together long enough to articulate any very well-developed sense of whether they were acquiring any distinctive characteristics as individuals, that is, a collective identity. Georgians were just beginning to attribute special defining qualities to themselves—"a Volatile, but kind people," in the estimation of Habersham; a people who were, "in general of very elevated Spirits," according to De Brahm; a people who, not caring "for a small profit" or a modest way of living, were prone, in the words of Boltzius, to "abuse . . . [their] freedom." But their sense of self was primarily expressed through their understanding of their physical and social landscapes.[49]

Especially in view of the destructive effects of the War for Independence in Georgia, the colony's many loyalists and two of its earlier historians, Anthony Stokes and Alexander Hewat, wondered why

Georgians put their new prosperity and positive identity at risk by joining the rebellion against Britain in 1776. "No country ever enjoyed a greater share of liberty than Georgia did from the time it became a King's Government, down to the breaking out of the Civil War," Stokes wrote in 1782: "Justice was regularly and impartially administered—oppression was unknown— . . . taxes . . . were trifling—and every man that had industry, became opulent." "The people there were more particularly indebted to the Crown, than those in any other Colony," he noted, "immense sums were expended by Government in settling and protecting—that country—troops of rangers were kept up by the Crown for several years—the Civil Government was annually provided for by vote of the House of Commons of Great Britain, and most of the inhabitants owed every acre of land they had to the King's *free* gift: in short, there was scarce a man in the Province that did not lie under particular obligations to the Crown."[50] Stokes did not understand that Georgians could never feel that they were equal to the other colonies until they had done exactly what he found so incomprehensible: shown that, like the others, they were willing to put all the prosperity they had gained at risk in behalf of the liberty they claimed as Britons, including their liberty to have slaves.

That Georgia's success in achieving a positive sense of self in the 1760s and 1770s was so heavily dependent upon the massive adoption of black slavery was thoroughly consistent with its entire colonial history. For one of the most interesting facets of the history of colonial Georgia, one that provides some consistency over the entire period, was that it seemed forever to be destined to be going against history. Started as a place that would be free of the social evils of other British American colonies, it had been reconstituted as an entity that would be as free as possible from the centrifugal impulses toward autonomy that, at least to metropolitan authorities, had seemed to make the colonies politically fragile and increasingly difficult to control. By managing to subvert both of these designs, Georgians had succeeded in placing themselves on an equal footing with the other colonies. But in thus thrusting themselves into and thereby showing that they belonged in the mainstream of British-American colonial history, they were at the same time once again going against much larger currents in Western history. For at the very time Georgia was moving so heavily into slavery, that institution was beginning—for the first time—to be widely condemned in western Europe as a moral evil that was inappropriate for civilized societies. Although this movement seems to have created no problems for Georgians during the colonial period, the rapid triumph of the point of view it represented, which was nearly as sudden as, and far more revolutionary than, Georgia's rise to prosperity, would soon put Georgians at the same point they had found themselves repeatedly: on the defensive. No doubt the Earl of Egmont and the other authors of the Trustees' Georgia plan would have found this development disquieting, as they would have found almost everything else that happened to their colony. But they might also have gained a certain amount of satisfaction to know that their early forebodings over slavery had not been without foundation.

NOTES

1. Américo Castro, *The Spaniards: An Introduction to Their History* (Berkeley, 1971), 127.

2. This larger study, still in process, is tentatively entitled *Paradise Defined: Studies in the Emergence and Changing Character of the Plantation Self in Virginia, Jamaica, and South Carolina, 1660 to 1815.*

3. "Some Account of the Designs of the Trustees for Establishing the Colony of Georgia in America," *Coll. GHS*, 20:4–6; "Reasons for Establishing the Colony of Georgia," ibid., 1:216–17, 224, 226; Francis Moore, *A Voyage to Georgia Begun in the Year 1735* (London, 1774), in Trevor R. Reese, ed., *Our First Visit in America: Early Reports from the Colony of Georgia, 1732–1740* (Savannah, 1974), 99; Henry Newman to Reverend Mr. Samuel Urlsperger, May 18, 1733, in George Fenwick Jones, ed., *Henry Newman's Salzburger Letterbooks* (Athens, 1966), 44–45.

4. [Jean Pierre Purry], *A New and Accurate Account of the Provinces of South-Carolina and Georgia* (London, 1732), in Trevor R. Reese, ed., *The Most Delightful Country of the Universe: Promotional Literature of the Colony of Georgia, 1717–1734* (Savannah, 1972), 124, 127, 143–44, 147; "Reasons for Establishing," 205–6, 208–12, 216, 223; Newman to Urlsperger, May 18, 1733, Jones, ed., *Newman's Letterbooks*, 44–45; "Some Account of the Designs," 4, 6.

5. "Some Account of the Designs," 6–7; "Reasons for Establishing," 223–24; [Purry], *New and Accurate Account*, 127; Newman to Urlsperger, November 21, 1732, May 18, 1733, Jones, ed., *Newman's Letterbooks*, 31, 43.

6. Moore, *Voyage to Georgia*, 99.

7. "Some Account of the Designs," 6. The definitions in this paragraph are taken from Samuel Johnson, *A Dictionary of the English Language*, 8th ed., 2 vols. (London, 1799).

8. "Some Account of the Designs," 5–6; "Reasons for Establishing," 214,

221, 225–26; Newman to Urlsperger, May 18, 1732, Jones, ed., *Newman's Letterbooks*, 44–45; Moore, *Voyage to Georgia*, 99–100.

9. "Some Account of the Designs," 4–7; "Reasons for Establishing," 216, 218, 221–22.

10. See, esp. Isaac Kramnick, *Bolingbroke and His Circle: The Politics of Nostalgia in the Age of Walpole* (Cambridge, Mass., 1968). The quotation is from *State of the British and French Colonies in North America* (London, 1755), 67.

11. "Some Account of the Designs," 5–6; "Reasons for Establishing," 231–32.

12. "Some Account of the Designs," 6; Robert G. McPherson, ed., "The Voyage of the *Anne*–A Daily Record," *GHQ*, 44:222; Newman to John Vat, October 10, 1735, Jones, ed., *Newman's Letterbooks*, 175.

13. James Oglethorpe to Trustees, December 1733, Francis Piercy to Rev. Forster, June 1, 1735, and Phillip Thicknesse to His Mother, November 13, 1736, in Mills Lane, ed., *General Oglethorpe's Georgia*, 2 vols. (Savannah, 1975), 1:27–30, 180–81, 282; George Fenwick Jones, trans., "Commissary Von Reck's Report on Georgia," *GHQ* 47 (1963):100.

14. Jones, trans., "Commissary Von Reck's Report," 101; Robert G. McPherson, ed., *Egmont's Journal*, 71, 307; Moore, *Voyage to Georgia*, 98; "Travel Diary of Commissioner Von Reck," Samuel Urlsperger, comp., *Detailed Reports on the Salzburger Emigrants Who Settled in America . . .* , ed. George Fenwick Jones et al., 7 vols. to date (Athens, 1968–), 1:142; "Daily Register," ibid., 2:193.

15. See John Brownfield to Trustees, May 2, 1737, Lane, ed., *General Oglethorpe's Georgia*, 1:305–9.

16. E. Merton Coulter, ed., *The Journal of Peter Gordon, 1732–1735* (Athens, 1963), 49–51, 59; Brownfield to Trustees, March 6, 1736, May 2, 1737, Lane, ed., *General Oglethorpe's Georgia*, 1:248–50, 306–9.

17. William Stephens, *A State of the Province of Georgia* (London, 1742), in Trevor R. Reese, ed., *The Clamorous Malcontents: Criticisms and Defenses of the Colony of Georgia, 1741–1743* (Savannah, 1973), 3–5, 8, 10–11, 14; [Benjamin Martyn], *An Account Showing the Progress of the Colony of Georgia . . .* , (London, 1741), in ibid., 224–25; [Thomas Christie], *A Description of Georgia* (London, 1741), in Peter Force, comp., *Tracts and Other Papers Relating Principally to the Origin, Settlement, and Progress of the Colonies in North America*, 4 vols. (Washington, 1836–46), 2:3–4.

18. Patrick Tailfer, Hugh Anderson, and David Douglas, *A True and Historical Narrative of the Colony of Georgia*, ed. Clarence L. Ver Steeg (Athens, 1960), 4–5, 40–41; Coulter, ed., *Journal of Peter Gordon*, 25; Inhabitants of Savannah to Trustees, November 22, 1740, Hugh Anderson and Others to Trustees, December 2, 1740, Petition to George II or Parlia-

ment, December 29, 1740, Joseph Avery to Harman Verelst, January 31, 1743, Lane, ed., *General Oglethorpe's Georgia*, 2:486–89, 492, 513, 519, 522–23, 654; [Thomas Stephens], *A Brief Account of the Causes That have retarded the Progress of the Colony of Georgia, in America* (London, 1743), in Reese, ed., *Clamorous Malcontents*, 287.

19. Coulter, ed., *Journal of Peter Gordon*, 53–54, 56–59; Tailfer and Others to Trustees, August 27, 1735, Petition to Trustees, December 9, 1738, Hugh Anderson to Oglethorpe, January 9, 1739, Inhabitants of Savannah to Trustees, November 22, 1740, Hugh Anderson and Others to Trustees, December 2, 1740, Petition to George II or Parliament, December 29, 1740, Avery to Verelst, January 31, 1743, Lane, ed., *General Oglethorpe's Georgia*, 1:225–27; 2:372, 374, 382–83, 489–90, 494, 513, 515, 519–21, 656; [Stephens], *Brief Account of the Causes*, 279–80, 284.

20. Coulter, ed., *Journal of Peter Gordon*, 51–53; Inhabitants of Savannah to Trustees, November 22, 1740, Petition to George II or Parliament, December 29, 1740, Lane, ed., *General Oglethorpe's Georgia*, 2:490, 517–18; [Stephens], *Brief Account of the Causes*, 275–76, 281; Robert Pringle to James Henderson, June 22, 1739, Walter B. Edgar, ed., *The Letterbook of Robert Pringle*, 2 vols. (Columbia, 1972), 1:101; Tailfer, Anderson, and Douglas, *True and Historical Narrative*, 8, 17, 52–54, 58–59, 129–30, 141; [Thomas Stephens], *The Hard Case of the Distressed People of Georgia* [London, 1742], in Reese, ed., *Clamorous Malcontents*, 266.

21. Tailfer, Anderson, and Douglas, *True and Historical Narrative*, 3, 17, 20; Coulter, ed., *Journal of Peter Gordon*, 52; Tailfer and Others to Trustees, August 27, 1735, Inhabitants of Savannah to Trustees, November 22, 1740, Hugh Anderson and Others to Trustees, December 2, 1740, Lane, ed.. *General Oglethorpe's Georgia*, 1:225, 2:489–91, 496.

22. Tailfer, Anderson, and Douglas, *True and Historical Narratives*, 3–4.

23. Coulter, ed., *Journal of Peter Gordon*, 54; Petition to Trustees, December 9, 1738, Hugh Anderson to Oglethorpe, January 6, 1739, Inhabitants of Savannah to Trustees, November 22, 1740, Petition to George II or Parliament, December 29, 1740, Avery to Verelst, January 31, 1743, Lane, ed., *General Oglethorpe's Georgia*, 2:372, 382, 384, 487–88, 518, 656; Tailfer, Anderson, and Douglas, *True and Historical Narrative*, 4–5, 40, 67–68; [Stephens], *Hard Case of the Distressed People*, 260–62, and *Brief Account of the Causes*, 279–81, 283, 288.

24. [Benjamin Martyn], *An Impartial Enquiry into the State and Utility of the Province of Georgia* (London, 1741), in Reese, ed., *Clamorous Malcontents*, 126–47; [Martyn], *Account Showing the Progress*, 191–92; Urlsperger, comp., *Detailed Reports of the Salzburger Emigrants*, 3:311; Tailfer, Anderson, and Douglas, *True and Historical Narrative*, 103.

25. [Martyn], *Impartial Enquiry*, 127–29; [Martyn], *Account Showing the Progress*, 187, 217; Stephens, *State of the Province of Georgia*, 11;

[Christie], *Description of Georgia*, 6; *Egmont's Journal*, 71; Tailfer, Anderson, and Douglas, *True and Historical Narrative*, 17, 21, 39–40, 59, 158.

26. [Stephens], *Hard Case of the Distressed People*, 267; Leo Francis Stock, ed., *Proceedings and Debates of the British Parliament Respecting North America*, 5 vols. (Washington, 1924–41), 5:140–41, 151–52, 164, 167.

27. [Edward Kimber], "Itinerant Observations in America," *Coll. GHS*, 4:15–19; Klaus G. Loewald, Beverly Starika, and Paul S. Taylor, eds., "Johann Martin Bolzius Answers a Questionnaire on Carolina and Georgia," [March 19, 1751], *WMQ* 3d ser., 14 (1957):242, 246–50, 252, 254, 15 (1958): 232, 243, 250.

28. John Oldmixon, *The British Empire in America*, 2d ed., 2 vols. (London, 1741), 2:525–41; [Kimber], "Itinerant Observations," 19; John Harris, *Navigantium atque Itinerantium Bibliotheca*, 2 vols. (London, 1748), 2: 323–47.

29. Alexander Hewat, *An Historical Account of the Rise and Progress of the Colonies of South Carolina and Georgia*, 2 vols. (London, 1779), 2:18.

30. Ibid., 2:165; Louis De Vorsey, Jr., ed., *De Brahm's Report of the General Survey in the Southern District of North America* (Columbia, 1971), 141; William Douglass, *Summary, Historical and Political, of the first Planting, progressive Improvements, and present State of the British Settlements in North-America*, 2 vols. (Boston, 1749–51), 1:207.

31. [Edmund Burke], *An Account of the European Settlements in America*, 2 vols. (London, 1808), 2:311; Hewat, *Historical Account*, 2:165; De Vorsey, ed., *De Brahm's Report*, 142; Jonathan Bryan to Earl of Halifax, April 6, 1756, *CRG*, 27:114–15; Douglass, *Summary*, 1:207; "On Governor Ellis's Arrival in Georgia," [1757], *Coll. GHS*, 20:942; Anthony Stokes, *A View of the Constitution of the British Colonies in North America and the West Indies, at the time the Civil War broke out on the Continent of America* (London, 1783), 115.

32. John Huddlestone Wynne, *A General History of the British Empire in America*, 2 vols. (London, 1770), 1:315, 318; Henry Ellis to Board of Trade, August 1, 1757, January 1, 1758, January 29, 1759, and to William Pitt, August 1, 1757, *CRG*, 28, pt. 1:41–42, 44, 104, 178.

33. Hewat, *Historical Account*, 2:165; James Wright to Board of Trade, February 22, 1763, December 23, 1763, *CRG*, 28, pt. 1:406, 455.

34. "Report of Sir James Wright on the Condition of the Province of Georgia," September 20, 1773, *Coll. GHS*, 3:160, 167; Wright to Board of Trade, April 15, 1761, *CRG*, 28, pt. 1:309; Wright's Answers to Board of Trade's Queries, February 15, 1762, and 1766, ibid., pt. 2:186; De Vorsey, ed., *De Brahm's Report*, 162.

35. "Journal of Lord Adam Gordon," 1765, in Newton D. Mereness, ed., *Travels in the American Colonies* (New York, 1916), 394–95; Wright to Board of Trade, June 24, 1765, Wright's Answers to Board of Trade's

Queries, February 15, 1762, and 1766, *CRG*, 28, pt. 2:94, 180; James Habersham to Earl of Hillsborough, April 24, 1772, *Coll. GHS*, 6:173; "Report of Sir James Wright," September 20, 1773, ibid., 3:160; De Vorsey, ed., *De Brahm's Report*, 153, 158, 161.

36. Wright's Answers to Board of Trade's Queries, February 15, 1762, and 1766, and Wright to Board of Trade, June 8, 1768, *CRG*, 28, pt. 2:183–86, 251, 258; "Report of Sir James Wright," September 20, 1773, *Coll. GHS*, 3:167; Habersham to Ellis, January 27, 1772, and to John Nutt, July 31, 1772, ibid., 6:162, 196; De Vorsey, ed., *De Brahm's Report*, 163–64; Harry L. Carman, ed., *American Husbandry* (New York, 1939), 351; Hewat, *Historical Account*, 2:266–67.

37. Wright to Board of Trade, April 23, 1765, October 21, 1766, *CRG*, 28, pt. 2:92, 172; Habersham to Hillsborough, April 24, 1772, *Coll. GHS*, 6:173–74; De Vorsey, ed., *De Brahm's Report*, 142; Guillaume Thomas François Raynal, *A Philosophical and Political History of the Settlements and Trade of the Europeans in the East and West Indies*, trans. J. O. Justamond, 2d ed., 6 vols. (New York, 1969), 6:69–70.

38. Ellis to Board of Trade, April 24, 1759, and Wright's Answers to Board of Trade's Queries, February 15, 1762, and 1766, *CRG*, 28, pt. 1:207, pt. 2:185; De Vorsey, ed., *De Brahm's Report*, 140, 150; Carman, ed., *American Husbandry*, 345, 357; Hewat, *Historical Account*, 2:267; Stokes, *View of the Constitution*, 116.

39. Loewald, Starika, and Taylor, eds., "Bolzius Answers a Questionnaire," *WMQ* 3d ser., 14:254; Verner W. Crane, ed., "Hints Relative to the Division and Government of the Conquered and Newly Acquired Countries in America," May 5, 1763, *Mississippi Valley Historical Review* 8 (1922):371–72.

40. Ellis to Board of Trade, January 1, 1758, March 15, 1759, *CRG*, 28, pt. 1:101, 193.

41. Stokes, *View of the Constitution*, 137; Crane, ed., "Hints Relative to the Division and Government," 367–73; "Journal of Lord Adam Gordon," 396; Habersham to William Knox, October 28, 1765, *Coll. GHS*, 6:46; Wright to Board of Trade, January 15, 22, February 1, 1766, May 15, 1767, *CRG*, 28, pt. 2:133–36, 217.

42. Wright to Board of Trade, June 8, 1768, *CRG*, 28, pt. 2:253; Habersham to Nutt, July 31, 1772, *Coll. GHS*, 6:197; "Report of Sir James Wright," September 20, 1773, and Wright to Lord Dartmouth, August 24, 1774, ibid., 3:164, 180; *S.C. Gaz.*, September 12, 1774, February 27, March 5, 1775.

43. Stokes, *View of the Constitution*, 113, 115; Ellis to Board of Trade, August 1, 1757, William Knox's Memorial to Board of Trade, December 7, 1762, Wright's Answers to Board of Trade's Queries, February 15, 1762, and 1766, *CRG*, 28, pt. 1:41, 385, pt. 2:187; De Vorsey, ed., *De Brahm's Report*,

163; Hewat, *Historical Account,* 2:267; "Report of Sir James Wright," September 20, 1773, *Coll. GHS,* 3:167.

44. Robert Rogers, *A Concise Account of North America* (London, 1755), 142; Hewat, *Historical Account,* 2:16–17, 151; [Burke], *Account of the European Settlements,* 2:304–5, 307–8; Raynal, *Philosophical and Political History,* 6:65–67; Wynne, *British Empire in America,* 1:311.

45. Carman, ed., *American Husbandry,* 343; [Burke], *Account of the European Settlements,* 307–12; "Report to Sir James Wright," September 20, 1773, *Coll. GHS,* 3:158; Ellis to Board of Trade, April 24, 1759, Wright to Board of Trade, June 10, 1762, December 23, 1763, June 15, 1767, Knox's Memorial to Board of Trade, December 7, 1762, Wright's Answers to Board of Trade's Queries, February 15, 1762, and 1766, *CRG,* 28, pt. 1:207–8, 377, 384, 455, pt. 2:179, 232.

46. De Vorsey, ed., *De Brahm's Report,* 160; Wright's Answers to Board of Trade's Queries, February 15, 1762, and 1766, *CRG,* 28, pt. 2:179; Rogers, *Concise Account,* 145; John Mitchell, *The Present State of Great Britain and North America* (New York, 1767), 178, 184–85, 188–91; Hewat, *Historical Account,* 2:259.

47. Wright's Answers to Board of Trade's Queries, February 15, 1762, and 1766, *CRG,* 28, pt. 2:185; Habersham to Wright, February 17, 1772, *Coll. GHS,* 6:166–67; De Vorsey, ed., *De Brahm's Report,* 143–44; "Journal of Lord Adam Gordon," 395; Carman, ed., *American Husbandry,* 345.

48. Carman, ed., *American Husbandry,* 335–37, 344–45, 351; "Journal of Lord Adam Gordon," 396; Wright to Board of Trade, June 8, November 24, 1768, *CRG,* 28, pt. 2:258, 309; Habersham to Ellis, January 27, 1772, to Wright, February 17, 1772, *Coll. GHS,* 6:162, 167; De Vorsey, ed., *De Brahm's Report,* 150; Stokes, *View of the Constitution,* 115.

49. Habersham to William Symonds, December 4, 1765, *Coll. GHS,* 6:51; De Vorsey, ed., *De Brahm's Report,* 143; Loewald, Starika, and Taylor, eds., "Bolzius Answers a Questionnaire," *WMQ* 3d ser., 15:243.

50. Stokes, *View of the Constitution,* 137, 139.

The Contributors

LEE ANN CALDWELL is a Ph.D. candidate at the University of Georgia and coordinator of the Department of History and Political Science at Paine College. She has published in the *Georgia Historical Quarterly*, the *Georgia Journal*, and *Richmond County History*.

EDWARD J. CASHIN is chairman of the Department of History, Political Science, and Philosophy at Augusta College. His books include *Augusta and the American Revolution* (with Heard Robertson), *A History of Augusta College*, and *The Story of Augusta*.

KENNETH COLEMAN is professor emeritus of history at the University of Georgia. His publications include *The American Revolution in Georgia, 1763–1789*, *Georgia Journeys, 1732–1754* (coauthored with Sarah B. Gober Temple), *Colonial Georgia: A History*, *A History of Georgia* (general editor and coauthor), four volumes of *The Colonial Records of the State of Georgia* (coedited with Milton Ready), and the *Dictionary of Georgia Biography* (coedited with Charles Stephen Gurr).

JACK P. GREENE is Andrew W. Mellon Professor in the Humanities at the Johns Hopkins University. He has authored and edited a number of books and articles on British-American colonial history, including *The Quest for Power: The Lower Houses of Assembly in the Southern Royal Colonies, 1689–1763* and *The Diary of Colonel Landon Carter of Sabine Hall, 1752–1778*.

The Contributors

CHARLES M. HUDSON is a professor of anthropology at the University of Georgia. He is the author of *The Catawba Nation, The Southeastern Indians,* and *Elements of Southeastern Indian Religion.*

LARRY E. IVERS is a lawyer in Eagle Grove, Iowa. While in the service he spent time in Georgia and prepared the operational war plan for the defense of the southeastern states. This research resulted in several publications, including "The Battle of Fort Mosa" in the *Georgia Historical Quarterly* and *British Drums on the Southern Frontier.*

HARVEY H. JACKSON is chairman of the Division of Social Sciences at Clayton Junior College. He is author of *Lachlan McIntosh and the Politics of Revolutionary Georgia* and coauthor of *Georgia's Signers and the Declaration of Independence.* His articles have appeared in the *William and Mary Quarterly,* the *Georgia Historical Quarterly,* and *Southern Studies.*

GEORGE FENWICK JONES is a professor of medieval German and comparative literature at the University of Maryland. He is translator and editor of *Henry Newman's Salzburger Letterbooks* and seven volumes of the *Detailed Reports of the Salzburger Emigrants Who Settled in America,* as well as the author of *The Salzburger Saga: Religious Exiles and Other Germans Along the Savannah.*

B. H. LEVY received his J.D. from Harvard Law School. He is president of the Georgia Historical Society, state chairman of the Georgia Semiquincentenary Commission, and on the Executive Council of the American Jewish Historical Society. He is the author of *Savannah's Old Jewish Community Cemeteries* and numerous articles on Jewish history.

MILTON L. READY is chairman of the Department of History at the University of North Carolina at Asheville. He is author of *The Castle Builders: Colonial Georgia Under the Trustees* and coeditor of *The Colonial Records of the State of Georgia.* His articles have appeared in the *Georgia Historical Quarterly, Agricultural History,* and *Urban Growth and Urban Life.*

JOHN W. REPS is a professor of city and regional planning at Cornell University's College of Architecture, Art, and Planning. He is the

The Contributors

author of *Cities of the American West: A History of Frontier Urban Planning, The Forgotten Frontier: Urban Planning in the American West Before 1890, Cities of Stone, Tidewater Towns, Town Planning in Frontier America, Monumental Washington,* and *The Making of Urban America.*

W. CALVIN SMITH is professor of history and chairman of the Social and Behavioral Science Division at the University of South Carolina at Aiken. His articles on colonial Georgia and the Habershams have appeared in the *Georgia Historical Quarterly,* the *Florida Historical Quarterly,* and the *Encyclopedia of Southern History.*

PHINIZY SPALDING is a professor of history at the University of Georgia and former editor of the *Georgia Historical Quarterly.* He is the author of *Oglethorpe in America* and articles in the *Yale University Library Gazette,* the *Johnson Society Transactions, Journal of Imperial and Commonwealth History,* and other journals.

BETTY WOOD is a lecturer in the Faculty of History, University of Cambridge, and a fellow of Girton College, Cambridge. She has published articles on the history of slavery in colonial Georgia in the *Georgia Historical Quarterly* and *Explorations in Economic History,* and is the author of *Slavery in Colonial Georgia, 1730–1775.*

Index

Index

Firman, Thomas, 47–49, 53
Fitzwalter, Penelope, 188
Florida, 34, 153
Fort Argyle, 158
Fort King George, 153; built, 5–6
Fort Prince George, 157
French, 4, 7, 35, 152, 153; threaten South Carolina's Indian trade, 5, 6; Georgia's effect upon, 16; Huguenots in Florida, 35

Gage, Gen. Thomas, 236, 238, 239
Galphin, George, 237
Gee, Joshua, 9, 65
Georgia: petition for charter, 8; role of Bray Associates in, 8; named, 11; becoming like South Carolina, 72, 297–300; as a royal colony, 188, 191, 298; as depicted in promotional literature, 5, 48, 56, 65, 117, 281–82; population of, grows, 296; South Carolina planters move to, 297–98; conditions improve in, 301–2
Georgia plan, 50, 53, 54, 57, 81, 83, 84, 283–84, 304; failure of, 75; Egmont's commitment to, 86, 89; attacked by malcontents, 88–92; defended, 88–92
German Protestants, 219; as potential colonists, 6, 50; family alliances of, in Georgia, 221–23. *See also* Salzburgers
Gibbons, Joseph, 261, 272 (n. 28)
Gordillo, Francisco, 25
Gordon, Peter, 138, 186
Green, Ann, 192
Grierson, James, 245
Gronau, Rev. Israel Christian, 218, 223
Guale, 36, 37; missions attacked, 38–39

Gwinnett, Button, 253, 258, 261, 266, 267, 272 (n. 28)
Gwynn, John, 127

Habersham, James, Jr. ("Jemme"): partner of Clay, 205, 206; business activities of, 206–9; post-revolution problems of, 209–11
Habersham, James, Sr., 54, 55, 56, 253, 297, 299, 302; arrives in Georgia, 198; reasons for coming to Georgia, 198–99; relations with Whitefield, 198–99; partner of Harris, 199–204; moves to Savannah, 200; trading problems of, 200–203; opens direct trade to England, 202; on Board of Assistants, 203; emulates Charleston merchants, 203–4; and rice planting, 204; uses slave labor, 204; association with Rasberry, 204–5; helps Clay, 205; reenters commerce, 208–9; death of, 209; opposes Whig activities, 209; describes Crackers, 236; acting governor, 239, 241; on governor's Council, 254; supports Wright, 257
Habersham, John: clerk apprentice, 206; business activities of, 208–9; post-revolution problems of, 209–11
Habersham, Joseph (Joe), 73, 262, 263; partner of Laurens, 206; goes to London, 206; supports Whigs, 206, 209; business activities of, 205–6, 208; partner of Clay, 208–9; post-revolution problems of, 209–11; views on Whig factions, 251–52, 253; Whig leader, 252
Hales, Robert: relations with Bray, 7

318